The Stone Crusher's Daughter

The Implications of Being Made in God's Image

David Lundy

Disclaimer

The opinions expressed in this book are solely that of the author and do not represent the position or ideology of any organization, charity or individual.

Copyright

Printed and bound in Canada by Thistle Printing Limited

Acknowledgements

I owe any success to this writing venture in no small part to those who read my complete manuscript with a view to its improvement, including my wife, Linda. A word of appreciation is also due to Gary Corwin, Ivan Kostka and Greg Livingstone, among others, who read sections of the manuscript where their expertise provided invaluable insight.

Other Books by the Author

*We Are the World: Globalization and the Changing Face
of Missions*   1999
Servant Leadership for Slow Learners   2002
*Borderless Church: Shaping the Church for the
21st Century*   2005

Books Contributed to by the Author

*The Desert Is Alive: Stream of Living Water from Muscat
to Marrakesh*   2006
One World or Many?   2003
A Passion for the Impossible: The Life of Lilias Trotter   2003
Missiological Models in Ministry to Muslims   2006

How To Contact Author or
Purchase More Copies

The author can be reached at lundyconsulting2@gmail.com
Copies of this book may be ordered from the author by email
if in North America or on Amazon.com.

The Stone Crusher's Daughter: The Implications of Being Made in God's Image

Foreword

In some African cultures whenever a man or woman meets another person walking toward them they call out in a friendly voice: "Do you see me?" Culturally this is a way to say to another person that I value you as a person. I do see you and I need you to acknowledge that I too have a value in your sight. Imagine what it's like to be a Dalit in India? To know that for thousands of years you and your ancestors have not been a person of much value in the sight of others. This is a form of bondage and cripples the lives and dreams of such people. God calls us to find our true identity in Him, the One who made us in His image. When God looks at us, He does see us and He calls us to see others with His eyes of love and compassion. Lundy's heart searching book will open your eyes to the plight of those "not seen". You will not be the same if you understand the compelling truth of this book.

Dr. Bill Fietje, President of Associated Gospel Churches of Canada and Chair of Board of the Evangelical Fellowship of Canada

Introduction

Beaming proudly, the charming Indian young lady uttered astonishing words. In impeccable, if thickly-accented English, Meena[1] blurted out, "I am the first person in my family to graduate from school." She was a Dalit girl who had joined the Good Shepherd School to gain an English-medium education, an otherwise unaffordable luxury for her destitute family.

Her father was a stonecutter. He used a sledge hammer or pick 12 hours a day, six days a week, sometimes seven, back-breaking work, to crush boulders and rocks into gravel in the nearby gravel pit. His father had done the same thing. So had his grandfather. So had his great grandfather. As a Dalit, could he expect any better? Had not his karma from a previous life predestined him to such an existence? His caste was set in stone. Poverty and scorn were his family's lot in life.

"Now I am going to college to get a degree in commerce so that I can go into the banking sector", Meena went on, beaming. For Meena's family, this was unimaginable. Their daughter was twice discriminated against. She was a Dalit, an outcaste, first of all. She was also female. Without hope in this world. Probably not in the next, either. If she was lucky, to be married off at a pre-pubescent age. Or trafficked into the sex trade by parents desperate to make ends meet and prone to pressure

---

1   Names of children are changed throughout the book to protect their anonymity. But these are real people and true stories.

from unscrupulous people preying on the uneducated and the disenfranchised. But they had given this English medium education a chance, knowing that normally only high caste and middle class families could afford to send their children to such a school in order for them to go on to university—which throughout India was mainly in English, one of the legacies of British rule. This normally private school education had been offered almost free of charge to them at a Good Shepherd School established in a nearby village. They had to contribute 50 rupees per month and the school subsidized the rest of the cost.

Meena had proven gifted in mathematics. She had slowly mastered English. Her parents were proud of her and had observed the emergence of her self-confidence and self-respect. Should she go on to high school? No one in their family line, to the best of their knowledge, had ever completed secondary school, certainly not in English! So they did something culturally unconventional and let Meena continue in the school she had come to love, a respite from the grim world she inhabited in her village the better part of each day. Now she was ready to take the next step that eventually would mean a good job instead of stonecutting. She could soon support the family. Maybe even lift them from the endless cycle of poverty they had inherited from their forefathers. The stone crusher's daughter has discovered that she is a person of great worth in her Creator's sight, in fact that she is made in the image of God.

Ironically, the way humans often treat one another is counter-intuitive to the value the God of the Bible places on them, those he has described as being made in his image. Becoming aware of the plight of India's Dalits set me on a quest in 2011 to more fully ascertain what I accepted at face value as a follower of Jesus, that the Creator God made all human beings to have value and equality by virtue of being made in his image. When

I was faced with the sobering truth that the Dalits of India, over 200,000,000 of them, had been systemically mistreated through caste for three millennia, I wondered what hope there was for them. How could such seemingly wretched beings have God's image within them? Conversely, how could millions of others consider themselves as inherently superior to the Dalits and still be made in God's image? As I thought about it, I concluded that all cultures embrace hidden values that presume humans are created unequal—demonstrated by something as simple as the acidic bullying of teens on the Internet or virtual deification that postmodern culture projects onto celebrities. Or by the appalling way women can be dehumanized within the Muslim community or freedom of religion erased without a second thought. Hopefully this book will help you rediscover the centrality of the biblical message that all human beings are made equally in God's image.

Another of my aspirations for the book is that those who think Christianity is irrelevant will crack the cover of the book—although they are not my primary audience. As well, I trust that as I delve into the richness of the truth about our innate human dignity, made as we all are in God's image, followers of Jesus will be refreshed in their souls; and non-believers will find a rationale for comprehending their own significance.

This treatise also is meant to help the church champion the cause of all people on earth being treated with justice and respect. The church has been too distracted by the consequences of the fall on humankind to major on the implications of its polar opposite truth, the infinite value and potential of human beings as image-bearers. Chapter 6 is especially for you if this is your primary interest in reading this book.

Although I lived for about six years in the 1970s in India, and have made 25 trips back there since, the Dalits' existence was hidden to me until recent years. For that reason, I suppose, I seek some kind of atonement here. I seek to shine a spotlight on a people I was blind to nor helped when I lived in India. This book is about giving a voice to the voiceless. Providing hope for the despairing. Lifting up the downtrodden to a place of equal opportunity. Restoring to all of us an awakening to the thrilling implications of why we are made in God's image.

Why should I, as a North American, presume to speak about Indian or Muslim societies? While recognizing that there are injustices and disparities to confront in my own country, such as among aboriginal peoples, which I pull no punches about in chapter 4, I take as my marching orders Proverbs 31:8-9: "Open your mouth for the mute, for the rights of all who are destitute. Open your mouth, judge righteously, defend the rights of the poor and needy."

While I hold much in Islamic, Indian and Western culture in high esteem, my global travels in 50 countries and spiritual pilgrimage as a follower of Jesus have convinced me that only the Bible accurately explains reality, earthly or ethereal. Christians have historically and in every generation been guilty of obscuring the intrinsic value of people of certain ethnicity or ethos, so I hope you do not find me self-righteous or triumphalist about what I share, since I too undoubtedly have blind spots. But these caveats do not detract from the fact that in our world people are being transformed as they learn that they are made in God's image. Some indeed believe in Jesus and are transformed even more from the inside out into a virus-scrubbed fuller version of all they were meant to be in their humanness as they take on Christlikeness. We will see the worst and the best of image-bearing among the Dalits, Muslims and postmodern Westerners.

If you are not interested so much in theology, or already have your thinking sorted out on what it means to be made in God's image, you might prefer to skip chapter 1 and delve into chapter 2. Similarly if you are interested in a particular worldview's position on this subject, you may want to jump right to that chapter.

CHAPTER 1
The Amazing Truth of Being Made in God's Image

What Distinguishes Humans from Other Animals

Observing the grace and dignity of Meena, the stonecutter's daughter, in contrast to the degradation and hopelessness of the rest of her family surely leads to the question of how a young lady like her could be transformed while living in such a demeaning life situation. The Bible offers an answer that may be akin to the unlocking of the secret of ancient languages that the Hammurabi tablets triggered. Christian scripture maintains that humankind is made in the image of God. All human beings possess the *imago Dei*. Right in the first chapter of the first book of the Bible, Genesis 1:26 captures God's lofty intentions for human beings in these words: **"Let us make mankind in our own image, in our likeness"**.[2] After God had made all of the animal and marine life to grace the planet, he finished his creative activity by fashioning human beings.

A majestic lion is an animate being, a marvelous one. But it is not a person, in spite of what people say about Cecil, the butchered lion in Zimbabwe. Its behaviour[3] is circumscribed by

---

2   Unless otherwise noted, the 2011 *New International Version* of the Bible as published by Zondervan is quoted.

3   Canadian English is used throughout—which involves a combination of British and American spellings, as here, where "behaviour" follows British spelling.

instinct and conditioning, not insight and compassion. What distinguishes us from animals and accounts for our dominance over them, in part, is the difference between being made in God's image and not being made so. On the other hand, that is not to say that all differences between animals and human beings are attributable to humans being made in God's image nor that animals are insignificant, nor that they fail to have degrees of 'intelligence'. God sees the little sparrow fall. All creatures of this earth matter. Nonetheless, this qualitative difference between humans and animals in God's ordering of creation is evident also in Genesis 2 where God parades the animals before Adam and then is fascinated to observe what he would name them. According to the poet W. H Auden, the human species is the only one where animals work, laugh and pray.[4]

Why make this seemingly self-evident point? Well, because evolutionary philosophy and Marxism-Leninism-Maoism, to name two ideologies, would not distinguish qualitatively between animals and humans. If creation does not explain apparent differences between our two species, then there should be no special rights granted to humans over animals. I have sisters-in-law who treat their cats with so much pampering that their cats might as well be humans. The cofounder of People for the Ethical Treatment of Animals was following the logic of a materialist worldview when she declared: "A rat is a pig is a dog is a boy."[5]

In John Calvin's magisterial work, *Institutes of the Christian Religion,* in his opening comments, he writes: "Nearly all the wisdom we possess, that is, true and sound wisdom, consists of two parts of knowledge of God and knowledge of ourselves.

---

4   Cited in Philp Yancey, *Finding God in Unexpected Places,* 245.
5   Cited in Ibid, 199.

But as these are connected together by many ties, it is not easy to determine which of the two precedes, and gives birth to the other."[6] In investigating how we as humans are like God, we will discover this difficulty because although God is the proper starting point, the source of all life, since we are his image-bearers, whether we look at God or ourselves, we find insights relevant to the subject of this book.

The Creation Account and God's Image

The main thing that separates humans from the rest of the animal kingdom is found in this revelation in Genesis: human beings are made in God's image (1:26-27). The first chapter of the Bible assigns the incredible status to humans of divine image-bearing.

> Then God said, "Let us make mankind in our image, in our likeness, so that they may rule over the fish in the sea and the birds in the sky, over the livestock and all the wild animals, and over all the creatures that move along the ground. So God created mankind in his image, in the image of God he created them; male and female he created them."

However, although all human beings have been made in God's image, the Scriptures are also clear that we can realize our potential as human beings only by becoming like Christ, the process which begins when we embrace Jesus as our Saviour. As we shall see, it is Jesus Christ whom we are to become like and whom we are to look at if we want to see what God has created us to be like, so to speak. Christ, in his earthly existence, it turns out, is the exact representation of the invisible God (*eikon* in Col. 1:15) and so when we gaze on Christ we see who the Father is (John 12:45; 14:9). Christ was the *prototokos* or "the firstborn among many brothers and sisters" (Rom. 8:29b), the first-born from the dead (Col. 1:18), the prototype of redeemed

---

6   Henry Beveridge (translation), 37.

Christians who, at Christ's second coming, are given their new bodies and perfected (glorified) character in fully becoming like Christ. Such an outcome is only possible because, in the first place, humans have been created in God's image.

Another way of drawing this distinction is that whereas Christ **is** the image of God (2 Cor. 4:4), we are **in,** or, made **according to**, God's image at birth quite apart from whether we have a re-birth (there is always a preposition in front of "God's image" when humans are described in relation to God's image, but not with reference to Christ who is God – cf. Gen. 1:26-27; 5:1-3).[7]

We have to be careful in ascribing content to what God's image in humankind is because it is a term found rarely Scripture and without clear definition. We might think, as many theologians have, like Augustine and Luther, that to be made in God's image has to do with our moral capabilities, our reasoning, or our creativity. But to define "image" in such ways is to deduce something that is not actually stated in Scripture. It is far better to say that all human beings are created in God's image while only some are recreated in Christ's image. In fact, as we shall postulate, the degree of education, the degree of moral uprightness or the pedigree of family has no bearing whatsoever on whether one is made in God's image: all human beings are presently, whatever their condition, fully found in God's image. The implication of this universality of our status, then, is that there is no justification for discrimination on the basis of gender, caste, race or religion when it comes to human beings' status as divine image-bearers. Whether we are found living up to what God's intentions are is an entirely different issue from whether we are created and found in his image. That latter status is a done deal for all human beings. Acknowledging

---

7   John Kilner, *Dignity and Destiny: Humanity in the Image of God*, 88-91.

this truth frees us to treat all human beings—including those very unlike us—as equals, as those deserving our respect.

Our human instinct has predictably been to judge character and form opinions about people based on outward characteristics. The Israelites chose their first king based on his physical height, leading to the statement from God himself that "people look at the outward appearance, but the Lord looks at the heart" (1 Sam. 16:7). Racial discrimination led Europeans to view Africans they kidnapped and forced into slavery as a lesser grade of human being, if that. Some were considered as God's image bearers and some not. But the thesis developed here is that all human beings have been given the same starting line in the race of life by virtue of equally being found in God's image at birth, without any slippage along the race course. Christ's death and resurrection may have broken down the barriers between Jew and Greek functionally in the Body of Christ (Eph. 2:11-22) but already they had been levelled in another and profound sense because of equally being found in God's image from birth onwards.

Living up to God's reason for creating us in his image, on the other hand, requires us to act on the knowledge that we are in a state of fallenness (rebellion against our Creator) and so we need to discover that Christ is our salvation and hope. When we believe on Jesus we begin a lifelong journey of being transformed into the image of Christ (2 Cor. 3:18). We might compare being made in God's image and being transformed into Christ's image as the difference between being drafted to play baseball by a major league baseball team and actually playing for that team. Many players get drafted while they are in high school or college but never make it to the major leagues. Being drafted by a major league team and actually reaching the major leagues as a player are related but two very different things. Both are professional baseball players. Only major leaguers realize the potential they had when drafted. Similarly, although from the outset we have been fashioned in God's image, we do not realize God's aspirations for us to become like him nor our purpose for living until we believe in Christ. Being made in God's image means that we alone of all created creatures have the capability, indeed are designed, to be in relation with our Creator in a special way, made possible through Christ.

In unveiling the story of the creation of humans, the Bible specifically reveals the role of gender on this subject: "God created mankind in his own image, in the image of God he created them; **male and female he created them** "(verse 27; cf. Gen. 5:1-2). So "man", or *Adam*, the Hebrew word used, includes "female". We'll have more to say about the gender aspect later, in chapter 3. But it is an important distinction to make here because among the ideologies discussed in this book only Christianity and postmodernism assign to the female sex the high position they actually have in the created order. At any rate, this disclosure of the significance of humankind does not mean that to be god-like is to be god. Merging the two is what Hindu thought boils down to: a Hindu would claim that, like a spider weaves the spider-web from its own spittle so that the web is really an extension of the spider, we humans only need to look within themselves to find the reality of our oneness with ultimate being, that we are indeed the centre of the universe. The Bible, on the other hand, teaches that the Creator and the created are entirely separate. The Creator God fashioned us out of nothing. God was self-sufficient and complete before we were "made in his image". He did not need to create us. We did not always exist within him. We were created out of nothing and so to be made in the image of God, if we did not realize it already, does not mean that we are divine, coming out of his essence and being. We are part of the animal kingdom biologically but unique because we are made in God's image. We should not, then, be Deepak Chopra-like, believing in our own divinity.

Although we are not divine, it is not wrong to think that in looking at God's nature as revealed in Scripture, and particularly in the person of Christ, we cannot understand something of what God created us to be like. That is, in looking at God's character and acts in history we understand something of what it means to be made in the image of God. J. I. Packer, considered by many to be the greatest evangelical theologian in the English-speaking world of the 20th century, described the Godward glance this way:

> The biblical way to think of God is, not indeed as a man, but as an analogy of man—in other words, as having in him, alongside that which transcends us, that which corresponds to everything in us that is properly human. The God who is said to dwell in darkness too thick to penetrate or in light too bright to look on is also said to hear, see, smell, perceive, think, touch, and speak. In other words he is pictured in Scripture as if he were man. Why? Not to teach us that God is manlike, but rather to convince us that man is godlike.[8]

The most obvious way to understand *tselem* in Hebrew in Genesis 1, translated as "image" there, is that it connotes approximation or resemblance. When we say, he is the spitting image of his mother, we are not saying that the son corresponds precisely to his mother. We mean that there is a family resemblance. Some people say that my son is obviously my wife's son, but he has blue eyes while she has green (and I have brown). Nevertheless the similarities are unmistakable.

The word "image" is actually a little stronger in the text of Genesis 1:26-27. This early biblical disclosure about the special uniqueness of humankind is not implying that we are God. But there is elasticity in how the word and its NT equivalent, *eikon*, are used (*eikon* is also the Greek word used in the Septuagint, the Greek translation of the OT, to translate the Hebrew word *tselem* here). Whereas "image" refers to Christ in the NT, as

---

8   *Christianity: The True Humanism*, 142-143.

in Colossians 1:15, there being instructed that "the Son is the image of the invisible God", from the immediate context we can see that really what is meant is that Christ is exactly the same as the Father in essence, for we read in verse 19 that "God was pleased to have all his fullness dwell in him {the Son]." 2 Corinthians 4:4 as well specifically calls Christ "the image [*eikon*] of God". The theologian Philip Hughes captures the nuanced range of meanings in this term when he comments: "In common usage, the noun 'image' frequently signifies no more than a copy of or reflection which is something other than the reality it represents, such as the head of a ruler imprinted on a coin—as in Luke 20:24, when Jesus asks concerning a denarius, 'Whose image does it bear?' It however may stand for the reality, the real substance as distinct from a copy or an insubstantial shadow."[9] In Genesis 1, the term as it relates to humans means "approximation" whereas in Colossians 1, with reference to Christ, it means "the same as".

What we might miss in the text, thinking that verses 26 and 27 of Genesis 1 communicate somewhat different things, is that the passage is an excellent example of Hebrew parallelism. Verse 27 is actually repeating the same thing as verse 26 but in slightly different words so that the cumulative effect is emphasis. Moreover, the text in verse 26 uses two different words to describe humans: "image" translated as *tselem*, and "likeness" translated as *demuth*.

We have the same sort of literary device in English. To highlight the humour behind our friend's clumsiness, we might say in one sentence that she had a pratfall. Then in the next, while describing her embarrassment, we might add "she fell flat on her face" so as to accentuate our observation. We describe the same event using different words. All this to say that there

---

9   *The True Image: The Origin and Destiny of Man in Christ*, 24.

is something distinctive and special in God's creation about humankind in comparison to the rest of the created order and we dare not miss this distinction in the Genesis account. It is strongly emphasized in the text. Whatever it means to be made in God's image, it is something extraordinary and lofty.

Are Human Rights Self-Evident?

As we drill down, looking at what the Bible explicates about humankind and its Creator, the dignity, equality and rights of all human beings as understood by the world *writ large*, now pretty well universally affirmed, are not exactly self-evident. It is only through the self-revelation of the Creator God, in the Bible, that what many people and societies observe to be true experientially and believe in uncritically can be accepted *prima facie*. Biblical revelation distinguishes humanity from all other forms of creation by stating that humans are made in God's image, unlike anything else created, thus granting them an elevated status within the created order.

Differences in intelligence, education, ethnicity, colour, physical well-being, or the myriad of things that make up the diversity of the human race do not detract from our common heritage of being equally special people because of our exalted status with our Creator by virtue of being those found in his image. Although frequently the image of God is treated as being marred, lost, or damaged by the 'Fall', the Bible nowhere actually states that sin has had any impact on our created status as image-bearers.[10]

---

10   This is a very important point made in John Kilner, *Dignity and Destiny*. His premise is that Genesis 3 (where the fall is described in detail) is about human beings, not their status as divine image-bearers, which is the thrust of Genesis 1. He then goes on to make the point that when in Genesis 5 it declares that God created Adam in his image there in verse 1, the text goes on to say that Adam had a son, Seth, who was in Adam's "image". This context for the use of "image" verifies that the "image" was not lost after the fall, it seems to me (pp. 135-37). We will defend this viewpoint in other ways, too.

Sin has not marred or eradicated God's image; it has marred humans. God is unchangeable in the sense of his perfection in terms of who he is, with all his unmatchable attributes, whereas humans are not: "all have sinned and fall short of the glory of God" (Rom. 3:23).

An example of where appearances can be misunderstood, as they often are when thinking about fallen humanity in relation to God's image, would be in evaluating someone's state when suffering from ALS (Lou Gehrig's disease). A family friend died recently of ALS. As he deteriorated, and I visited him from time to time, I could see that he had reached the stage where he no longer seemed to be there consciously. He could only communicate by blinking his eyes in response to questions. Looking at him in what appeared to be an almost vegetative state, I felt that the real man was no longer with us, that only the shell of the man was alive. However, in spite of his physical inertia and unresponsiveness, the same person was there, trapped as he was in a diseased body. Similarly while it appears that human beings have lost God's image in them because of their fallenness and sinfulness, they have not. If all human beings are thus created equal because they are divine image bearers, then fundamental human rights as enshrined in the United Nations' charter are universal, and therefore owed to every human being.

A Dose of Humility Is Warranted

This book unabashedly asserts that the Christian view of what it means to be human, taking the Bible as the basis for our authority, is true, and if so, the only fully valid description of humanness.[11]

---

11 I do not mean by that statement, of course, that we should expect the Bible to be a scientific textbook. What we need to know from God about our "humanness" in the context of biblical revelation is not biological detail. This is as we should expect since God is personal and humans are personal and so he communicates to us in ways that we need understand, according to the context.

Notwithstanding that claim and this book's defense of it, Christians have a lot to be humble about. It is important that I state this principle because I am critiquing other worldviews and religions as an outsider. Mahatma Gandhi is reputed to have asserted that he loved and believed in Jesus but he could never become a Christian because he did not see enough Christians who were like Jesus. Even though Christians claim to know that all human beings are equal in God's sight and try to live out that truth, we can be the most spiteful, mean-spirited and discriminatory of people. We need to acknowledge that we do not always practice what we preach. History is strewn with human wreckage caused by the Church in spite of its claim to be all about love. However, just because Christians killed Muslims in the Crusades or engaged in manic witch-hunting in the Middle Ages does not invalidate the treasuring of human life the way the Bible teaches or the way most practicing Christians live out that truth compassionately day by day. Human nature being what it is, we are always trying to throw out the baby with the dirty bath water. We specialize in straining gnats and swallowing camels.

Of all people, those who have been touched by God's saving grace through Christ should be the most charitable to people **not** like us. Because we know that all human beings are made in God's image, Christians should be setting the pace in championing human rights and justice for the poor or marginalized of this world. Furthermore, as recipients of God's undeserved forgiveness, we know that we are fallen creatures, like all other human beings, and that, like the Korean proverb goes, "Pat any person and dust will fly". We may be made righteous by God's grace but we are still sinners and therefore we have no cause to be self-righteous around people who may have a different set of moral values than we do. Sin has damaged human beings but not God's image in them.

Moreover, Christians would do well to recognize where we have common ground with people of other faiths—or of no faith. For example, because of our high view of human life Christians form a natural alliance with Muslims and religious Jews when it comes to a pro-life stance. Similarly, post-Christian and postmodern agnostics or atheists yearn for meaningful community—and Christians identify with them in that quest. That quest partially explains the success of social media. It is just that ours is found in the church and theirs in the pub or the fitness club. Indians, whether caste-bound or otherwise, esteem the family and the elderly; Christians should admire these core values of Asian culture. Philip Yancey puts it well: "Communicating faith to skeptics usually works best when it emphasizes how we are alike, not how we are different. I am learning to resist the tendency to see others as opponents or targets and instead look for common ground, places where we can stand together".[12]

This tolerant attitude is engendered in the concept which the Bible calls *oikoumene*.[13] The usual translation for it into English is "world" but that is such an ambiguous word that we might prefer something like "universal family". It appears 14 times in the NT, one relevant occurrence for our purpose here being in Acts 17:31: "... for he [God] has set a day when he will judge the *world* with justice by the man [Christ] whom he has appointed ..." (italics mine to identify where *oikoumene* is found in the text). The word connotes the idea of "the brotherhood of humankind" so to speak. We are all in the gene pool of Adam and Eve. We all are fallen human beings too (Ps. 14:1-3; Rom. 3:23). Someone has said that Christians are not perfect, only forgiven. Christians have no basis for being self-

---

12 Philip Yancey, *Vanishing Grace: What Ever Happened to the Good News?* 55.
13 Chapter 4 on postmodern culture will devote a section to the difference between 'tolerance' and 'persuasion'.

righteous; God's image resides in all of us in the human race. In a very real sense, we are all brothers and sisters of one another (distinguishing though between that use of biological kinship and that of the spiritual family of God, which is on the basis of faith in Christ – Eph. 2:18-19; John 1:12). Let me be clear, which will be expanded on later, non-Christians are created in God's image just as much as Christians are.[14] Where we differ is that upon regeneration by the Holy Spirit at the time of entrusting our life to Christ, we begin the slow but certain journey of being transformed into the image of Christ.[15] And being transformed into the family likeness exhibited by the God-man, Christ, is why God created all human beings in his image.

Implicit in this passage in Acts 17 where it talks about the universal human family, it is worth noting, is the principle that diversity among humans does not imply a hierarchy of human worth for earlier in the same speech in which the statement in verse 31 is found, Paul, the speaker, declares that "from one man he [God] made all the nations, that they should inhabit the whole earth" (v. 26). We all have the same origin. Furthermore, as we shall see, the possibility of diversity and sameness in two different human beings should not surprise us because that dynamic is rooted in the very being of God who is both one (Deut. 6:4) and three-in-one (Matt. 28:19), nor should it necessarily lead to a hierarchy of worth due to the difference.

The One God of the Bible is a Three-Person God

At the heart of the nature of the one God who created the universe is not a monad, but three distinct Persons who together, and inseparably, are as one essence God: God the Father, God the Son and God the Holy Spirit. Historically, Christians have

---

14   This position is well developed theologically in John F. Kilner, *Dignity and Destiny*.

15   This theme will be picked up again in chapter 5 in a fuller way.

given this Three-In-One God the title of "Trinity" or "Triune God". The Bible speaks of the love between the Father, Son and Holy Spirit as between co-equals and yet who inseparably are of one essence. Thus Jesus, in speaking to his disciples of the love he had for the Father and the Father had for him, could say that "I am in the Father and the Father is in me" (John 14:11). Similarly, in John 10:30 Jesus declares that "I and the Father are one". Jesus is not saying here that he and the Father are one person but that they are one nature. How do we know that? Well, the Greek word translated as "one" is not *eis,* which is the masculine of "one", but *en,* which is the neuter form and therefore means "are of one essence or nature".[16]

Wait a minute. Can something be one entity and at the same time more than one? Certainly Muslims think not as they seek to defend the Oneness of God. There are many imperfect analogies in nature—such as the sun existing as light, energy and heat. Or in speaking of eating a fried egg for breakfast, as I routinely cook for myself Saturday mornings, I do not expect my wife to assume when I tell her "I had my usual fried egg this morning" that I meant that I ate the egg shell along with the egg white and egg yolk. But we think of all parts of an egg and of its individual parts as being an egg. Yet these are imperfect examples because, for example, the first illustration of the sun implies that there are three functions of the one sun, whereas reducing the Trinity to three functions is to do injustice to the three distinct persons in the godhead. This approach gives rise to the heresy of modalism.[17]

The Bible itself understands oneness in different ways, too. There are nine different Hebrew words that refer to "oneness". For example, *echad* is used in Genesis 3:22 to convey the idea

---

16   Robert Morey, *The Trinity: Evidences and Issues,* 445.
17   Alister McGrath, *Christian Theology: An Introduction,* 256-7.

that Adam and Eve became one with God in a new way but in so doing it did not mean that they lost their individual personhood, swallowed up by God.[18] That use of "one" means a compound oneness. This word for "oneness" is used repeatedly with regard to God—such as in the famous Shema in Deuteronomy 6:4: ""Hear, O Israel: The Lord your God is *one*".

With reference to "one" meaning absolute singularity, *yachid*, the Old Testament (OT) Hebrew word for that concept, is never used to describe God. The word is translated as "solitary" in Psalm 68:6 in the *Authorized Version*; "God setteth the solitary in families" and from the sentence itself we see how oneness is to be understood. Surely this discriminating use of various Hebrew words for "one" in the original text lays out theologically the groundwork for the Trinitarian understanding of the one God.

We will cite one other example of plurality in the context of oneness in the very words of Scripture. Right in the first verse of the Bible the plural form of *El*, *Elohim*, is used to introduce and name the Creator and One God. It is the most common word for "God" in the OT, used hundreds of times. While some scholars have tried to dismiss the use of *Elohim* for "God" by arguing that its presence, as in Genesis 1:26 (Then God said, "Let **us** make man in **our** image"), is an example of the royal we in play. However, there apparently was no use of the plurality of majesty during biblical times in the Hebrew language.[19]

So we return to the idea of personhood in describing the one God. Since God is a plurality-in-unity, God is personal in his essence. As Hughes puts it: "To be personal, otherness must be present together with oneness, the one must be confronted and must interact with another, for personhood is a reality only

---

18   Robert Morey, *The Trinity: Evidences and Issues*, 88.
19   Ibid, 95-6.

with the sphere of person-to-person relationship. To be solitary is to lack identity."[20]

The Persons of the Godhead are relational with each other and always present when the other one is: "God was in Christ reconciling the world to himself" (2 Corinthians 5:18). You could say that the God who exists is communal. To have authentic community you have to have more than one person and you have to have a desire to be one in the sense of togetherness. Since God is Love (1 John 4:8)[21], of course then we should not be baffled to find that unfathomable depth of love and commitment to community within the godhead.

C. S. Lewis grapples with the idea of the one-and-yet-more-than-one God by comparing the idea of the Trinity to a cube:

> On the divine level you still find personalities; but up there you find them combined in new ways which we, who don't live on that level, can't imagine. In God's dimension, so to speak, you find a being who is three Persons while remaining one Being, just as a cube is six squares while remaining one cube. Of course, we can't fully conceive a being like that: just as, if we were so made that we perceived only two dimensions in space we could never properly imagine a cube. But we can get a faint notion of it.[22]

Should it not make sense, if we look at the nature of God by looking at our human selves and working back to God, that we can see what is unique about us in comparison to the rest of the animal kingdom? To the extent that the copy resembles the original, we come to see God more clearly and what is magnificent about being human. Although this is a somewhat anthropological approach to talking about God, and does not do justice to the unique way in which the unity of God transcends

20 *The True Image*, 5.
21 But the Bible does not teach that 'love' is 'god'.
22 *Beyond Personality*, 16.

our notion of personhood vis-à-vis community, Scripture itself is our test when it talks about God's nature in such a way that it squares with an extrapolation from our own nature. Without seeking to defend this premise, one thing that distinguishes us from the rest of the animal world is our self-consciousness. That is, we are aware of ourselves in counter-distinction from 'the other', other 'persons'. We are created to be in community. We communicate with others. We love and hate. We are personal beings. This drive within us to know God personally is a passion which does not escape Hindus, who through a devotional, *Bhakti*-style worship of *avatars* like Krishna or Ram, or *Sufis* (mystical Muslims), seek for a solution to what otherwise are rather impersonal religions. Ravi Zacharias, noted Christian apologist, observes the substantive difference between the personal God of the Bible and that of other major world religions when he comments: "Even atheistic religions like Buddhism and pantheistic religions like Hinduism, though they deny a personal, absolute God, still smuggle in ways of worship in which a personal being is addressed, only because the isolation within drives the self to a transcendent personal other."[23] No man is an island unto himself, as John Donne famously observed.

What Is Personhood?

It is relatively easy to distinguish between 'inanimate' and 'animate' objects. A 'stone' is 'inanimate' and a 'stonecutter' is animate. One has self-consciousness, the other does not. Moving on, what's the different between an animate 'dog' and an animate 'human being'? We are more than instinctual and conditioned bulls looking for the cow in heat with which we can mate or the dog that looks intently up at its master while

---

23 *Jesus among Other Gods: The Absolute Claims of the Christian Message*, 92.

waiting to be given that treat for fetching the slippers. We are not simply a set of biological responses.

Or to put it another way, why should Kumar, one of the leaders of Dalit Freedom Network's partner in India, which started the Good Shepherd Schools, as a child be so dismayed when his cricket opponent called him a 'dirty Dalit dog' after an encounter on the pitch? Let me explain. As a young teenager, Kumar enjoyed playing cricket in his village in Karnataka State, like any Indian boy. It united villagers across caste and creed—like Bono does globally with his music. But one day, he accidentally touched a player from the other team who was a high caste lad. In anger, the offended boy lashed out at Kumar with the epithet that he was a 'dog'. Angered, Kumar wacked the boy with his cricket bat.

Kumar half-believed he was sub-human because his mother told him that such was the condition of the Dalits in the village. "We are really dogs", she lamented. The question is: why should Kumar have been offended if he unconsciously did not know he was more than a dog? The theme of this book really revolves around the idea that Kumar innately knew something of his unique value because, in fact, like all human beings, he was made in the image of God and therefore knew that he was somehow different than the rest of the created order. That difference only needed to be awakened like when a mother bear realizing something moved too close to her young bear cubs springs into protective action. Kumar was a person who was conscious of himself in relation to other human beings and as distinct from those others.

That story is not finished. The high caste boy went home to parents who were enraged at a Dalit boy's presumptuousness to touch their son. They rallied other high caste families in the village and a mob descended on Kumar's home. An ultimatum was given to Kumar's family. They were forced to flee the village, abandoning their home, within 24 hours.

Some years later, his brother, Chelladurai, came home from his wanderings, and announced proudly to Kumar that he had found joy and purpose in life by becoming a follower of Jesus. He had discovered, he went on to say, that God had created him with dignity and value.

"How is that possible?" Kumar blurted out.

Turning to the first chapter in the Bible, Chelladurai pointed out that the Christian book stated that all human beings were made in God's image, not just high caste people. Amazed, Kumar asked Chelladurai to take him to the people who had told him this story and so remarkably changed his demeanor and values. Thus began a journey that transformed Kumar's life and led him in 2012 to tell his story in impeccable English to a spellbound audience in Toronto. Kumar had risen to prominence in Indian Christian circles, managing the All India Christian Council, appearing before the House of Lords in the UK and the United Nations, among other things, in the cause of helping to free the Dalits socially. He had come to realize that he as a person was made in God's image and had been transformed through Christ.

The root of this concept of personhood in Christian history is attributed to Tertullian who posited that a person is a being who thinks and acts—developing the train of thought found in the original Latin word, *persona*, used to describe the masks (personas) worn in Roman theatres to indicate the role actors were playing in dramas.[24] Personhood came to be understood as the individuality of a human being, in relation to others through communication and behavior with them. It involved intelligence, emotion, volition and awareness of the 'other'.

---

24   Alister McGrath, *Christian Theology: An Introduction,* 209.

That said, "person" is in New Testament (NT) Greek found as the word *prosopon* and its cognates (e.g. "God accepteth no man's person – Gal. 2:6 *Authorized Version*); such a word only was seen to make sense as describing distinct identity if done so in relationship to another. Today personhood has evolved in usage to refer to the lone individual, not in reference to others. The autonomous person is not reflective of the Godhead of self-giving love between the Persons of the Godhead, though.

Do you see where I am headed with this line of thinking? While individuality does not require social relationships, "personality relates to the part played by an individual in a web of relationships, by which that person is perceived to be distinctive by others."[25] We use the word "person" to refer to somebody in counter-distinction to but related to another human being; we use "individual" as a stand-alone word to describe a separate human being. In many cultures, to this day, the individual does not take her frame of reference in terms of self-consciousness apart from her web of human relationships, starting with immediate family, then extended family, then community, city or village, etc. Westerners have made too much out of their individuality.

When a Christian makes the seemingly ridiculous and scandalous claim, as perceived by non-believers in the West and by Muslims, as the case may be, that she knows God personally, she is merely saying that she can have a connection with her Creator which is analogous to what we have with another human being. She is saying that she has a personal relationship with God in some same way that she does with her brother. She talks to him and he communicates with her. They can have rational interaction about which is the best shampoo to use for their inherited dry scalp. They argue at times but they love one

---

25   Ibid.

another to the point of being willing to die for each other. What she is really saying is that because she is made in God's image she can have a person-to-Person connection.

Indeed, our personhood is related to our being made in God's image since it is only a human being that we find the Creator God speaking to out of all the created beings in the creation account (Gen. 2 and 3, with a few notable exceptions like to Balaam's ass!) with the expectation that the human person will communicate back in kind. Because humankind is made in God's image, we are persons. And we have the capacity to know God. We have been programed differently than the rest of creation.

God Is a Person but also a Spirit

When Jesus encounters the Samaritan woman by the well (John 4), he reveals something profound about the nature of God. Although as the second person of the Trinity, the Son of God, taking on human existence, thus becoming the only genuine God-Man, to be explored later as it relates to other faiths, and having a human form, he drops the bomb, "God is spirit" (verse 24; cf. 1 Tim. 6:16).[26]

Now we tend to think of spirits as being less than personal. Like zombies. Ghosts. But, not in this context. Here 'spirit' means that God the Father has no body but that does not make God any less a person. Flesh and bones a spirit does not have (Luke 24:39) but, in the context of Jesus' comment, the word *pneuma* (spirit) appears first in the sentence, grammatically then as a

---

26 When the second person of the Trinity came to earth and became a human being through Mary, he did not forsake his divinity. Orthodox Christian theology understands the Lord Jesus Christ to have been fully human and fully divine while on earth. Furthermore, after his death, resurrection and ascension to heaven, we understand, from numerous Scriptures, that he continues as the second person of the trinity but now in heaven in human form. This aspect of Christology will be considered more fully in Chapter 5.

substantive; it describes God's essential being and not just as an attribute. Therefore we are to assume that Christ was making reference to the personhood of God as much as he was to a non-physical entity. Why is the God who is spirit seeking true worshipers if he is just an impersonal force when our spirit seeks connection with the divine spirit?

You regularly hear Christians speaking about knowing God personally and talking to him. I make that claim and say it partially describes my experience, not a cultural Americanism which some may think errs on the side of over-familiarity with the divine. If God is personal, albeit so great in comparison to me that the Bible speaks of the transcendence of God, it should also be true that he is immanent. The former refers to his other-worldliness and his infiniteness compared to our finiteness. The latter refers to his active engagement with us and our world, not only in carrying out his purposes in history but in intimate interaction with us who know him individually, as one Person to another person. We have known his intervention in our lives, sometimes in answer to specific prayers we make and so we believe he is there and he is not silent. For us to speak of knowing him presupposes that we have responded to him as we would any other person. We open ourselves up to that person. We communicate with him or her, whether by texting or face-to-face or however; on the emotional, cognitive, physical and verbal levels.

The infiniteness and yet personhood of God is difficult enough for Christians to grasp. For the Hindu, though, this divine dynamic is virtually impossible to fathom because personhood implies differentiation, which implies limitation.[27] We will consider pantheistic worldviews in chapter 2.

---

27 Nancy Pearcey, *Total Truth: Liberating Christianity from its Cultural Captivity*, 147-148.

When one responds to God in the way the Bible teaches us to, first accepting that we have to deal with the sin barrier, which has been removed by Jesus' sacrificial death on the cross, the promises of God are fulfilled as his Holy Spirit comes and resides inside of us as we take that step of faith in Christ. It is that quickening by the Spirit, which in theological language is called 'regeneration', which enables us to sense God's nearness, and gives us assurance that God is our Father and that we have access to his presence as we pray and praise. As Scripture indicates: "The Spirit you received brought about your adoption to sonship. And by him we cry, "Abba [Daddy], Father!" The Spirit himself testifies with our spirit that we are God's children" (Rom. 8:15b, 16). It is then that we know the Personhood of God and that we have discovered our purpose as human beings to commune with our Creator in a love relationship that unlocks our full humanity, much as turning the key on a music box reveals that the music box is more than an ornament.

While we are dealing with 'God' and 'spirit', let us make an aside here that the Holy Spirit is not just an impersonal force, as Christians, and others, have struggled to resolve. The Holy Spirit is fully divine and fully personal: He is the third member of the godhead. Here are a number of Scriptural references that defend His personhood:

- The Holy Spirit is "grieved" when we sin (Isa. 63:10)
- The "fellowship of the Holy Spirit" as a Trinitarian benediction also implies personhood (2 Cor. 13:14)
- The Holy Spirit talks (Mark 13:11)
- The Holy Spirit hears (John 16:13)
- The Holy Spirit teaches (John 15:26)
- The Holy Spirit comforts (John 16:14)
- The Holy Spirit convicts (John 16:8)
- The Holy Spirit witnesses (Acts 5:32)

- The Holy Spirit intercedes (Rom. 8:26)
- The Holy Spirit guides (John 16:13)
- The Holy Spirit "searches all things" (1 Cor. 2:10)
- The Holy Spirit wills (1 Cor. 12:11)
- Personal pronouns are used with reference to the Holy Spirit (John 15:26)

There is much more to say on this subject of God's personhood (and the Holy Spirit) but we will put that aside for now, and pick it up on in Chapter 5 on Jesus as the One who humans are to become like in order to express our proper humanity. The only other thing we will add at this juncture is that we agree with this assessment as it relates to God's gender (or lack thereof): "The use of masculine personal pronouns for God conveys the connotation of God's personal qualities and secondarily any distinctive functional responsibilities males may have."[28] At the same time, in Scripture we definitely see feminine qualities ascribed to God: "Jerusalem, Jerusalem, you who kill the prophets and stone those sent to you, how often I have longed to gather your children together, as a hen gathers her chicks under her wings, and you were not willing" (Matt. 23:37; cf. Isa. 49:15; 66:13).

Are Only Christians Found in God's Image?

To repeat, although Christians may feel that they are found expressing what it means to be made in God's image more than the general population, the Bible clearly states that all human beings are made with the divine image intact. Christians are not more in God's image than other human beings are. It is the special status placed on humankind *writ large* that explains why capital punishment was required in the OT when murder

---

28 Gordon Lewis, "Attributes of God" in Walter Elwell (Ed). *Evangelical Dictionary of Theology*, 451-452.

occurred: "Whoever sheds human blood, by humans shall their blood be shed; for in the image of God has God made mankind" (Gen. 9:6). Flipping over to the NT, we read the same thing about all human beings having the divine stamp upon them. James 3:9 makes this clear: "With the tongue we praise our Lord and Father, and with it we curse human beings who have been made in God's likeness." Commenting on this matter of cursing people, one scholar observes: "It is wrong [to curse] because it tears down people who are made in the image of God. People themselves—not anything in particular about them—are connected with God's image and so, in a special way, with God. There is no suggestion that some attribute in people is at issue here."[29] In other words, there is no hierarchy of human worth that determines whether one is found in God's image or not. It is not only good, educated or powerful people who should be talked to respectfully. Or Christians only. No apartheid was introduced into creation—except a benign one between humans and the rest of the created order on earth (Ps. 8).

What is confusing, as we have just considered, but which is worth repeating, is the impact of what Christians refer to as "the Fall". Scripture interprets the Fall in ways that we know only too well from experience, that humankind is blemished by sin as surely as malware corrupts a computer. Over the centuries, the misunderstanding has not been overcome easily whereby some Christians conclude that only redeemed humans (those regenerated by the Holy Spirit through believing on Christ – Titus 3:3-5) retain or regain this lost image. My grandparents had this old bedroom chest of drawers with a mirror attached to the top so you could look at yourself while you were dressing. Unfortunately the silver backing had somehow worn away and so you could only see yourself fuzzily in the mirror. The

---

29   John Kilner, *Dignity and Destiny,* 95.

Fall has done that to us spiritually, or, to use another analogy, it has ravaged our soul and behaviour much as you see the facial features of an alcoholic negatively impacted, to change the analogy. The face still appears in my grandparents' mirror. But the full beauty of that humanity will never be seen in this life although significantly transformed by the re-creation those who have faith in Christ begin to experience (2 Cor. 5:9). Although a crude example, we could compare Christ and the regenerating power of the Holy Spirit to the role of the silver behind the glass in the mirror. Once Christ is believed on and the Holy Spirit enters us, it is like the silver lining being replaced. The mirror then reflects our true image (of course we know from experience and from Scripture that the renewing happens slowly so the analogy is imperfect). While the Fall deflected us from reflecting God's image, Christ actually and in intention always reflected God's image and that is why Christians are to reflect Christ's image. We have God's image now but will not fully reflect Christ's image, God's purpose in investing us with his image, until we reach heaven (sanctification gives way to glorification). In the meantime, it is quite another thing to say that those who are not believers in Christ do not possess the image of God. That theological stance is a fallacy.

In understanding that all human life is to be treasured, we find justification, for instance, in the work of a Jean Vanier. He is a Canadian Roman Catholic priest who founded L'Arche in the 1960s to succor and support mentally challenged people. Speaking of his love for these people, Vanier maintains, "They are beautiful people, people of the heart. It is great to be together." Or we think of Mother Teresa who cradled dying beggars from the streets of Calcutta. Or of my son working with a 35 year-old man who stopped developing mentally and emotionally at the age of 16 because he was joy-riding and fell off a car he was riding on the roof of onto his head, almost dying. Why shouldn't such people be treated with dignity? After all they are as fully in God's image as the best of the world's physical and mental specimens.

People are equal the way pennies are equal, philosophized G. K. Chesterton. Some pennies are worn, others freshly minted. Some pennies are scratched, others look unused, with many different dates on them. But all are equal in value because all bear the image of the sovereign ruler. So too are humans who although as different as there are kinds of snowflakes, are equal in value because bearing the image of God.[30]

Sundeep's Story

Graduating from Amedupur Good Shepherd School in India in 2015, Sundeep is going to the local college to pursue a degree in electrical engineering. Given his misery as a child, you would not recognize him today. His mother was widowed while Sundeep was still a baby. With no family support and shunned in her village as a Dalit, it was a tough row to hoe for Sundeep's mother. She had no land, no money, and no education. Then she met one of the teachers at the Good Shepherd School just started in a nearby village. There she got a job which really saved her family from destitution. 14 years later, her son, now having gone his whole school life to this English-medium school, is preparing for higher education. Sundeep exclaims, "If it was not for this school I would be a poor agricultural worker today." In the hour of moral classes he took weekly in addition to his regular studies, he learned that the God who made him created him in his image. Sundeep has been transformed by his education and by the knowledge that he has special value in God's sight and is not inferior to other human beings. If his

---

30 Cited in Vinoth Ramachandra, *Subverting Global Myths: Theology and the Public Issues Shaping our World*, 104.

potential had not been perceived through realizing he was created in the image of God he would have resigned himself to a debased existence.

Untouchability in the New Testament

As the post-resurrection church began to form, the NT reveals that there was a tension between Jewish Christians and Gentile believers. The Jewish church questioned whether the message of salvation through Christ was really for non-Jews, and if it was not, then surely Gentile believers must adopt Jewish customs and mores, they argued, such as circumcision and eating kosher food. Today we might dismiss such a conflict as redundant. Of course, we maintain, the Gospel is for everybody; there should be no racial discrimination in the church. Christ is a universal Saviour.

Few people in Bramalea Baptist Church in the Greater Toronto Area, my home church, give a second thought to the fact that over 60 nationalities are represented amongst its 1,300 attenders—and as far as I know there is nary a Jewish-Canadian believer in their midst. Furthermore, informed Bramalea members are aware that there are followers of Jesus in every nation on earth. Even before his death, they know, Jesus surveyed the temple in Jerusalem and called it the house of prayer for all nations. So of course racial discrimination is not acceptable, the way the average Christian thinks.

Yet, the book of the NT narrating the history of the early church, Acts, devotes almost two of its 28 chapters to this very issue as it tells the story of Peter's unusual vision. You see, Jews felt that because the OT scriptures were revealed to the Jews, the prophets being given to them, and Jesus himself being born into a Jewish family in Palestine, then any Gentile person of faith should adopt Jewish culture and OT practices (Rom.

2:12-3:2). At the epicenter of this lengthy narrative is a bold statement that explains why Peter had the vision he did: "God shows no partiality" (10:34). There is no untouchability in God's sight might be another way of phrasing the impartiality of God's character. Jew and Gentile alike can be part of his forever family.

However, the idea of a hierarchy of human value has long held an insidious grip on our self-understanding. Aristotle concluded that some people are born to be slaves. He especially contended that the degree of rationality set one person above or below the next.[31] Throughout history, the seesawing between treating all humans as equal versus treating them as unequal has been like the waves going in and out on the seashore. The Ku Klux Clan. Martin Luther King and the Civil Rights Movement. Adolph Hitler and the Nazis. Nelson Mandela and the breakup of apartheid. Both ends of the continuum have had their champions. The biblical worldview comes down decisively on the side of the sacredness and intrinsic value of all human beings. There is no justification theologically for untouchability. There is no justification for a doctrine of inherent inequality among humankind.

The Bible has a habit of leveling many distinctions and judgments we humans tend to mount against each other. James 1:9-11 pricks the balloon of self-importance in exhorting: "Believers in humble circumstances ought to take pride in their high position. But the rich should take pride in their humiliation—since they will pass away like a wild flower. For the sun rises with scorching heat and withers the plant; its blossom falls, and its beauty is destroyed. In the same way the rich will fade away even while they go about their business."

---

31 Aristotle's *Politics* is his classical treatise on how human being should be treated in society.

Seeking to translate this head knowledge about equality and its corollary, justice, into heart knowledge, James, a little later on, condemns rich church members who hold back wages from their employees (5:1-6). Impartiality is engendered also in terms of where people should be allowed to sit in church (2:1-7). The way attendees are dressed should not influence where they are permitted to sit. Rich believers should not expect favoritism over the poor in their midst. Such equal treatment of human beings stems from our being made in God's image without exception.

Creativity and the Image of God

There is a difference between God's creativity and ours. My mother was very artistic. One of her skills was making pottery in her own kiln and painting the sides of her creations as part of the process. But she used existing clay and worked from photos or artwork she had seen in some antique shop or arts and crafts shows. Christians accept that God created the universe out of nothing whereas human beings only create from existing substances or ideas. This higher power of creativity in God whereby he creates things *ex nihilo* is taught in such passages as Hebrews 11:3, Psalm 148:5 and Romans 4:17. While there is nothing conclusive that points to creativity being one of the distinguishing marks of persons being God's image-bearers, it is something all human beings have in common which distinguishes us from other creatures.[32] While spiders spin complex webs, those webs pale beside the beautiful and intricate architecture of the Taj Mahal. Furthermore, 'creativity' in the animal world is a function of instinct whereas humans create spontaneously, such as Picasso in his paintings. It is reputed that when the world-

---

32 Philip Yancey and Paul Brand, *Fearfully and Wonderfully Made,* is an excellent book contrasting God's amazing and unmatchable creativity and ours as humans.

class cellist Yo-Yo Ma visited a dying Steve Jobs and played Bach for him, Jobs tearfully said: "Your playing is the best argument I've ever heard for the existence of God, because I don't really believe a human alone could do this."[33]

Who has not felt a chill go down their spine in the presence of some great artistic feat? When I was a teenager, growing up in an evangelical Christian home, and rebelling against my spiritual underpinnings, my mother dragged me to a performance of the Messiah during the Christmas season. As I viewed the London (Ontario) Symphony Orchestra play and the mass choir sing the stirring composition of Handel, I felt the presence of God and knew at that moment that Christ really was the Messiah. Don't ask me to explain it or to make sense of it theologically. But I suspect it had something to do with humans being able to create great things because of being made in God's image, and that truth, made real in space and time, reflected back to who God is. And how he had created us. We will reflect further on the attributes of God and how that may relate to his likeness in humans throughout this book.

The Creativity of Love

Just as creativity is spontaneous and unforced, so is love. It is evident both in the OT and the NT that the God who created us desires a love relationship with human beings. That is why he created us in his image. The quality of our relationship does not determine our degree of being made in God's image. Just as our degree of creativity does not determine how much of God's image we have. An active love relationship has to do with our re-creation in Christ. Love cannot be forced. God's love, as manifested in Scripture, in Christ, and in reflection on the example of the triune God, is an unselfish love, unforced, not

---

33   Cited in Yancey, *Vanishing Grace*, 141.

the by-product of a power play, seeking instead to give to the other as much as to receive, or even without the expectation of getting something back. Love emanates from God to the creature made in his image for the creature's sake not only for the pleasure our loving response brings to God. As Volf expresses it, "God loves, and seeks to creatively transform an ungodly person into a godly one. God loves, and in loving God brings forth from the unlovable creature the beloved object of God's delight."[34]

Being made in God's·image explains our predilection to seek out community. God is in plurality in unity which explains why we humans are social beings. To be in relationship through marriage, family, friends, church, society, and civilization is natural and normal because we are made in God's image. We are meant to love more than our individual selves. It explains why the most debilitating form of torture is prolonged solitary confinement. The extreme individualism of the 21st century warps our humanity.

In summary, we contend here that the Bible teaches that all human beings are made in the image of God. That image does not vary from Muslim to Christian, from Dalit to Brahmin, from the middle-aged marathoner with a resting heartbeat of 60 to a homeless alcoholic who looks as old as the runner but is two decades younger. A family that once visited the famous Grand Coulee Hydroelectric Dam in Oregon was surprised to see the visitors' centre in darkness. There were no lights on inside. Not one of the displays was working. The power was off. Only a few hundred feet from one of the world's most powerful electricity-generating dams, there was no evidence that the dam delivered on its promise. Similarly, humankind is like the darkened visitors' centre, created in God's image, with the potential to know

34   Miroslav Volf, *Allah: A Christian Response*, 172.

him, to discover human purpose in line with divine intentions, and yet, without Christ, unable to deliver on the promise. The resolving of that gap we will turn to in a later chapter, but for now, in the next three chapters, we will ponder how three large swaths of humanity, while being made in God's image, distort that biblical truth.

CHAPTER 2
God's Image and India's Dalits

There is so much to love about India.[35] How else would you explain me living there for some years as a young man and making frequent trips back? I love the gentleness of the Indian people. I love the sense of timelessness about the land—'eternal India', where everything somehow seems unchanged, immutable, like the pungent smell of cow dung fires hanging thick in the air as you descend from the plane in New Delhi in the dead of winter. Or the splash of radiant colours in the sarees worn by graceful and bare-footed, henna-stained Rajasthani women. I love the crowded trains and the cacophony of cries from chai wallas and newspaper vendors screaming for attention at each train stop along the way. Just as the Muslim call to prayer defines the sounds of Muslim majority countries, also competing for one's attention in India, the blaring sounds of Hindi pop music and Hindu weddings dominate the street sounds wherever you go.

There is a lot about India to love, not only sentimentally, but in the sense of admiring. The centrality of the extended family and honour for the aged have not been lost, as essentially they

---

35   India and Hinduism are made almost synonymous in this book because, of the 982,000,000 Hindus worldwide, close to 95% of them live in India even though Hindus make up only 82% of the country's population. That said, it can be argued that "Hindus did not develop a strong sense of themselves as members of a distinct religion until there were other religions against which they needed to define themselves" (Wendy Doniger, *The Hindus: An Alternative History*, 24).

have been in Western civilization. India's inherent religiosity and tolerance is a given—in spite of its great diversity of religions, caste-based communities and regional uniquenesses. There is much about *hamare Hindustan* to love and cherish.

India Is a Great Civilization

India is a great civilization. Here is one largely unknown illustration, symptomatic of how that greatness is unrecognized, by and large, in the West. India was long the foremost cotton-textile producer in the world. Its silk sarees are still without peer. Although Great Britain was renowned in its industrial age as a producer of iron and steel, as late as 1842 the number of blast furnaces in India was about fifty times the number found in the UK and ten times the number in the peak year of 1873.[36]

Indian engineering graduates each year are double the number graduated by North American and European institutions combined. The eloquence of its novelists, in English alone, is on a world-class level with writers like Arundhati Roy, a Booker Prize-winning novelist. Testifying to India's advanced scientific community is the fact that it is a member of the nuclear bomb club of nations. Venkatraman Ramakrishna won the Nobel Prize for Chemistry in 2009, one of 10 Indian-born people to have won a Nobel Prize in the past century.

India's citizens have a long history of being altruistic. Some of the most tolerant people I know are high caste Hindus, well-educated and pacesetters in many fields. Globally admired are towering figures like Mahatma Gandhi. Pandita Ramabai. Prime Minister Nehru. Kailash Satyarthi won the Nobel Peace Prize in 2014, a singular achievement. He is a longstanding children's rights' advocate and activist against child labour. He founded the Bachpan Bachao Andolin in 1980, an organization that has

36   Vinoth Ramachandra, *Subverting Global Myths*, 225-226.

intervened and protected the rights of over 83,000 children in 144 countries. So many renowned figures are the product of a civilization four millennia old.

The India that dominates Western media coverage is about the half of the Fortune 500 companies that outsource their information technology work to megacities like Bangalore and Hyderabad. It is about how India's economy has grown about 8% per year for most of the past two decades. India is where the burgeoning middle class has caused multinational corporations to choke on their own saliva as they dream about their prospects in the new India. India today is a new world power that has its own space program. It is the third newly emerging global power along with China and Brazil.

Here are a few other notable achievements of the country. 'Bollywood' has become a household word in the same breath as 'Hollywood'. It is the largest film industry in the world.

India is the world's largest democracy. Freedom of religion is enshrined in a secular constitution adopted in 1950. These realities in themselves are incredible accomplishments.

In many respects, though, this ancient civilization of 1.3 billion people is a caste-based society. Caste-based religion has been compared to a high-rise condominium tower with no staircase, no elevator and no entrance. Every condo dweller has to live and die on the level, if not the same apartment on that floor, in which they were born. There is no upward mobility or migration between castes allowed in this life, between stories (floors) of the building. So wrote B. R. Ambedkar, the main author of India's constitution and himself a Dalit. Only one's karma in a previous existence determines what you are reincarnated into in this life, it is believed.

Caste is integral to an understanding of India. It is the glue that has held Indian society together for over 3,000 years. In one of India's sacred and ancient indigenous scriptures, the *Rig Veda*, in Sukta 90 Book X it describes primeval man whose body upon being sacrificed by the gods was divided into four *varnas* (castes) of humankind as well as the entire universe.

- His mouth became *Brahmin* (priests)
- His arms *Kshatriya* (soldiers)
- His thighs *Vaishya* (traders)
- His feet *Shudra* (servants)

In *The Laws of Manu*, we read these words: "... from his [Manu's] mouth he created the priest, from his arms the ruler, from his thighs the commoner, and from his feet the servant."[37]

It is understood by the West but not necessarily the case within Indian society that the most revered and popular Hindu scripture is the *Bhagavad-Gita*.[38] This 6th century AD scripture (date could be as early as the 1st century AD) is first of all the story of Lord Krishna's interaction with Arjuna, a kind-hearted prince, revolving around a battle Arjuna was reluctant to engage in because it was against his cousins, the Kauravas. In its 4th chapter Krishna plainly states: "The four castes were created by me" and in the 18th and final chapter, it reiterates earlier scriptures, such as *The Laws of Manu*, in dividing society up into four castes with roles of each caste clearly specified, including the duty of the *Shudras* to serve the three higher castes.[39] There it distinguishes between four castes and associates the status of inequality on the basis of nature: "O Parantapa, the activities of

---

37 *The Laws of Manu* are Hindu scriptures regularly protested against by the scheduled castes (Dalits) and this is a translation of chapter 1 verse 31 by Wendy Doniger and Brian Lewis, 6-7.

38 Wendy Doniger, *The Hindus: An Alternative History*, 25. She also makes the point that there is no commonly-accepted Hindu canon of scripture.

39 Shakuntala Sastri (translator), *The Bhagavad-Gita*, 4:13

the Brahmanas, the Ksatriyas, the Vaisyas and of the Sudras are distributed by strands which prevail in their nature."[40] In other words, caste has a longstanding presence and predominance within Indian culture.

At least in the West, most people would know about the *Brahmins*. They are the highest of the "forward" (as opposed to "backward") castes, as they are often referred to. Only they are authorized to be priests in Hindu temples. That said, many Brahmins are not priests, instead dominating the intellectual and political arenas as scholars, media personalities and members of parliament. To this day, as a generalization, they have the most prestige and influence of any group within Indian society.

The second forward caste is the *Kshatriyas*. They were historically tasked with ruling the country, forming the army, etc. To them belonged the lion's share of political power.

The third forward caste is the *Vaishyas*. The function of this caste is to run the economy and businesses of the country. To them belongs financial clout. Mahatma Gandhi came from this caste, interestingly. They are also known as *baniyas*.

The *Shudras*, the lowest of the four castes, function as servants and manual laborers for the three higher castes. Speaking on this caste, *The Law of Manu* states: "The Lord assigned only one activity to a servant; serving these (other) classes without resentment."[41] They provide cheap manual labour, such as farming, for the forward castes. The *Shudras* are also popularly known as OBCs (Other Backward Classes) as the government sought to acknowledge that affirmative action programs and reserved political seats should be given to these backward

---

40   Ibid, 18:41.
41   Ibid, 1:92.

castes, and not considered as the preserve of the forward castes.

And then there are the outcastes, previously known as untouchables, or *Harijans*, as coined by Gandhi, but today commonly referred to as *Dalits*[42]. The lower you go in the caste hierarchy the more likely you are to pollute the person from a high caste if touching that person. Some sub-castes (*jatis*), like the *Mahars*, the *jati* Dr. Ambedkar was from in Maharashtra State, had to tie brooms to their waists to sweep away their contaminated footprints lest a Brahman walked on them by mistake, as recent as 150 years ago.

Fascinatingly, before we forget about Ambedkar, who fashioned the analogy about being born in an apartment building and not being able to change floors, and who was the architect of the Indian constitution, it is generally unknown outside of India that Ambedkar is more revered in India, especially among the scheduled castes, than Mahatma Gandhi. His statue is more in evidence in India's villages than Gandhi's. He is always portrayed as holding a book, and that book is not Vedic Scriptures, but the Constitution. In that document, freedom of religion and equal opportunity are enshrined.

Periodically, Dalits and OBCs have risen up in protest against caste discrimination. Ambedkar was not the first enlightened leader among the backward castes. It was Mahatma Jotiba Phule who became the modern era pioneer of backward caste renaissance, calling his movement *Satya Shodhak Samj* (the community of truth seekers) in the late nineteenth century. He

---

42 *Dalit* as a term to describe the untouchables below the official caste system has its origins in the Marathi language meaning "crushed, broken". Made popular by Ambedkar in the 1940s and 50s and then the fame of the Dalit Panthers in Maharashtra in the 1970s, the term is now preferred by the vast majority of outcastes all over India. It symbolizes their brokenness and degradation in light of the caste system.

was a Shudra (OBC). In his treatise, *Slavery*, he minced no words in dismissing the idea of caste: "The shudras and [Dalits] ... can understand what it is to be a slave and what joy it is to be released from the chains of slavery. Now the only difference between them and the slaves in America is that whereas the blacks were captured and sold as slaves, the shudras and [Dalits] were conquered and enslaved by the Brahmans."[43]

Lest we minimalize the magnitude of the Dalit problem, we should note that 16.6% of India's population is Dalit, according to the 2011 India census. This share of India's population is growing since the same census revealed that while India's decadal population grew by 17.7%, it was less than the 20.8% growth rate for the Dalits.[44]

Caste and the Image of God

How does a caste worldview conflict with the biblical worldview we delineated in chapter 1? Essentially, it undermines the biblical account that all human beings are made in God's image and so have equal value in his sight, as they should in everybody's sight therefore. Caste has a sharply defined hierarchical view of human worth. Its perspective is that humans are created unequally. It historically has resulted in the virtual enslavement of the Dalits and Other Backward Castes—albeit with invisible chains. Instrumental as he was in the abolition of slavery in the 1800s in the Western Hemisphere, William Wilberforce nevertheless considered British treatment of Indians in their

---

43 Jotirao Phule, "Slavery" in G. P. Deshpande (ed.), *Selected Writings of Jotirao Phule*, 40.

44 Cited in *Forward Press*, June 2013, 32. There is some dispute over whether currently there are 250,000,000 or 210,000,000 Dalits. If you include the Scheduled Tribes (ST), the SC and ST make up 250,000,000 people. Alternatively if you include Muslim and Christians who ancestrally were Dalits and who still face discrimination today due to that and who do not qualify for the reservation privileges, there are at least 250 million Dalits.

colony in South Asia as "next to the Slave Trade, the foulest blot on the moral character of our country" and caste discrimination in India as institutional slavery without the name.[45]

Untouchability

One of my greatest experiences in India was taking train journeys that lasted more than 24 hours. These lengthy trips occurred a number of times, such as between Delhi and Bombay, or Ahmedabad and Allahabad, in the 1970s. Today, super express trains and airplanes have substantially reduced travel times between key cities. But long train trips are still a way of life in India. When you sit for hours across from people in a reserved sleeper coach you get to know them. You make friends. It always touched my spirit when a high caste Hindu, someone who engaged you for hours in animated conversation, invited you to share their *chapattis* and *subzi* with them. In doing so, they were breaking caste requirements. It was a supreme gesture of friendship and acceptance.

However, the whole concept of untouchability is not dead in the culture. Much of this discrimination continues unabated in the villages of India, much as it did at the time of the birth of Christ. Caste discrimination rarely makes headlines—but it did, for instance, when a temple in Madhubani was washed after the Chief Minister of Bihar, Jitan Ram Manjhi, himself a Dalit, paid a visit there in September 2014.[46]

Can anything more degrading and dehumanizing be imagined than to have to carry a spittoon around your neck to trap your polluted saliva? Such scenes may not be commonplace around India a generation after Ambedkar but the attitudes are still

---

45 Eric Metaxas, *Amazing Grace: William Wilberforce and the Heroic Campaign to End Slavery*, 227.
46 Abhay Kumar, "Untouchability Dies Hard", 34.

there and still dehumanizing. Forward caste men, all too many, feel they have undisputed access to the bodies of Dalit women, whether through prostitution, rape, molestation on crowded buses or 'eve's teasing' (public taunting of a sexual nature).

Justification for untouchability is seen in this one of numerous similar verses in *The Laws of Manu*: "If a man of inferior caste tries to sit down on the same seat as a man of superior caste, he should be branded on the hip and banished, or have his buttocks cut off."[47]

Untouchability in the villages of India means that if your very shadow falls across the path of a high caste person, that person will have to go home and take a bath to overcome ceremonial uncleanness. Yet, ironically, most of the brothels of India, which cater to all types of men, are largely filled with Dalit women. You can sleep with a Dalit woman but you can't let her shadow fall across you on the street.

A survey conducted by the National Council of Applied Economic Research and the University of Maryland in 2014 unearthed the fact that one in four Indians still practices untouchability and that this social reality spans all regions, religions and social strata.[48] Caste discrimination was banned in 1950 when India's constitution was implemented, and that has gradually had some impact on practice, but such discrimination is still deeply embedded in the Indian psyche. Cultural practices and laws on the books can be two different things.

---

47   8:282.
48   Atif Rabbani, "No End to Untouchability", 32-35.

The Invisibility of Dalits

Ashamed I am to admit that during the two years I lived in Bombay[49] in the 1970s I did not realize that the servants who with crude straw brooms cleaned the floors and toilet bowls of the guest house where our family lived were Dalits. I never spoke to these sweepers as they went about their work. I never really saw them. They were invisible. They were Dalits. Only in the last decade have I come to realize what their social status is and that they are invisible to many Indians, too.

How unlike the interaction between my recently-deceased elderly mother with the care-givers in her home. Although from talking to them you realize that they may not be too well educated or high achievers, they are real people and my mother related to them on the same level as anyone else. They are not invisible ... or voiceless. They are heard. They are respected as equals.

The silence about the Dalits and caste in the West by the Indian diaspora is partly a function of shame or denial. But to be fair it is also a function of ignorance. Wealthy and well-educated urban Indians whose families migrate to the West are often living in a middle class bubble there where the servants who clean their condos, cook their meals, drive their cars, and do their grocery shopping may not be associated as being from a particular caste. The well-off do not interact with them to any great extent. Servants are all but invisible. The children in private schools are taught that untouchability is no longer legal in society even though caste still functions on a practical level. Their world and predilections are largely family-oriented, consumer-driven and globalized. When they migrate to the West and hear about the scourge of caste back home they

---

49   Bombay changed its name to Mumbai in 1995.

are puzzled or hostile, thinking it is just propaganda for some Greenpeace-like social agenda by do-good Westerners.

Case in point. A couple of weeks ago (at the time of writing this) my wife took an envelope to the post office to be registered and sent to "Dalit Freedom Network". Angrily, the post office clerk, someone originally from India, glared at my wife and contended with her that there was no such thing as caste in India and that she should not be mailing this to an address with that name.[50]

You Can Change Your Class but Not Caste

On the face of things, caste appears to be no more a problem than class. You can be upwardly mobile in a society where class is culturally important—as in Great Britain well into the 20th century. But whereas class can be ameliorated by merit there, you cannot change caste in India. We don't understand caste in the West. We have a democratic heritage even though we might be blind to people different than us who we, in attitude if not in action, subtly discriminate against. You are stuck in the caste you are born into in India, as *The Laws of Manu* make clear: "[A priest] may make a servant do the work of a slave, whether he is bought or not; for the Self-existent one created him to be the slave of the priest. Even if he is set free by his master, a servant is not set free from slavery; for since that is innate in him, who can take it from him?"[51] One's caste is determined, supposedly, by one's karma in the previous life (most Indians believe in reincarnation).

Indians themselves and Westerners are told that caste discrimination and the practice of untouchability have ended with the founding of modern India. Untouchability was abolished

---

50   It was a good thing she did not report him or he might have lost his job by seeking to interfere with the post.
51   8:412-413.

when India gained its independence and established its modern constitution over a generation ago. But there is a difference between what is legally forbidden (e.g. untouchability) and that which is institutionally and culturally practiced (often full-blown caste discrimination). Tell the Dalit woman who has to trudge two kilometers to the nearest stream because she is not allowed to draw water from the village well in that to do so would pollute the well for caste Hindus that she should take her discriminating villagers to court; it would be unthinkable to do so in her mind. There would be too many negative repercussions.

Tell that to Dalits in the over 600,000 villages of India who are not allowed to set foot inside temples lest they pollute the worshippers and deities there. So they set up their own shrines.

Tell that to the millions of manual scavengers, all outcastes, who clean human feces from dry toilets and streets since it is one of the jobs assigned to their gradation in the caste system (even though it was outlawed in 1996 it is estimated that there are still over a million manual scavengers today).

In the four castes are hundreds of sub-castes (*jatis*) that are based along hereditary occupational lines. Thus the *Chamars* traditionally were assigned according to their *jati* the tanning of leather, not a sought-after vocation. Conversely, plum and influential business jobs are corralled generally by high caste people. Seven of the top ten billionaires in India are from the merchant caste, all of them CEOs in major corporations.[52] Although only 6.4% of the population according to the last census to track caste (1931), *Brahmins* hold about 70% of government jobs, 49% of the media elite, and of course the entire priesthood in the temples.[53]

---

52   Arundhati Roy, "The Doctor and the Saint", introduction to B.R. Ambedkar, *Annihilation of Caste*, 28.
53   Ibid, 30-31.

Most of the world thinks that caste is a racial division of people. However, as Ambedkar concluded: "The caste system is a social division of people from the same race." Then he goes on cheekily to observe: "Assuming [caste], however, to be a case of racial divisions, one may ask: What harm could there be if a mixture of races and of blood was permitted to take place in India by intermarriages between different castes?"[54] Those courageous words were written two generations ago, long before the multicultural and globalized contemporary world specialized in inter-racial marriages with barely an afterthought. But inter-caste marriage in India is still taboo and often leads to honor killings (we'll consider honor killings in chapter 3).

Marriage across the caste divide is taboo because marriage in Hinduism is endogamous (sub-castes only marry among themselves). Sub-castes are often so rigidly maintained that, sociologically, it might be more accurate to think of India as being divided up into more people groups than missiologists estimate (people groups are usually identified by cultural, religious and linguistic criteria).[55] In western cultures, we do not grasp this kind of distinction easily: we make social distinctions quite often on the basis of religion, whereas in India one can be a Hindu but be in a social silo, cut off from fellow Hindus on the basis of caste or kinship.

While caste may have been officially thrown off with laws on the books declaring this, caste remains in the mindset of the average Indian. Yes, you can live in a suburban Mumbai condo sector with a name like Regency Park and wear the latest Levi designer jeans but important decisions related to marriage and

---

54 Ambedkar, *Annihilation of Caste*, 5.3.
55 Mark Pickett makes this case in his article, "Ethnicity, Kinship, Religion and Territory: Identifying Communities in South Asia", *The Journal of the International Society of Frontier Missiology*, 23-36.

daily ritual remain solidly caste-based.[56] Such westernization may only be skin-deep.

Education in English in India

Reinforcing the perpetuation of the glass ceiling between castes is the frowning on of education for the backward castes. Non-education actually serves the power holders as a solution to retaining and consolidating their privileged place in society. Enlightenment through education brings power to change, we know. Why should one encourage a brick-making Dalit on the blazing hot Gangetic plains the opportunity to discover through reading as he gets educated that actually he is not obligated to send his son to the brick kiln like his ancestors before him had always assumed that their sub-caste required? Fine, let Dalits go to elementary and secondary government schools in local languages, but that's as far as they should go, too frequently is the attitude among the forward castes. Limit their access to English-medium education and they will not go to university and on into professions and occupations that are the preserve of high caste people and where a lot of money can be made. Interestingly, more than twice as many Indians speak English as there are people in the United Kingdom, the English language's birthplace. But English is the language of the privileged and the well-educated in India.

One might not realize that education is universal in India. This is a commendable thing. Government-run elementary and secondary schools are taught in the regional languages, as you would think they should be. So in Rajasthan elementary school is taught in Hindi. In Andhra Pradesh, elementary school is taught in Telegu. However, the word on the street is that if you want to get ahead in India you need to know English. The main

---

56   Pavan Varma, *The Great Indian Middle Class,* 44.

reason for this is not so you can get a job in Bangalore working for a multinational company so much as it is because college and university education are primarily in English. English is the portal to higher education. Therefore children of middle class and high caste families invariably send their children to private and expensive English-medium schools to prepare them for college or university—which will function in English. Dalits, and often OBCs, rarely can afford such a thing.

The obsession in India with knowing English is apparent in the male search for a suitable bride. Matrimonial advertisements commonly have a unique term in them: "convented". It is probably not used this way anywhere else in the world. Young ladies who are "convented" are very eligible marriage partners for the aspiring young man. To be "convented" is not to have been sent to a nunnery. It means that the young lady had an English-medium education in a Roman Catholic school. This assures that the educated and upwardly mobile groom will have a Westernized and sophisticated bride to host his business clients.[57]

It is not only the word on the street that influences those who can afford it to send their children to a private school functioning in English. Education may be a legal right for all children but only three in every four children complete grade 5. Government schools often face the issue of teachers not showing up for work. Classes are overcrowded (only 60% of schools across the country have a ratio as low as 30 students per teacher, as mandated by law).[58] It is the aspiration of every parent to send their child to a quality private school. However, such schools are out of reach financially for most scheduled caste families. Little wonder that Dalit parents pull their children out of school

---

57   Ibid, 156-157.
58   Charu Sudan Kasturi, "Learning Curve", *Hindustan Times*, 12-13.

at an early age to work alongside of them in the fields or stone quarries.

Yes, generally, those from the lowest official caste, the *Shudras*, and the *Dalits*, the outcastes, cannot afford to send their children to such schools. What good does it do to tell them that there are university entrance spots reserved for them if their children cannot pass the entrance exams in English? In fact, 71% of scheduled caste (SC)[59] children never matriculate.[60] The majority of girls leave school once they begin to menstruate.

Over a century ago, Phule saw the futility of trying to break the caste barrier for the lower rungs of society without education. He observed: "The shudras and {Dalits] have been saved from the physical slavery of the brahmans[61] since the advent of the British [written in 1873]. But at the same time we are extremely sad to note that the benevolent British government has ignored the problem of the education of the shudras. And as a result, they remain ignorant and captive in the mental slavery that the brahmans have perpetuated through their books [scriptures]."[62]

To break through this glass ceiling, Dalit Freedom Network partnered with Operation Mercy Trust to start English-medium schools, called Good Shepherd Schools, primarily for Dalits, beginning in 2002. Indian Christians and others who understood the power of transformation through education responded affirmatively to Dalit leaders' request for such help, which we shall tell the story of shortly.

---

59 *Scheduled Castes* refers to the officially designated disadvantaged people in the caste system, which are the Dalits.

60 Ibid, 33.

61 "Brahman" is one of the spellings in Hindu Scriptures for what is normally written today as "Brahmin".

62 "Slavery" in G. P. Deshpande (ed.), *Selected Writings of Jotirao Phule*, 45.

The Reservation System

Sekhar listened respectfully while I explained to him how I was involved with a charity that had helped fund 107 schools with 26,000 children for mainly Dalits in them to help overcome the disadvantages caste culture trapped them in. As a high caste Indian he found it disconcerting that a Canadian was assuming that caste still was a factor in Indian society.

"Don't you realize that Dalits and other backward caste people now have the same opportunities to get a higher education as anyone else in India? We have had a reservation system for 60 years. This means that every stratum of society is given the opportunity to go to university," he countered.

I replied, "Respectfully, what good does it do if a Dalit boy or a tribal young lady cannot pass the university entrance exam in English?" Sekhar did not know what to say; he looked like a kid with his hand caught in the cookie jar.

With much disincentive to finish high school, necessary to be eligible for the reservation policy, it is not surprising to discover that according to the 2001 census, only 2.24% of Dalits are university graduates. Yes, the rare ones, like their hero Ambedkar, overcome the horrendous hurdles to become doctors, lawyers, scholars and civil servants—but they are as likely to succeed as the proverbial camel can pass through the eye of a needle.

Further Problems with the Reservation System

What if you are a Dalit from a Christian or Muslim background? There is no allotment of university spaces for you. It is okay if you are a Buddhist, Sikh or Hindu from the disadvantaged members of your community (all Indians are told from an early age what caste their ancestors came from even if they have left the Hindu fold, such is the socio-cultural hold of caste). There are reservation quotas for you. These people are designated as scheduled caste (SC) people—which means they have access to certain potential perks in education or employment as do the forward castes. The modern governmental category of "scheduled caste" excludes Christians and Muslims, however, who were, for the most part, Dalits or Shudras ancestrally. To this day, except in a few states, educational or vocational reservations are not available for Muslims or Christians. If they were included in the Dalit populations totals we would be looking at closer to 250,000,000 Dalits instead of around 210,000,000.

Baudh is a budding scholar who would like to apply for a government grant to do his Ph.D. as a SC Dalit. That means he must submit a certificate to prove that he is a SC Dalit. But his parents never applied for one after they became Buddhist because they did not want their outcaste ancestry to stigmatize their children in high caste-dominated north India. This prevents Baudh from availing himself of caste-based quotas for employment or education unless he goes through the process of getting legal certification of his Hindu Dalit background, although he grew up as a Buddhist.[63]

Baudh ended up refusing to apply for his SC certificate because he sees the discrimination against religious minorities as the denial of a fundamental human right. He is fortunate because if he were a Dalit who professed Christ or Allah, he would be denied SC status and therefore access to the reservation scheme at all. In this way, non-Hindus are pressured (tempted) to renounce the Islam or Christianity of their forefathers and return to the Hindu fold. *Hindutva* sees India becoming a Hindu

---

63   Sumit Baugh, "In the Conversion Noise, the Silence", 99.

country once again as the only true expression of being Indian.[64] Thus, some laws and customs subtly discriminate against religious minorities.

The idea of caste-based reservation in education and jobs has been around for about one hundred years. It was first introduced into Indian society by the Shudra king of Kolhapur in 1902. Its primary ambition has been to break the stranglehold Brahmins have held on Indian bureaucracy, from being chief ministers of state governments to village clerks.[65] It has been addressed in different ways at different times, from India's inception to Mandal's Report in 1990—none of the attempts at providing a level playing field for all Indians in the face of endemic caste sentiments being sufficiently successful.

That said, primary and secondary education is universally available to all Indians. So one might wonder if Dalit Freedom Network, Operation Mercy Trust and other partners should invest in English-based education for the Dalits when Indians live and breathe the local languages of where they reside. Interestingly, Christians have historically been at the forefront of the drive to respect and preserve India's indigenous languages. A Ph.D. thesis by Dr. Babu Verghese a few years ago proved that 73 modern Indian literary languages were created by Bible translators using the dialects of mostly illiterate Indians.[66] For example, the famous William Carey, over two centuries ago, translated the Bible into Bengali. Henry Martyn, another early English missionary, translated the NT into Urdu and thus gave grammars and dictionaries for the enduring welfare of hundreds of millions of people.

---

64 *Hindutva* according to the Wikipedia entry on this term is an ideology of Hindu nationalism. According to this viewpoint, India should be a Hindu country.
65 Ashok Yadav, "OBC Quota Division: States' Job, Not Centre's", *Forward Press*, 10.
66 Vishal Mangalwadi, *Why Are We so Backward?* 128.

In response to the Indian Christian community's request to meet with top Dalit leaders from around India in 2001, 800 Dalits leaders gathered with a cross-section of Christian leaders to discuss ways to alleviate their sense of being trapped in no man's land socially, economically, spiritually and politically. Unanimously the Dalit leaders said: "It is too late for us but save our children by providing them with an English-medium education and educate them about the Christian worldview." The Good Shepherd Community Schools, as they are now called, were the result of that convention. These schools are not the result of do-good, we-know-better foreigners imposing their development agenda, but the fruit of the Dalit community's initiative. And secondarily of the Indian Christian community. The schools express the indigenous communities' felt-needs.

The remarkable story of how a massive educational program for the Dalits is chronicled in the book by one of the movement's founders, Joseph D'Souza called *Dalit Freedom: Now and Forever* and also in *Why Not Today* by Matthew Cork. Let me give you an abbreviated version here.

Good Shepherd Schools

Once Dalit leaders learned to trust the Christian leaders they were in dialogue with, literally scores of meetings taking place between their leaders and Christian leaders, in late 2001 they asked in one meeting of 800 participants if quality English-medium education could be given to their children. "It is too late for us", they said. Dalit freedom from caste discrimination must change a deep-seated mindset, in their communities. As one of their spokespersons and presently a member of parliament, Udit Raj, declared: "Caste inferiority must be taken out of the minds of our children and our people. That is where the work must be done."[67] The Dalits urged the Christian community in India to start 100,000 such schools for them, not only with an English-medium base but with a Christian worldview. "We have heard that your god created all humans equally", they said.

Responding to this request was Joseph D'Souza and his leaders from one Indian charitable entity. And so the first Dalit Education Centres, as they were first called, were born. This band of brothers and sisters committed to a long-term goal of establishing 1,000 schools (250 by 2025) and a separate entity specializing in education was created, called Operation Mercy Trust. One by one the schools were started, first in diverse places like Lucknow area and south Tamil Nadu. By 2011, the first 100 schools had been birthed. Along the way, to mobilize resources and capture the groundswell of interest in the West for this contemporary anti-apartheid movement, Dalit Freedom Network organizations were created. First in the USA, which had a particular interest in justice advocacy. Then in the UK, which has had a focus on anti-human trafficking. And then in Canada in 2006 with a particular commitment to the initial vision to bring about empowering Dalit children through education. Today there are about 15 major global partners with this indigenous Christian ministry which has morphed into a multi-faceted set of entities that encompasses economic development and health care as well as the schools.

As of 2015, there were 107 schools with 26,000 children in them. In the June 2015 graduation classes of the schools, 440 students graduated from secondary school. The preference is to start the children in lower kindergarten and then graduate them after the 10th standard, the next step being two years of Junior College before passing their entrance exams for university.

---

67   Quoted in Joseph D'Souza, *Dalit Freedom: Now and Forever*, 78.

Schools are constructed from one-time gifts. Dalits and local communities provide the land normally. Funds for construction are raised abroad primarily, and then local materials and people are hired to do the actual construction, thus providing employment to local people. Schools are only started where the Dalit community has invited in what are now called Good Shepherd Schools, fully aware that these are Christian-registered schools where a biblical worldview will be taught alongside the government educational curriculum. Amazingly, there is a lengthy queue of groups of villages with a high concentration of Dalits that have asked for a school. Not only are the schools popular, but in keeping with the biblical worldview that God favors no one race or ethnicity, about 20% of the student spaces are kept available for those not from the Dalit Bahujan[68], such as high caste Hindus.

The hunger for a quality education and the popularity of these schools can be observed in Raju's life. Raju just became a teenage this year and is in Grade Eight in a Good Shepherd School in Rajasthan. He has to walk four miles to school and four miles back home each day. That would not be too difficult if it were not for the fact that he also has to cross a river on foot to get there. During the monsoon season the river is in full spate and it becomes treacherous for Raju to cross it. But he does. He has been studying in this school since Lower Kindergarten. It is an escape from an alcoholic father and an illiterate family.

There is no electricity supply in his village. His family depends on the battery-powered street lamp near his house for feeble light at night. Quite often Raju will sit under the street light and do his homework. He is the most educated person in his village

---

68   "Bahujan" means majority and so when used as the term "Dalitbahujan" means the majority of Indi's population that includes the Dalits (SC), the OBCs and the Tribals (ST). Together they account for 52% of the population, although that aggregate is disputed.

for not only does he know how to read and write but he can also do it in the coveted English language.

This educational movement is such a massive undertaking, logistically and financially, that the schools are built in three phases. Each phase costs about $175,000. Initially, eight classrooms are constructed to take the children through to Grade 5. Then Phase Two allows for six more rooms to be built to provide separate classrooms for Middle School. Then Phase Three enables a High School to be added, usually being a second floor on top of the Elementary School. All told, each school, when brought to maturity, has 20 rooms, for 12 years of schooling, plus other needed rooms like a principal's office and an assembly hall. 500 is the targeted ideal enrollment.

The daily cost of keeping the students in school is met through $33 per month sponsorships of individual children. That paltry amount covers each student's share of their teacher's salary, their uniform, their share of wages for maintenance staff on site, and student books and supplies.

The medium-term goal is to have 250 schools fully functional and providing excellent education by 2025. Why not 1,000 as per the original goal?[69] Simply because global partners with Operation Mercy Trust have had to make some hard choices. Do they want quantity without quality? Better to complete each school and give the smarter children a fighting chance to make it to college or university rather than abort their schooling just to open another school before all grades are offered in schools already started, it was decided. All sorts of issues go into each school's effectiveness. Continuing education for teachers.

---

69   Actually Operation Mercy Trust only promised 1,000 schools. Others will have
      to step up to help shoulder the larger vision.

Establishing school libraries and computer labs. Creating a Good Shepherd Teachers' Training College, now fully functioning.[70]

Annika, the Movie Star

Mention Oscar winning movie, *Slumdog Millionaire*, and everyone knows what you are talking about. Determined to make a Christian and Hollywood-standard version of this eye-opening film about the realities of the slums and trafficking in India, Friends Church and their network in California made a feature length film, *Not Today*, which premiered in about 20 cities in the USA in 2013.[71] It tells the story of an American tourist in India who meets a tiny girl begging. He gives her some loose change but then meets her father by chance and learns of the family's destitution. Later he discovers that the father has trafficked his daughter, Annika, reluctantly, out of desperation. The movie follows this American returning to India to track down and rescue Annika.

What most people do not know is that the girl who plays Annika really stole the show with her skillful acting and well-spoken English. Nor are they aware that the movie director discovered her in a Good Shepherd School where she had developed self-confidence and facility in English although coming from a humble Dalit family. Annika is now back in school. I guess you might call this empowerment through education.

---

70   All teachers hired must have their teachers' certificate, know English and the local language of the schools they serve in.

71   Matthew Cork and Kenneth Kemp, *Why Not Today* (Chicago: Moody Publishers, 2013).

Bribery as a Way of Life Discriminates Against the Poor

One of the first words I learned in India in 1972 was *baksheesh*. It has somewhat broad connotations but loosely is translated as "tip", a euphemism for placing in the outstretched hand, sometimes figuratively, an undeserved gift, such as a bribe. We might call it "greasing the palm" in English—and certainly that is rampant enough in North America, or anywhere in the world, for that matter. To be fair, it also refers to "charitable giving", so when a beggar stretches out her hand in a crowded bazaar in Nagpur, and plaintively utters *baksheesh*, passersby will not assume there is anything unethical in what she is doing. In fact, such charitable giving is religiously-sanctioned behaviour in Muslim-dominated countries as one of the five pillars of Muslim practice, the term originating in the Persian language. And in India, Islam claims 12% of the population—equal to the second largest Muslim population in the world found in any nation.

Begging is an accepted part of the culture. By both Hindus and Muslims. However, bribery, as opposed to begging, is a refined art in India. It is estimated that in the 1950s India's black market economy was 3% of the GDP, 40% by 1995 and about $1 trillion annually today.[72] While globalization, with its emphasis on free market economies, education and democracy, has loosened caste hold on the disadvantaged OBCs, claims one Indian commentator, "corruption continues to barricade [our] people into backwardness."[73]

The dilemma here for the Dalits and the OBCs is that to get ahead by greasing the palms of the local officials for paper work that you have a right to, such as a deed to property your

---

72 Estimate from social scientist Arun Kumar, *Forward Press,* 67.
73 Ibid, 83.

ancestors have owned but which cannot be found, is impossible because of their poverty. So the rich get richer and the poor get poorer. Cultural practices in this case favour forward rather than backward caste peoples. Bribery exacerbates a hierarchical view of humankind.

Furthermore, laws are applied to the poor and outcastes but not to the rich, who can talk their way out of danger—'talk,' as in proffer a bribe, to have a traffic ticket overturned or even a murder charge dismissed. Societies that do not function on the basis of the rule of law (as long as the laws are good and fair) do not respect the fact the humankind is made in God's image.

The importance of justice prevailing in all situations was driven home to me in a fresh way recently when my wife and I took in the Hollywood movie, *The Judge*, starring Robert Duvall and Robert Downey, Jr. The upright and stern judge of a small town in Indiana was soon to retire. He had alienated his son, Hank, a successful lawyer now in Chicago, because of his severe outlook on life, exemplified by his law and order reputation in the courts. But his wife had died and so the son came home for the funeral.

One night, coming home in the dark, seemingly drunk, the father hit and killed a pedestrian. When, eventually, his unappreciated son, the lawyer, realized that his dad had killed this man because of the dent in the car's hood, and because the police had questioned him about the hit and run, and then charged his dad, Hank, the son, decided to delay his return to Chicago to defend his father. The proud judge seemed to undergo a fierce internal conflict about defending himself against the manslaughter charge for drunk driving leading to death but finally admitted to Hank that he was dying of cancer. It was disorientation from the chemotherapy and not alcohol that had caused the accident.

A moving point comes in the final moments of the trial when the judge reconciles himself to having to go to prison. Looking intently at Hank he says, "Without the law, it is impossible for there to be justice." What he was really saying was that laws were put in place to be followed and so, unless there were consequences to his own hit and run manslaughter charge, the family that had lost their husband and father would not find justice. It was now time for him to practice what he had preached as a judge. Justice, as we will explore later, is as necessarily a logical consequence of living in the light of being made in God's image, who is a just God (e.g. Psalm 89:14; Isaiah 51:4), as grabbing for a glass of water follows from feasting on Indian curry.

The Gang Rape of a Gender

The gang rape of the 23-year old woman in New Delhi in 2012, which sparked global outrage, was just the tip of the iceberg. What is not so well known is that lower caste and outcaste women and girls are the ones mostly picked on. In 2012 alone, 1,574 Dalit women were raped, or at least reported their rape.[74] Probably at least ten times as many go unreported. Women not included in this statistic, made in God's image, can be stripped naked and paraded through the streets of their village for some alleged misdeed, thousands of them in the course of a year across the country.

Seemingly symptomatic of male indifference to women's dignity in India was the banning of the British documentary of the above-mentioned rape, which revealed the unrepentant and chauvinistic attitude of one of the accused rapists interviewed in jail. *India's Daughter* was banned, revealing once again the discrepancy between theory and practice over women's rights.

---

74   http://www.prospectmagazine.co.uk/features/indias-shame

But the heart of the issue is that women are downtrodden in India because its primary faith does not rise to the level of the Bible in its view of women as being made in God's image. As we saw in chapter 1, the notion of humans being created in "the image of God" in Scripture clearly states that both males and females are equally fashioned in God's image (Gen. 1:27).

Brahminical notions of purity operate at home not just in the temple. Men are not to help in the kitchen, where 'dirty work' is done. An ideal woman in the forward castes does not eat in the presence of men. Exercising patriarchal authoritarianism is considered spiritual. Where do such attitudes and practices find their locus of influence? In the Vedic scriptures themselves. Here are some examples of the second-tier place that the female has in the grand scheme of things:

- Krishna is an avatara[75] who had eight wives. But his wives did not have other husbands.
- Women whose husbands died before them were expected to commit suicide (suttee) by throwing themselves on the funeral pyre of their cremated spouse (banned now but still reputed to be practiced rarely in some rural areas). Several queens commit suttee in the epic *Mahabharata*.
- Although the god Brahma's wife, Saraswati, is said to have invented Sanskrit, she was illiterate. Women were not allowed to have a formal education until Savitribai Phule was educated by her husband and eventually together started the first school for girls in the 1800s.[76]

---

75 *Avatara* is similar to the Christian view of the incarnation. It refers to the divine spirit which takes up abode in a human being. While Hinduism has several incarnations of gods, they seem to move back and forth between either human or divine states whereas the Christian view of Jesus is that while he was on earth he was in both states simultaneously and always. See Chapter 5.
76 Kancha Ilaiah, *Why I am Not a Christian*, 72-74.

- Lakshmi, the wife of the god Vishnu, is portrayed as being the goddess of wealth, but is fully dependent on Vishnu for her well-being. Brahmin women are not allowed to own property, interestingly enough.[77]

Feticide is another barometer of a country's moral health. It is estimated that 40 million female fetuses have been aborted in India—although this practice is a commonplace scandal in many other Asian cultures too (China in particular). If not aborted, millions of new-born babies are killed right after birth because of their gender in certain parts of the world. More about that in chapter 6.

Female children are assumed not to need a rudimentary education in the same way boys are, even though education in India is available to all. Indians led the way for this understanding in India, it needs to be pointed out. It was Savitribai Phule (1837-1897), wife of social reformer, Jotirao Phule, who in the 19th century advocated for education for girls and low caste children to be opened up.[78] Savitribai and her husband were Shudras and so in that day and age not able to avail themselves of a proper education. They became the first-ever Indians to open a school for girls and did so for all caste ones at that. Although initially it was a struggle to get Dalit girls into the Good Shepherd Schools, they now make up close to 50% of the students.

That this sex selection discrimination is not an ancient cultural practice but still current is borne out by some startling research making front-page headlines in the most-read Canadian newspaper and entitled "Where have all the girls gone".[79] In that article the reporter refers to 4,400 "missing girls" from Canada's

---

77 Ibid, 75-77.
78 Thom Wolfe and Suzanne Andrade, *Savitribai: India's Conversation on Education*.
79 Jonathan Forani, *Toronto Star*, A1, A11.

Indian-born parents—although in actual fact these missing children are abortions. In the second trimester of pregnancies, Canadian mothers are told the gender of their fetuses. Information complied by Statistics Canada and the Institute for Clinical Evaluative Sciences in Toronto between 1990 and 2011, and 1993 and 2012 respectively, determined that 196 boys are born in Ontario for every 100 girls by Indian-born mothers who already have two daughters as opposed to 104 boys for every 100 girls by Canadian-born mothers who already have two daughters. Indian-born mothers living in Canada with two children had 138 boys for every 100 girls. These skewed ratios cannot be accidental statistical anomalies and indicate that a male child is still the preferred gender for many Indian families.

"We Don't Want a Religion that Only Rejects Us"

Ghar Wapsi is an expression that the Hindu radical groups RSS[80] and VHP[81] use to describe their "reconversion" efforts. It euphemistically means "homecoming". The RSS unit in Aligarh district (county) of Uttar Pradesh, a largely Muslim area of north India, claimed to have reconverted 40,000 primarily Dalits back to Hinduism through special ceremonies, including 2,000 Muslims in 2014. Vishal, one of those allegedly reconverted to his ancestral faith—even though he had never left it—was heard to complain: "We don't want a religion that only rejects us. We know we are Dalits. Everyone treats us as outcastes even now [after the reconversion ceremony]".[82]

---

80   The RSS stands for *Rashtriya Swayamsevak Sangh* and is a national organization of volunteers founded in 1925 which embraces Hindutva ideology and has 7,000,000 members in 50,000 branches.
81   VHP stands for *Vishva Hindu Parishad* which means *The World Council of Hinduism*, founded in 1964, the activist arm of the RSS. Its youth wing is called *Bajrang Dal*, founded in 1984, which is notorious for targeting Christians and Muslims.
82   http://indianexpress.com/article/india/india-others/dont-want-a-religion-that-only-rejects-us.

The experience of the Dalits, who form the majority of members in the 3,800 Good Shepherd Community Churches emerging across India, drives their quest for an alternative to virtual slavery. Sometimes they are harassed because of their new-found faith. When asked why they would risk losing benefits and face persecution in leaving Hinduism, they retort: "Why should we return to a religion that only mistreated us; at least Jesus loves us and the Christian Bible tells us we have dignity because we are made in God's image." Freedom of religion, without undue pressure to remain in one's family's faith or choose a faith of one's own, is critical to a prospering India. In a climate of fear and repression people do not thrive in other spheres of life either. It is also necessary if a society accepts that all human beings are made in God's image.

As it is, since the Dalits cannot worship in the temples, cannot handle Hindu Scriptures on their own, and are shunned in daily social intercourse by those in the three top castes, they do not necessarily think of themselves as Hindus. Such is the testimony of Kancha Ilaiah, who was a Shudra, born into the Kurumaa subcaste in Andhra Pradesh state (Kurumaa is the shepherding subcaste) when he observes: "I was not born a Hindu for the simple reason that my parents did not know they were Hindus. This does not mean that I was born as a Muslim, a Christian, a Buddhist, a Sikh, or a Parsee. My illiterate parents, who lived in a remote South Indian village, did not know that they belonged to any religion at all... . My parents had only one identity and that was their caste: they were Kurumaas."[83]

Thinking negatively about the Shudras, Dalits and Tribals is kind of like adopting a Theory X instead of a Theory Y style of leadership. Leaders who basically trust people's instincts and motivation in decision-making and workplace behaviour, whether that be to

---

83   This is the shepherd sub caste.

work hard or not steal from their employer, exhibit a Theory Y style of leadership. It is affirming and optimistic. People generally thrive in such a workplace atmosphere. Theory X style leadership assumes the worst about people and so their decisions are second-guessed, they are highly controlled, and productivity is reinforced through fear of being shamed publicly. Little trusted with responsibility, OBCs and Dalits are treated for the most part with Theory X style attitudes by other elements in the Indian population.

Persistently, fundamentalist RSS leaders charge Christians with inducing conversions to their faith through unscrupulous tactics such as the promise of a wife or through offer of money. But that is not happening. In fact, as *Ghar Wapsi* reveals, if any groups in India are guilty of "proselytization" it is the ones who need to get the log out of their own eyes. Joseph D'Souza on this subject strikes this tone: "The most poignant aspect in the whole debate on conversion across the Indian nation is that there is no place in the Christian faith for forced, fraudulent conversions. Jesus never forced anyone to follow Him. God never forces, compels or tricks people not following Him. True discipleship involves a free will decision to follow Jesus and worship Him."[84] In the same vein he exclaims that "the Hindutva lie is that Christian love always has an ulterior motive—conversion. We love the Dalit-Bahujan people unconditionally."[85] We will address this issue of the importance of respecting the volitional powers of human beings as an ethical response to humankind being made in God's image in the next chapter, when we focus on Islam.

Moving in the opposite direction to this sentiment of D'Souza, the states of Gujarat, Rajasthan, Madhya Pradesh, Chhattisgarh, Odisha (Orissa), Himachal Pradesh, and Arunachal Pradesh

---

84   *Dalit Freedom: Now and Forever*, 70.
85   Ibid, 52.

have passed anti-conversion laws. These laws are really meant to arrest the conversion of Hindus to other faiths.

One has to fear for the probability of continued religious freedom in the land when a mob of 60 Hindu fundamentalists attacked two Christian schools in Hararibagh, Jharkhand, demanding to know why they do not have a statue of Saraswati, Hindu goddess of learning.[86]

The Dignity of Labor... or at Least Some Labor

How is a caste-oriented India to successfully become an economic powerhouse if all labor is **not** treated as respectable? Why should certain jobs have to be done on a caste basis? Are Indian *dhobi wallas*[87] from other than the Dalit community? Can you open a saree shop in the center of cosmopolitan, affluent Mumbai if you are not from the Vaishya caste? Ambedkar expressed the indignity of work forced on the Dalits in a more succinct way. He observed that "the caste system is not merely a division of labour. It is also a *"division of laborers."*"[88] What we really hear from Ambedkar is the heart-cry of someone made in the image of God. God created us, as we will explore in more depth later, in chapters 4 and 6, to not just find significance in *being* but in *doing* (Gen. 1:28-30). He did not simply create the earth to be fruitful and productive on its own, but designed humans to bring order and development to it, which is sometimes called the "cultural mandate".

The story is told of an English gardener, Cockney in fact, who was showing off his beautiful and lush garden to the local pastor. Admiring the gardener's handiwork, the pastor broke out in

---

86   https://barnabasaid.org/news/Hindu-activists-storm-two-Christian-schools-in-India-demanding-closure.

87   People who wash clothes for others by hand in rivers, running tap water or ponds for a small price.

88   B.R. Ambedkar, *The Annihilation of Caste*, 4.1.

praise to God. The gardener seemed not to be fully pleased that God got all the credit. And so be blurted out: "You should 'ave seen this 'ere garden when Gawd 'ad it all to 'isself."[89] Bingo. In point of fact, the gardener had it right. God gave us the threads but left it up to us to make a beautiful carpet. So not to allow some members of society to have the right to do meaningful work is to tell them they are not made in the image of God.

An unintended consequence of India's rush to modernize and become a global economic juggernaut is that some of the infrastructure needed is done on the backs of children and the Dalits as a group. A few years ago *The Toronto Star* newspaper did an investigative feature on child labour in India and told the story of ten-year-old Muna Behera in Orissa who spent 14 hours per day in a stone quarry stacking 40 kilo piles of stone in a basket and then carrying them on his head to a machine that crushed the stone into gravel for use in road construction. He began working in the stone quarry three months before he was interviewed because his father, Ganga, then 55 years old, began to suffer paralysis in his legs, a symptom of silicosis, which is a common ailment among quarry workers. Although such child labour is banned, it is often overlooked, in part because of India's rush to meet such goals as laying 20 km of roads a day, whether super highways or to widen 6,300 km of its single lane highways.[90]

A few years ago, along the road between Hyderabad and Nagpur, my taxi driver, taking me to view a property purchased to build another Good Shepherd School, stopped on the way so that I could take a close look at a gravel pit operation in the countryside. As we climbed a rocky hill on the barren terrain, in withering heat, we happened upon an encampment of huts.

---

89   John Stott, *Volume 2, Social and Sexual Relationships in the Modern World*, 28.
90   Rick Westwood, "Modernizing India on Backs of Children", *The Toronto Star*, A25, A26.

Squatting there were some women and children, trying to find shade in the blazing mid-day 45 decree C heat. Their huts were cobbled together with corrugated metal, pieces of wood, newspaper and wire, kind of like a human version of birds' nests stitched together by bits of debris. Dalits, their husbands were over the next hill breaking down boulders into gravel with manual tools. Stone crushing. What we introduced the book with a story about. Their back-breaking daily routine was sort of like trying to run a marathon in the middle of a heat wave and in urban sprawl with toxic air to breathe. Brutal. Diminishing. Unfit conditions for those made in the image of God. The inherent dignity of labour had been stripped away from them. Meena, whose story was told in the introduction to the book, had been fated for the same sort of grueling and dehumanizing life's work were it not for her Good Shepherd School education.

Although India's GDP grew 7.5% in Modi's first full year as the Prime Minister, India has the second largest labour force in the world and roughly half of them work in the fields on extremely small plots of land subdivided over many generations. To change India into a huge manufacturing and service-based economy is a gargantuan task, especially if it is to be inclusive of the Dalits.

More about Child Labour

Most Americans will associate cotton-picking with Afro-American slavery in the Deep South. But consider the 21st century cotton-growing industry in India. According to the India Committee of the Netherlands, one million children are involved in cottonseed-production, with 200,000 of them being under the age of 14.[91] While there are new laws in place to curtail child labour and multinational companies like Bayer

---

91 http://newint.org/blog/2015/07/31/india's-forgotten-cotton-picking-child-labour/.

pressured to prevent such employment, shockingly the number of children in the cotton-picking employment has increased by 100,000 since 2010. This is mostly in the states of Rajasthan and Gujarat where acreage given over to cotton-growing has increased. Parents of children in the fields and factories accept a lump-sum payment for their children to be employed in this way and so the children must complete the contract, a bonded labour type of entrapment. The children work in Dickensian conditions, often eight to ten hours a day. Need it be stated that most of these helpless and miserable children, usually forced out of school to comply with the long working hours, are Dalits.

Manual Scavenging

Like China leaping from a pre-industrial society to a post-industrial society in half a century, it will be a massive adjustment for India's Dalits to go from manual scavenging to owning manual drive cars in one generation. Who will clean the dry toilets of India if the Dalits are no longer willing to do so? Can modern plumbing be introduced to all 600,000 villages that quickly? Although manual scavenging was outlawed in India in 1993, it is estimated that there are still 2,000,000 of them in India, mostly in rural areas (close to two-thirds of Indians still live in villages).

Peddanna is an Andhra Dalit man who understood from early years that, like his ancestors before him, he was destined to be a manual scavenger. This means that each day he collects human feces from dry toilets in a basket which he carries on his head to a dumping ground on the outskirts of town. Every morning Peddanna and five *Thoti*[92] workers clean dry toilets in homes using a crude scooping tool, like a trowel. With half of the homes in the country not having indoor toilets (67% of

---

92   *Thoti* is the name of the Dalit sub-caste whose assigned job in life is to be manual scavengers.

Dalit homes according to the 2011 Indian census), there is no shortage of demand for this low-paying, filthy work. Peddanna and his co-workers have no masks and no rubber gloves. When it rains, the excrement leaks down onto their bodies. Like many *Thotis* Peddanna has chronic problems with stomach and intestinal bugs. He finds it hard to keep the lingering foul smell from his clothes. Ashamed and depressed by his lot in life, Peddanna has turned to homemade liquor to ease the pain.[93]

God's design for humankind includes finding dignity in our work. Our place of work is not only a way to put food on the table but a way to glorify God. Whether we are doing data entry or passing legislation, our work, if done in a way to please God, takes on meaningful dignity. Colossians 3:23 exhorts us that "whatever you do, work heartily, as for the Lord and not for men". We draw attention to our God's goodness instead of our misery when we are thankful in all circumstances (1 Thess. 5:18). Employees are to work hard and not undermine bosses (Eph. 6:5-7). We are to work for a living and not be dependent as a life-style choice on the backs of others (2 Thess. 3:6-8). Every work situation is filled with positive purpose if understood to be done for God (and family – 1 Tim. 5:8). In this spirit, Bradley Nassif maintains the following:

> Our workplace is not only a means of livelihood, but can become a place of redemption. It's not that that work redeems us through the deeds themselves, as if we could somehow earn our salvation just by being nice or honest in our dealings. Rather, each person's work is a sacred task given them by Providence in order to achieve Christlikeness. Our daily tasks and personal relationship become the hands of God to shape and fashion us into the image of his beloved Son.[94]

---

93   This story is recounted in Joseph D'Souza, *Dalit Freedom—Now and Forever*, 48-49.
94   "The Meaning in the Monotony", *Christianity Today*, 54.

However, redeeming work in this way is possible only if the culture acknowledges a God who creates everyone with equal dignity. A corollary of such equality is the right to choose one's vocation.

You cannot say that all Indians have the right to an education but then tell the high school graduates that because of their birth they are consigned to making bricks like their ancestors have always done. Universal freedoms cannot be cherry-picked. Principles of justice require that a society does not take away with the right hand what the left hand has given. Vishal Mangalwadi, himself a Shudra ancestrally, rightfully contends: "Freedom is an indivisible and organic entity. It is like a tree. You cannot demand that a tree grow only upward, not downwards. Freedom will either grow in all dimensions or be stifled."[95]

Should We Expect Democracy to Last?

Is it possible for democracy—which assumes the equality of all people—and caste thinking to co-exist indefinitely? Vishal Mangalwadi, outspoken Indian, thinks not: "As a philosophical idea, democracy is antithetical to the... belief that castes are born to rule because of their good karma in a past life, while the others are born to serve due to their bad karma. Democracy assumes equality and freedom for every individual."[96] But a question remains. If there is universal suffrage, but the same Dalit who votes freely does not have the protection of the police when she is forced to sell her *bhindi* (lady fingers or okra, the vegetable) at the village market at half-price because the high caste buyer bullies her into the lower price on the basis of his ability to make life difficult for her, what does the future hold?

---

95   *The Quest for Freedom and Dignity*, 99.
96   Vishal Mangalwadi, *Why Are We Backward?* 32.

Or is the enforcement of law leveling the playing field for the Dalit who is forced to clean railway tracks of human feces manually, the Indian Railway being one of the biggest employers of manual scavengers in India, when such scavenging has been outlawed (an estimated 172,000 open-discharge toilets empty their waste onto 65,000 km of tracks per day although the obvious way to comply with the law would be to have toilets storing waste treated chemically to be disposed of in a sanitary way at stations).[97] A society that does not enforce its laws, over time, no matter what is written on paper, becomes a state without sufficient rule of law. Elections then become a farce. The people are unable to speak their mind through the ballot box.

On one level, it cannot be disputed that forward caste Indians are progressive and productive out of proportion to their share of the population. Centuries of marrying within one's own *jati* or *Varna* have created social, economic and other inequalities through heredity. A woman's realizing of her equal rights to an education and professional advancement will depend on hereditary, conditioning, social and other factors. Equality in society is a fiction. But equality must be accepted as "a governing principle".[98] Equal opportunity is the issue. The image of God resting in all people equally dictates this sort of response.

Psycho-Social Needs Met

As we consider what it will take to release the oppressed from the specter of caste in the future as it relates to the young generation of those educated in English-medium schools, for example, it is not just a matter of giving Dalits a foot up through an English-based education, for there are other benefits which

97 Arundhati Roy, "The Doctor and the Saint', 36.
98 B. R. Ambedkar, *Annihilation of Caste*, 14.5.

may be as thorough-going in reform. One reason why outcastes do not continue until graduation in the public (government) school system is that they face what we in the West call "bullying". It can take the form of not being allowed to use the school toilets if you are a Dalit. Or you might not be permitted by forward caste kids to eat your lunchtime meal in the same room as them. Sometimes the hostility will be expressed physically.

Therefore, the psycho-social blessings of being in a school where all children are treated equally, as in the Good Shepherd Schools, are great. Respect for all students by the teachers breeds self-assurance in the Dalits and OBCs registered in the schools. Heading off to school every morning becomes a happy experience and, for many, the bright spot of the day in an otherwise dreary and sad existence. In school they know that the few high caste children will be taught to play with them in the school yard. They know that they will not be forced to sit on the floor but can pay attention to the teacher while seated at desks like all the others. Over several years the clouded eyes give way to hopeful eyes. Education becomes the pathway to enlightenment. The dream of the Phules has become a reality.

This sense of well-being increases for Dalit children in the Good Shepherd Schools if they have come to school enrollment as malnourished children. The Community Health Workers (CHW) who are being hired, a goal of one per school, with now 85 of the 107 schools having a CHW on-site fulltime, discovered early in the first decade of the schools that many children were not concentrating well in class and were performing poorly in their subjects. They were listless and depressed-looking. These CHWs discovered through bloodwork and other tests that 40% of the students were malnourished. Teachers observed that some students were arriving at school each day without a lunch from home, or with rotten food, often simple rice and dal with a chili pepper, which had to be thrown away. As a result of these discoveries, gradually a feeding program for malnourished students was implemented. A glass of milk, a banana and/or egg is given to 4,200 of the students daily. Further nutritional advancements are in store.

Over time, many of these malnourished students become playful and improve in their studies. Little wonder since it is common medical knowledge that chronic human hunger ravages the body in staggering ways, slowing down processes of mind and body to compensate for the lack of energy. Malnutrition stunts brain development, cycling before long through whole generations. For the Dalits to thrive instead of merely survive, sufficient and nutritious food must be their portion. It is estimated that one in four children in developing countries is underweight.[99] In fact, of seven countries that are neighbours to India, like Bangladesh, India actually has the highest percentage of children under five who are underweight (43%).[100] It is the Dalitbahujan children who make up the vast majority of this high proportion of malnourished children in India. So the law of unintended consequences of private education here is that improving the education of Dalit children led to their nutritional needs being met and therefore their emotional well-being.

An Uphill Battle

It would be presumptuous and triumphalist to declare that Dalits will be empowered and released from caste discrimination simply by being educated. The damaged psyche of three millennia cannot be overcome in one generation. Just as Afro-Americans would contend that emancipation from slavery at the end of the Civil War in the mid-1800s did not end racial discrimination, so Dalits will need time to heal.

---

99   Richard Stearns, *The Hole in Our Gospel*, 134.
100 World Health Organization's statistics found in "Good Shepherd Health Initiative Update" (April 2015), 4.

The grinding poverty and abominable living conditions found among the Dalits is not something that can be swept aside by the wave of a magic legislative political wand. The Census 2011 data revealed that although 91% of all Scheduled Caste (SC) families reside in livable residences, 78% of all SC households live in a dwelling place of one or two rooms.[101] The boom of the middle class has left untouched the vast majority of Dalitbahujans. For instance, the lauded software development and IT service industry employs no more than one percent of the Indian labour force so in itself is not the panacea to new wealth for the majority of the poor.[102]

We see this two steps forward, one step backward pattern in Jyothi's story. Jyothi was the child of Dalit rag pickers in Bangalore who lived on the streets and forced into prostitution. She was rescued and brought to Tarika, an anti-human trafficking Christian centre in the city where she stayed two years, learning English and embroidery. In 2014 she got a job in downtown Bangalore in a retail clothing store because of her ability to speak English. She married a man from her same background, a painter. For a year and a half her marriage seemed to go well. She gave birth to a baby girl. Unfortunately her husband has taken to drinking heavily and Jyothi is now pregnant again. Unhappy with this turn of events, unable to work outside the home, Jyothi has turned to the Tarika Centre again for support. She is determined not to give up and her newfound faith in Christ is giving her an abiding hope that God will intervene in her situation or give her the grace to deal with a difficult life.

It is said that one of the ways that Indians instinctively know what caste a stranger they meet is from is on the basis of body language. A Dalit will give himself away because his bearing will

---

101 Nagara Gopal, http://www.frontline.in/social-justice/dalit-nation/
      article7447625.ece.
102 Vinoth Ramachandra, *Subverting Global Myths*, 242.

not be self-confident nor will he look an upper caste person or a well-to-do person in the eye. Dalits are deeply wounded in their psyche. It may take more than a generation once they are given a level playing field before they rise to the maximum of their God-given potential. Until then, people may not view them as being made in God's image even though they already are!

They face overcoming the effects of conditioning like a circus elephant once freed does. While such elephants are young, they are shackled to deeply embedded stakes. Once older and able to play havoc in a circus tent, they nonetheless do not try to break free and pose no danger to curious onlookers. The shackled elephants have been trained never to leave their chained circle around the stake, even though they have the strength to ramble off with the jerked-out stake to which the chain is tied trailing behind them. Eventually they can be left unshackled with only a small and unattached bracelet on their legs. They are unaware of the freedom they now have. Similarly, emotional trauma and conditioning do not disappear overnight for the Dalits even when given unprecedented opportunities.

Added to the battle in discovering a healthy self-image, as has been suggested in different ways throughout this chapter, the Dalits continue to face subtle but stressful discrimination, even in the more cosmopolitan cities. That has been underscored by the suicide in 2016 of Ph.D. Dalit student, Rohith Vemula, in Hyderabad. Although Rohith grew up in an OBC home, he hid a secret from his university friends about the fact that his mother had actually been born to a migrant Dalit labourer family working on the railway tracks outside the home his mother was adopted into because that lady had just lost a baby daughter. This meant that Rohith was really a Dalit and not from one of the four castes. His grandmother really did not treat him well and used him as a servant in her home. Torn by the shame of his background, and bounded by upper caste university authorities, even though a brilliant student, Rohith took his own life.[103]

However, giving the oppressed their God-given dignity because they are divine image-bearers is a hope-filled proposition. The Dalits' identity will be more than the sum of their past memories and conditioning. As Volf puts it: "In terms of identity, *we are not fundamentally the sum of our past experiences* (as we are not fundamentally the sum of our present experiences). Our memories, experiences and hopes still matter; but they qualify rather than define who we are. If that is correct, the grip of the past on our identity has been broken."[104] Let us hope for a bright future for the Dalits, indeed, for they are made equally in God's image.

103 Sudipto Mondal, "Rohith Vemula: An Unfinished Portrait", http://www.hindustantimes.com/static/rohith-vemula-an-unfinished-portrait/index.html
104 Miroslav Volf, *The End of Memory*, 199.

CHAPTER 3
The distortion of the Image of God in Islamic Worldview and Practice

Enjoying the late afternoon sun as we stepped from the classroom, I found myself walking to the dining hall with Amir, one of the few non-Indians in the course I was teaching. "Why have you come all the way from Iran to study here?" I asked.

"I do not face as much scrutiny coming this way as going to the west," Amir responded.

"Do you face fearsome persecution for your faith like we hear about in Canada?"

"Well, I have not personally", Amir stated, "but my brother, also a believer, was released from prison two weeks before I came for these classes and he seems like a different person and won't talk about what happened to him. He is depressed and his family is concerned. We have learned to live with the uncertainty of our freedom but you would not believe how the church is growing in spite of that."

Amir was confirming what I had heard through back channels. Reliable sources suggest that there are 800,000 followers of

Christ inside Iran.[105] Far more than there were before the Islamic Revolution of the Ayatollah. This has been further confirmed through David Garrison's seminal research in *A Wind in the House of Islam*.[106]

When the champion of the Dalits, Dr. B. R. Ambedkar, pondered what religion to associate the Dalits with during his "Quit Hinduism" campaign in 1956, he looked to Islam at one point. However, he soon realized—both from his observation of Muslims in India and his studies—that Islam had an inferior view of what it meant to be human. Especially alarming to him was the way Muslims treated women.

Well documented in the secular press and in Christian missiological research is the reality of the widespread mistreatment of women within Islam. If it were only the matter of wearing the burkah, an outward symbol of seclusion and stigmatization to many in the West (e.g. France with its banning of it in government offices), it could perhaps be challenged and defended by women as part of the dynamic of living in a multicultural world. Or if it were only the separating of women from men behind a screen in mosques, we could tolerate it as a cultural and religious custom devoid of much theological meaning. Furthermore, practicing Christians and feminists alike deplore the sexualizing of European and North American culture and thus empathize with Muslim disgust at the shocking pornography and rampant hedonism of the West.

But it goes much deeper than that. Theologically, Muslim revelation as found in the *Qur'an* and reinforced in the *Hadith* maintains that females are inferior to males. Fundamentally, Islam treats women as inferior to men and this all traces back

---

105 Miriam Adeney, *Kingdom without Borders: The Untold Story of Global Christianity*, 145.
106 121-40.

to their failure to reckon with the biblical worldview that both male and female humans are made in God's image. Not without significance, given the long history of brutish male oppression of women worldwide, is the second statement in the Bible on what the image of God in humankind is. There in Genesis 1:27 we are told that "God created man in his own image; in the image of God he created him; <u>male and female he created them</u>."[107] In other words, both females and males are divine image-bearers.

The Devaluing of Females within Islam

Erun Aisar stood up for her rights as a Muslim woman one Friday in a Regina, Saskatchewan mosque. She took off her shoes, covered her head and joined about 50 men already praying in front of her. After the *imam's* sermon (*khutbah)*, while the prayers were continuing, several men came up to her and told her to leave, but she refused. Not giving ground while the men quoted from the *Qur'an*, supposedly giving them justification to insist that she pray in another room apart from the men, she was allowed to continue. Subsequently, a white curtain was hung at the back of the main meeting hall and the women who came to pray were asked to pray behind that curtain.[108]

An exception to the rule? Not in the half dozen mosques I've visited in Canada during prayer times over the years—in cities as diverse as Calgary, Edmonton and Toronto. If Muslim women are treated this way in a non-Muslim country, what are they treated like in the about 50 countries with a Muslim majority? Let me add a caveat here. There is much in Muslim culture that is admirable with regard to protecting women and in enjoining modesty between the sexes. But, as in the caste system in India,

---

107 Underlining mine.
108 H. Mazurkewich. "Veiled Threats?" *Homemakers,* 45-53.

considered in the previous chapter, in Islam it appears that not everybody is created equal. Females in Islam, no matter what moderate Muslims claim (and to be fair, often practice), generally are treated as inferior to males. It might be as simple as jumping ahead of women in the queue at the grocery store and then being sworn at by a man if you do not give way. My wife has experienced this behaviour toward her and observed it repeatedly in Toronto area stores. When it comes to sexuality, women are projected within Islam as being the weaker sex and more prone to sexual temptation. If Muslims were to view human creation as positioning humankind as made in their Creator's image, it is likely that the majority would not include females in that category.

A symbol of the secondary status of females in Islam is Malala Yousifzai. Being a Muslim girl in Pakistan who pursued an education and blogged about the need to offer educational opportunities to Muslim girls, she was resented by many Muslims, especially the Taliban. On October 12, 2012, a gunman boarded her school bus, asked for her by name and then shot her at point blank range in the head. Miraculously she survived and in the face of an international outcry was airlifted to England where, under the best of medical care, she survived and became an international celebrity, exposing the way girls are not given equal opportunity to the education Muslim boys have. This notoriety culminated with her becoming a Nobel Peace Prize winner in 2014.

Truth be known, most Muslim women do not possess anything close to a level playing field with Muslim men. For instance, girls entering puberty in a number of Muslim-majority countries like Somalia and Sudan undergo female circumcision in a barbaric rite of passage that leaves them in pain and susceptible to chronic health problems and difficulty in enjoying sex in marriage. The most brutal form of female genital mutilation involves cutting away the clitoris and labia and sewing together the scraped sides of the vulva, leaving a small hole. Surgical tools can be razor blades, scissors, or knives.[109] The assumption is that women need protection from their unbridled passions or from devilish men who cannot control theirs. Mutilation of female genitalia occurs surreptitiously in Western world lands as well.

While moderate Muslims say that they do not forbid their wives to work, cover their heads in public, or be subservient to men, such behaviour not being something proscribed in the *Qur'an,* they admit that others have blindly accepted restrictive views from certain religious leaders. However, it is not quite that simple. Based on Quranic tradition, it can be justified that women be portrayed as inferior to men. Here are a few examples:

- Beating is permitted according to *Qur'an* 4:34[110]
- Seclusion in your home is enjoined in *Qur'an* 33:33
- One-sided polygamy benefiting men is allowed – *Qur'an* 4:3, 129
- A woman's testimony in court is worth only half of a man's – *Qur'an* 2:282

Besides the *Qur'an*, Muslims hold in high regard, to the point of considering them almost inspired, the collections of sayings attributed to and stories about Muhammad, called the *Hadith*. The story of Muhammad wanting to marry a six year old girl, allegedly consummating their marriage when she was nine, has been used to justify child marriages in such countries as Yemen and Iraq. Sayings accepted at face value are "a man loves first his son, then his camel, and then his wife" and "a woman's heaven is under the feet of her husband."

---

109 Karen Mazurkewich, "Women's Rights, Women's Plights", *Homemakers*, 62.
110 The English translation used is by M. M. Pickthall.

Yet another way women in Islamic cultures are patronized, in the sense of having to be supervised by men in public, is the practice of guardianship. Stemming from the *Qur'an's* teaching in 4:34 that "men are the maintainers of women", the practice is presented as a way to protect women, but in essence it stifles women—so that they cannot do something as simple as shop for groceries without a male escort. This has reached the stage in fundamentalist states that women who go outside without a male chaperone are subject to beatings and arrests by roving moral police. ISIS is notorious for this sort of control of women.

Honour Killings

One final way Western society can overturn gender discrimination by Muslims, where females are clearly treated as though they are not made in God's image, is to punish severely those guilty of honour killings. This practice has gained significant attention in the West in the past decade. Just as terrorism coming to our soil has captured our attention like two dogs passing each other while being walked by their owners, so has honour killing because it is happening in our backyard. Canadians were riveted to their TVs in 2009 when a multimillionaire Afghan immigrant, Muhammad Shafia, cold-bloodedly locked his first wife and three daughters in a car near Kingston, Ontario and pushed it into the Rideau Canal because the girls were becoming too westernized in his view, and therefore bringing shame to the family. The one daughter had been dating a young man from Pakistan, much to the father's chagrin, as well. The media and public outcry brought the reality of 21st century honour killings front and centre to a culture not used to face or shame-based societies.[111]

---

111 Honour killings are not unique to Islam.

Honour killings resultant from a son or daughter fleeing home to marry out of love, and without parental assent, are widespread, but not the only issue negatively affecting women. There is also the very real mistreatment of women due to forced marriages.[112] We distinguish here between forced marriages and arranged marriages. One can be in an arranged marriage, as is the norm in the non-Western World, where there is negotiation with both individuals agreeing to live marital life with anticipation. However, a multitude of arranged marriages are coerced, involving emotional intimidation or physical violence, or both. It would be remiss to give the impression that forced marriages are the province of Muslims. They are also common among Hindus, Sikhs, and, really, wherever patriarchal and communal understanding of identity hold sway.

The Veil

Ironically enough, the most obvious symbol of Muslim identity for a woman, the *hijab* (head covering), is not required according to the *Qur'an*. One verse (Sura 24:31) enjoins modesty but the veil is actually spoken of in terms of being used to cover (disguise) women's breasts and does not refer to her head being covered. It therefore puzzles me why it should be so difficult for Muslim women to refuse to remove it for court appearances or citizenship ceremonies on the basis of religious reasons. Head covering may be a cultural custom but is it actually religiously required? That aside, the veil is seen by some within and outside of Islam as a symbol of female subjugation.

Certainly we have here (not so much in the head covering issue but attitudinally as a whole) a case of a world religion being clearly at odds with the biblical view of women and men being equally created in God's image. That fact of course does not

---

112 Singh, Nav, "Against Their Will", *University of Toronto Magazine*, 53.

mean that Muslims should have their religious freedom on fundamental faith issues denied; the Judeo-Christian worldview has shaped the laws of Western World and other countries but these are not Christian states per se.

Fatima's Martyrdom

Fatima was not the first martyr for her faith in Saudi Arabia. What singled her out in 2008 was that she was a well-known personality, recognized as an active blogger, and above reproach within the Saudi Muslim fold, coming as she did from a distinguished tribe. Over a period of time, as she searched the Internet in the privacy of her room at home, she discovered Christ and accepted him as her Saviour. She eventually came to the attention of Arabic-speaking Christians on the Arabic faith-based website called www.maarifa.org when she began to email staff and put up blogs on the website testifying to her new-found faith and how being a follower of the Messiah did not compromise her ability to be a patriotic Saudi. Eventually her brother found out and took her Bible and computer. Nevertheless she found a way to blog and told digital friends that if her voice went silent it meant her family had killed her to preserve her honour. Indeed it was discovered that her brother cut out her tongue and then killed her. This became a *cause celebre* on the Internet in the Arabian Peninsula, many using her as an example of the 'dangers' of the Internet, or in debating whether the family followed proper Islamic judicial protocol, but did not question whether she had become a follower of Jesus. This was the first time a Saudi was openly acknowledged within Saudi Arabia to have converted from Islam. Another thing this amazing story does is capture how repressed Muslim women can be, virtually sequestered in their own homes and not permitted to think or act for themselves. In Afghanistan this *purdah*, whereby girls and women are viewed as needing to be kept out of sight in the home, justifies girls being prevented from gaining a basic education. This seclusion is yet another evidence of how Islam does not really treat females as being made in God's image.

Can the Church Throw Stones When It Comes to Women's Rights?

Should Christians be quick to point fingers at Muslim mistreatment of women? No we should not. Men in so-called Christian societies denied women the right to vote until the 20th century. Without wanting to get into a debate about the theological merits of the complementarian or egalitarian interpretation of Scripture over women's right to lead or teach in the church, women have not been given sufficiently the opportunity to use their spiritual gifts in the Body of Christ. Christian men have been misogynists with the best of the Archie Bunkers of the world.

That said, it cannot be easily disputed that the Bible liberates the female sex in a way which has been counter-cultural historically. It started in Genesis 1 as we have seen. The Israelites had women leaders, such as Deborah. Jesus esteemed and affirmed women in a way that was unusual in the Palestinian and Roman society of his day. The gospel gave women the same status as men in Kingdom salvation (Gal. 3:28). The early church was advanced at least as much by women as men (e.g. Priscilla, the co-founder of an early church plant). The reality is that there has been a qualitatively different attitude and treatment of women within the Christian community in comparison to the prevailing Muslim community. Nine of ten countries that Freedom House calls "free" are identified as predominantly Christian and they are also cited by the World Economic Forum for best gender equality.[113] That is not a coincidence but a reflection of the

---

113 Philip Yancey, *Vanishing Grace*, 170.

worldview that assumes women are co-heirs with Christ and made in God's image.

Taking Away the Right to Choose Which Faith

Western world culture is swept up in lionizing human rights. The right to choose is paramount in my culture's understanding of inalienable rights. The right of women to choose whether their fetus lives. The right of the LGBT community to choose sexual orientation without being ostracized. The right to property. The right to a job. If you are an American, the right to bear arms and the right to pursue happiness. It is not a theological stretch to assume that one of the distinguishing marks of humans being made in God's image is their volitional powers. Right from the Creator's first recorded communication with Adam and Even in the Garden of Eden there is the presumption that humans have the capacity and responsibility to relate with God freely. They could choose to eat of the tree of the knowledge of good and evil or not. Respecting the right of humans to make decisions about what religion to believe in is to acknowledge that they are made in God's likeness with the capacity to think rationally and make choices based in their powers of reasoning, observation, intuition, cultural expectations, etc.

What you do not hear too much buzz about is radical Islam's intention to overthrow the right to freedom of choice about religion. ISIS[114] and Al Qaeda, to name just two radical Muslim groups, are euphemized by governments and the media as being fringe 'terrorists' or 'evil people'. Consider Barak Obama's

---

114 ISIS is short for the "Islamic State of Iraq and Syria". It has become the best known and wealthiest jihadist Muslim group in the world. Members used to be identified with Al-Qaida but that radical organization has now disowned them. ISIS gained notoriety by successfully releasing videos and websites which built up a following and recruitment from the West as well as the East, by beheadings of foreigners, and by forceable conversions. ISIS also set up its own caliphate under al-Baghdadi.

statement on September 10, 2014 shortly after the decapitation of Stephen Sotloff: "Now let's make two things clear: ISIL is not "Islamic". No religion condones the killing of innocents... . ISIL is a terrorist organization, pure and simple."[115] Jihadist Muslims often portray themselves as victims because America has sided unjustly with Israel vis-a-vis Palestinians, or as a result of a perceived wrong-headed American-led invasion of Iraq when Hussein was overthrown. Media have not always discerningly distinguished between the rightness and wrongness of causes of aggression, calling contributing factors root causes of aggression when the opposite might be true.[116]

It is true that most Muslims are moderates and want to 'live and let live' and that they live by portions of the *Qur'an* that call for an individualized and internal *jihad* in which the good wars against the evil in our spirits. The most famous injunction they adhere to is "let there be no compulsion in religion" – 2:256. And in the West, moderate Muslims also call on *Qur'an* 5:82: "The nearest in affection to the believers are those who say, 'We are Christians'".[117] All the same, *jihad* is also defined in the *Qur'an* in other sections in ways embraced by extremists that, at the end of the day, remove the human right to make free choices about what should be matters of the heart. We shall delve into those texts shortly.

In justifying forceable conversion, such Muslims make null and void a critical aspect of what it means to be human as a

---

115 Quoted in Ayaan Hirsi Ali, *Heretic: Why Islam Needs a Reformation*, 10.

116 There is balance needed in this discussion. Muslims do have grounds for being resentful of the West. We must be careful not to demonize Muslims stereotypically. For an empathetic overview of the need to avoid seeing a terrorist under every bush see Dudley Woodberry, "Terrorism, Islam and Mission: Reflections of a Guest in Muslim Lands", *International Bulletin of Missionary Research*, 2-7.

117 Andy Bannister in *Islam in Context* believes that only 15% of Muslims in the West are extreme, 15% very moderate and 50% in the middle who are highly suggestive to either extreme (pp. 34-35).

logical consequence of being made in the image of God. While the Bible does not ascribe the right to making free choices to image-bearing per se, it follows naturally. God has so created humankind that we have the capacity to make our own decisions, and he respects that right, too. God himself does not override our free will. True, he determines the consequences of some of our decisions. For example, he does not force us to believe in his Son. But he does set the consequence of the decision not to believe: "Whoever believes in the Son has eternal life; but whoever rejects the Son will not see life; for God's wrath remains on them" (John 3:36). God's sovereignty is not compromised by human freedom because God's purposes are worked out alongside of human responsibility (Eph. 1:11; cf. Phil. 2:12b, 13). God's omnipotence is not compromised either because God freely limited his power over us in order to make our volitional powers real and so as to elicit love, which is not love if not given freely; as a philosopher has said, "God cannot make square circles" because he cannot do that which is mutually exclusive and logically impossible."[118]

Furthermore, to possess free will does not imply that we have the freedom to choose all outcomes of our choices. Someone who wanted the freedom at age 15 to smoke cigarettes and then could not shake the habit for three decades cannot assume that breaking the habit guarantees that he will not die of lung cancer. The concept of total freedom in this life is naive. However, to restrict people's freedoms lightly devalues their dignity as special beings in the created order.

To restrict peoples' freedom of religion lightly also reveals Islamic failure to relate to Allah on a highly personal or intimate level. Part of personhood is the desire and ability to connect with other persons. Sometimes Muslims may quote Surah 50:16

---

118 Ravi Zacharias, *Jesus among Other Gods*, 117-118.

to imply that Allah is close to the human being relationally. There the famous verse speaks of Allah being closer than our jugular vein. But the context of this verse makes clear that the closeness is meant to stave off any rebellion against the God who will judge misbehavior on the judgment day.[119]

We cannot help asking if the disregarding of human rights through the mayhem and murder of extreme jihadists like Boko Haram and ISIS is a logical deduction of Muslim theology. Or, to put it another way, is this extremist element Muslim in name only, an aberration within Islam that should not tarnish the Muslim world as a whole? I would contend that these groups, while extreme and unacceptable to most Muslims, find the rationale for their behaviour within Islamic theology, albeit a minority view. At the same time, I implore the world not to marginalize or persecute Muslims for the faults of a minority within their *ummah* (community of faith). Thomas Friedman, though, renowned author and columnist in *The New York Times*, subscribes to the view that extremists should be understood as Muslim when in a 2015 editorial he argues as follows: "I... would never hold every Muslim accountable for the acts of a few. But it is no good for us or the Muslim world to pretend that the spreading jihadist violence isn't coming out of their faith community. It is coming mostly, but not exclusively, from angry young men and preachers on the fringe of the Sunni Arab and Pakistani communities in the Middle East and Europe."[120]

Likewise, longtime respected Middle East journalist, Daniel Pipes, postulates that political correctness has muted the objectivity of the debate: "Nearly universal falsification of jihad on the part of American academic scholars is an issue of far-

---

119 Andy Bannister and Tanya Walker, *Islam in Context*, 9.
120 Thomas Friedman, "The Problem is Islamism", *The New York Times*, January 23, 2015, 2.

reaching consequence."[121] He was musing on how to interpret 9/11 and reminding his audience that it is commonly accepted that Muhammad himself set the tone for aggressive, military advance of Islam by, in his estimation, engaging in 78 battles, of which only one (the battle of Ditch) was defensive.

Notable Middle Eastern scholar and commentator, Bernard Lewis, cautions that "the overwhelming majority of early authorities, citing the relevant passages in the Qur'an, the commentaries, and the traditions of the Prophet, discuss jihad in military terms. According to Islamic law, it is lawful to wage war against four types of enemies: infidels, apostates, rebels, and bandits. Although all four types of wars are legitimate, only the first two count as jihad."[122]

I would also contend that increasingly we are seeing that this radical interpretation of the mission of Islam is not quite so fringe as first imagined. The UN estimated in November 2014 that 15,000 foreign fighters from 80 countries have travelled to Syria to join the ranks of ISIL and other jihadists.[123] Furthermore, according to the respected Pew Research Center's surveying of attitudes in Muslim-majority countries, three-quarters of Pakistanis and two-fifths of Bangladeshis and Iraqis think that those who leave Islam should suffer the death penalty. More than 80% of Pakistanis and two-thirds of Bangladeshis and Iraqis consider *Sharia* law to be the revealed will of God.[124] A quarter of Bangladeshis and an eighth of Iraqis think that suicide bombing in defense of Islam is justified.[125]

---

121 Daniel Pipes, "Jihad and the Professors", www.danielpipes.org/498/jihad-and-the-professors
122 *The Crisis in Islam*, 24.
123 Cited in Ayaan Hirsi Ali, *Heretic*, 19.
124 17 Muslim-majority nations have made Islam the state religion. *Sharia* is the codified law of Islam as found in the *Qur'an*, the *Hadith* and the *Sunna* of the prophet Muhammed.
125 Cited in Ibid, 19-21.

Two Views of Jihad in the Qur'an

The *Qur'an* itself divides Muhammad's life as a prophet into two parts: his early ministry in Mecca and his later preaching in Medina. While in Mecca at the beginning of his work as a prophet, Muhammad's audience was not very receptive to his message. That resulted in a toned-down message compared to his later preaching in Medina where the local people were responsive. This contrast is no more apparent than in the Meccan versus Medinan teaching on *jihad*. In Mecca it was viewed more as an internal struggle between the forces of good and evil (e.g. Sura 49:15).[126] However, after fleeing to Medina in AD 622, his urging of the believing community to fight physically in the cause of Allah against their enemies, became more strident. These enemies were Arab polytheists throughout Arabia, hypocrites (Arabs who pretended to follow Muhammad's preaching), and people of the Book (Jews and Christians in the region).

Here are just two passages in the *Qur'an* urging Muslims to a 'holy war' if necessary:

> ➢ Then ... slay the idolaters wherever you find them, and take them [captive] and besiege them, and prepare for them each ambush. But if they repent and establish worship and pay the poor-due, then leave their way free" (Sura 9:5).

> ➢ "Fight in the way of Allah against those who fight against you, but begin not hostilities. Lo! Allah loveth not aggressors. And slay them wherever ye find them, and drive them out of the places whence you drove

---

126 M. M. Pickthall (translator), *The Meaning of the Glorious Koran.*

them out, for persecution is worse than slaughter"
(Sura 2:190-191).[127]

The *Hadith* (collected reports about the sayings and actions of Muhammad and considered almost of divine revelatory merit), called *Sahih Bukhari*, contains 199 references to *jihad* and every one of them refers to it in the sense of armed conflict against non-Muslims.[128]

Further complicating the issue is the Muslim doctrine of abrogation. It is used to justify the seeming acceptance of the Pentateuch, the Psalms and the Gospels of the Bible while attributing greater authority to the *Qur'an*. The latter revelation is said to supersede the former; it has been abrogated. It came centuries later on the scene. While this theory is not that widely known by the average Muslim, it carries a lot of weight among Muslim scholars such as those at the renowned Al-Azhar University in Cairo.[129] Abrogation as an interpretive tool for Muslim theology is problematic for moderates. After all, it is the hardline jihadist verses of their holy book which come later than the moderate texts.

Christians should learn from what is going on globally right now. Just as we do not want Christians in Egypt to be marginalized by the Muslim majority, we must not in the West, where Judeo-Christian heritage impacts law and morality, insist that only Christian perceptions of morality be upheld here; to do so is to undermine freedom of conscience and religious belief. We'll come back to this subject in the chapter on postmodernity and

---

127 It should be noted that while only the *Qur'an* is treated as inspired in the same way Christians treat the Bible, Muslims also submit to authority from several other sources too: the *Hadith* (canonical tradition), *ijma* (consensus of the Muslim community) and *qiyas* (analogy). These four sources converge to form the *Sharia* law.
128 Daniel Pipes, "Jihad and the Professors".
129 Mike Kuhn, *Fresh Vison for the Muslim World*, 194-195.

the chapter on practical applications about being made in God's image.

The question we must ask ourselves about Muslim extremists who force their views on others is why they cannot win the battle for the truth in the arena of rational persuasion. In 1972, I travelled the breadth of Afghanistan on my way overland from Europe to India. I had occasion to meet Christy Wilson, the famous pastor of the international church in Kabul, the church being the only physically visible and overt witness in the country. When I returned to Kabul three years later I discovered that this building had been razed to the ground; Afghanis did not want any open witness in their country, even if it was meant only for the expatriate community.

Christian proselytization[130] in Muslim-majority countries is virtually shut down. Why the fear? As far back as John Stuart Mill, the cogent argument has been made that without open discussion and presentation of alternative viewpoints, human beings may be deprived of exchanging error for truth. Without testing truth, there is the very real risk that beliefs will degenerate into superstition and unthinking dogma.[131]

Let me give you another illustration of a closed mind mentality too readily embraced in Muslim cultures. When traveling in the Arabian Peninsula in 2007, I had occasion to visit Sanaa, Yemen. My host, who had lived in the country for some years, gave me a tour of the city. He took me by the Grand Mosque, one of the oldest mosques in the world. He told me that one section was cordoned off and tourists were not allowed in there. What was

---

130 "Proselytization" is a word that people of most faiths shy away from. It is loaded with emotional baggage. I am using it here, tongue in cheek, because the modern use of the word implies aggressive witness, which just does not happen in Muslim-majority countries, as far as I have heard or observed.

131 Elmer Thiessen, *The Ethics of Evangelism: A Philosophical Defense of Proselytizing and Persuasion*, 134.

discovered buried in one of the pillars were allegedly sections of an ancient copy of the *Qur'an*. Apparently, the manuscript's text did not square with the accepted version of the Holy Book and there was an attempt to keep the whole thing under wraps while archeologists did further research. The word on the street was that this discovery would never see the light of day because it might bring doubt into Muslim minds about the reliability of the authorized text. Caliph Uthman in the mid-six hundreds is said to have commanded that different versions to his official text of the *Qur'an* be destroyed.

Quite a different attitude to Christian scholarship's efforts to bring to light all manuscripts of the Bible. The footnotes on each page in my Greek NT expose for all the world to see variants to what scholars believe is the original text.[132] What is there to hide if one is only interested in the truth? Truth will defend itself. It can even be contended that to interact in respectful disagreement, in this case let's say Muslim versus Christian claims about the inspiration of their respective scriptures, is to treat one another with dignity. As Thiessen puts it,

> The proselytizer, in attempting to convert you, to change your beliefs, is in fact upholding your dignity as a person who wants to know the truth. Further, the fact that a proselytizer resorts to persuasion rather than blackmail, for example, or outright physical force, is again a sign of respect. The proselytizer is appealing to your freedom to make up your own mind... . Proselytization is ... a moral activity, provided of course that it is not distorted in some way.[133]

---

132 Not one essential doctrine of the Christian faith is left in doubt by variations in the manuscripts for any given text in the Bible. An excellent introduction to this topic is found in F. F. Bruce, *The New Testament Documents* (London: InterVarsity Press, 1970).

133 *The Ethics of Evangelism*, 147.

Even-handed proselytization, as defined here, is in fact a demonstration of our conviction that the recipient of the message is made in God's image.

Martyrdom and the Image of God

The disregard for human life and freedom to make faith decisions, so as to trample on what it means to be made in God's image, finds expression in the Muslim view of martyrdom. While it may be fine for the Muslim expecting to gain paradise as a result of perpetrating a crime against humanity by killing innocent civilians in a suicide bombing, the barbarous act belittles what it means to be made in the image of God because of the taking of another's sacred life (Genesis 9:6) and by preventing that person slaughtered to live out their faith the way they want to. To kill another human being is tantamount to trying to murder God.

This is not a 21st century phenomenon, I hope we realize. Martyrdom in the course of advancing the cause of Islam is encouraged in the *Qur'an* (e.g. 33:23). This is not an isolated conviction among Muslims although most would probably abhor jihadist suicide. Another PEW survey, from 2011, unearthed the fact that about 180,000 American Muslims considered suicide bombings to be justified in some circumstances.[134] It could be argued that the first modern martyrdoms we heard about in the West revolved around the Iran-Iraq war of the late 1970s and early 80s. At least they were the first I heard about. We were shocked to hear of young boys being sent to the front lines and treated as national heroes by the Ayatollah Khomeini when they were killed in battle. We could not wrap our minds around a thirteen-year-old boy strapping explosives to his chest and blowing himself up underneath an Iraqi tank. 9/11 was not

---

134 Cited in Ayaan Hirsi Ali, *Heretic,* 185.

the beginning of such things. Jihadist martyrdom has a long history in Islamic practice.

This religious resoluteness to the point of embracing martyrdom is something Christians understand. The difference is that we stand up for our faith by not renouncing it under threat of death. We do not kill other people to advance Christian mission. We seek to be true to our conscience and to the Holy Spirit no matter what the implications will be for us personally. We do not take other people down with us. Daniel of old risked life and limb to be true to the living God but he did not use his courtly influence to overrun others' rights. Hebrews 11, that great catalogue of faith, includes in its list of giants of faith those who died for their faith ("They were put to death by stoning; they were sawed in two; they were killed by the sword" – verse 37a). The early church assumed there was a spiritual gift that enabled one to accept martyrdom as it faced virulent persecution from the Roman Empire. *Foxes Book of Martyrs* was a bestselling staple of Christian homes in the English-speaking world for several hundred years. We regularly meditate on the Lord Jesus Christ who "became obedient unto death, even death on a cross" (Phil. 2:8b) and so take to heart the words of the apostle Paul that we "are not [our] own [for we] were bought with a price" (2 Cor. 6:19b, 20a) and so do not "love [our] lives so as to shrink from death" (Rev. 12:11). The history of the global church is bloodstained with the martyrdom of millions of followers of Christ. Fanaticism for Christians is not about believing and acting blindly while committing intellectual suicide but it is the final, rarely required, act of being consistent with one's day-by-day thoughtfully and intentionally lived out relationship with Christ which may result in martyrdom.

Does Freedom of Religion Allow You the Right to *Change* or *Retain* Faith?

The Universal Declaration of Human Rights was adopted by the United Nations as a foundational document in 1948. But while it states that all humankind has the right to *change* religion, such an assertion did not get included in the document without a fight. Some Muslim nations, including Saudi Arabia, objected to the phrasing in Article 18: "This right includes freedom to change his religion or belief." Subsequent debate and lobbying have sought to change the meaning of freedom to *retain* from *change*.[135] This is not only an issue in Muslim countries. The problem is that if freedom is only defined in terms of being allowed to remain in one's ancestral faith, it presupposes that conversion to another faith has been induced through manipulative or coercive means, for example through the promise of a job or the imprisonment of family members. However, that is a one-sided and wrongheaded view of what happens normally in conversion and of what freedom means with respect to conversion to another faith. It is a disingenuous argument. When conversion involves any form of enticement, pressure or manipulation, it is immoral. It exerts undue pressure on the will. But most conversions do not involve that sort of thing.

This conservativism about freedom of speech so as to prevent conversion (unless it is to Islam) may have something to do with a mentality that seems to be engendered within Muslim countries where *Sharia* law holds sway. Ayaan Hirsi Ali, a Somali former Muslim who emigrated to the West and who has become a popular advocate for reform within Islam and women's rights, has this fascinating insight into the difference between her cultural roots and democracy as observed in the

---

135 Ibid, 232.

USA, where she now lives: "Whereas the rule of law in the West evolved to protect the most vulnerable members of society, under sharia it is precisely the vulnerable who are also the most constrained: women, homosexuals, the insufficiently faithful or lapsed Muslims, as well as worshippers of other gods."[136] She goes on to observe that "whereas Western laws generally set boundaries for what cannot be done, leaving everything else permissible, with sharia the system is reversed. The list of things that *can* be done is very small, while the list of what cannot be done overwhelms everything else—except for the list of punishments, which is even longer."[137]

Is Islamophobia or Christophobia More Prevalent?

The accusation that many Westerners are guilty of Islamophobia seems to be as frequently found in the media as outcries about homophobia. Lobbying groups like the Organization of Islamic Cooperation, based in Saudi Arabia, have been skillful at presenting the case that Muslims are victims of abuse in the West. And certainly they are. But do you hear much about the widespread severity of persecution and even killing of Christian minorities in Muslim-majority lands, which could be called 'Christophobia'? A case in point is as simple as the fact that in word processing this text, my spellcheck did not question 'Islamophobia' but it did not recognize the word 'Christophobia'. While the *Qur'an* itself grants a protective dispensation to "people of the book" (Christians and Jews), the influence of writers like Syed Qutb cannot be overstated. Qutb (1906-1966), who was a radical Egyptian Muslim who was implicated in an assassination attempt on President Nasser and eventually executed for his radical dissent over the Muslim status quo, was a prolific author who openly spoke of violence

---

136 Ibid, 142.
137 Ibid, 134.

for the good of the *ummah* and encouraged forceable *jihad* that inspired the Muslim Brotherhood. To this day, his commentaries on the *Qur'an* are influential and studied in thousands of Muslim homes and mosques throughout the Arab world, which associate Christians with the West and forbid Muslims contact with them because they are purported to lead the faithful astray.[138]

The world was shocked in February 2015 when the Islamic State posted a graphic online video revealing that 21 Christians in Libya had been beheaded in Libya. Clothed in orange jumpsuits, symbolic of their unlawful imprisonment, they were shown kneeling on a beach in Libya with several darkly-clad radicals standing behind them. One by one, these Coptic Egyptian Christians were beheaded.

Obviously, near the top of the media radar where this sort of violence against Christians was perpetrated between 2010 to this present day is the Boko Haram attacks on the Christian minority in northern Nigeria. While there has been longstanding tension and some violence between the Christian and Muslim sectors of Nigeria with its 160 million people, not until recently was it typical to see a radical Muslim group like Boko Haram go on a kidnapping, raping and murdering spree of Christian villages. Boko Haram in name means "Western education is sacrilege" and aims to establish *Sharia* law in the country. Over 2,000 children have been kidnapped by them in the past few years.

A similar slaughtering of Christians by Muslims has gone on in the Sudan unrelentingly in the twenty-first century. It was

---

138 Warren Larson, "How Islam Sees Itself", *Envisioning Effective Ministry: Evangelism in a Muslim Context*, 33-34. At the same time it needs to be stated that especially during the Middle Ages Islamic governments were more tolerant of Jews and Christians than so-called Christian governments were of Muslims.

at the heart of the genocide that took place in 2003 in Darfur. Sudan's Muslim president, Omar al-Bashir, has been indicted by the International Criminal Court in The Hague on three counts of genocide for these crimes against humanity. Granting of the Christian south independence in 2011 has not ended the kidnapping of children and targeted killings. It is estimated that there are one million displaced people in South Sudan, hidden from the world's view, but one of the greatest ongoing humanitarian tragedies of our day.

So too was the genocide a century ago in Turkey (during the Ottoman Empire's dying years) when a million Armenians were killed. Back in the early centuries after Christ's death and resurrection, Armenia became the first majority-Christian country in history. Yes, the Armenians slaughtered in 1915 were not Muslims, as 99% of Turks are, but Christian. To this day, Turkey refuses to call this mass betrayal genocide but the result of fighting in World War 1.

Most recently, at the time of writing, evidence of the systematic slaughtering of Christians has emerged from narratives concerning ISSL[139] in Syria and Iraq. As a first step to extermination of Christians it is well known that soldiers go through captured towns and villages marking a letter "N' in Arabic on homes where Christians live. The 'N' stands for "Nazarene', Jesus of course being from Nazareth (Matt. 2:23). Christians are marked people in the Middle East.

Former Muslim but not a Christian, Ayaan Hirsi Ali, now having found safe haven in the USA and teaching at Harvard, describes this Muslim outburst against Christianity in these words: "We hear so often about Muslims as victims of abuse in the West and combatants in the Arab Spring's fight against tyranny.

---

139 Also known as ISIS and Daesh.

But, in fact, a wholly different kind of war is underway—an unrecognized battle costing thousands of lives. Christians are being killed in the Islamic world because of their religion. It is a rising genocide that ought to provoke global alarm."[140]

In Pakistan, the Christian minority of 2% is relentlessly harassed. Periodically Christians are charged with blasphemy and sentenced to death. On November 4, 2014, Shahzad Masih and his pregnant wife Shama Bibi were savagely beaten and then burned to death by a mob of militant Muslims at a brick kiln near Lahore for allegedly committing blasphemy against Islam by burning pages of the *Qur'an,* although others close to the scene insisted the murder was over a money dispute.[141]

Human nature being what it is, liberal-minded humanists, thoughtful Hindus and Christians alike urge moderate Muslims and all fair-minded people to dissuade fundamentalist Muslims from thinking that forcible conversion is tantamount to genuine conversion. Such a trivializing of the human spirit and heart is like a political party conducting its own polls to prove that its leader is ahead in the popularity stakes. Coercive conversion does not mean anything in God's sight. Lip service to faith will not get one into heaven. Physical *jihad* is disgraceful and catastrophic to contemporary civilization. It flies in the face of the truth that we all are made in God's image.

Apostasy from Islam and Its Consequences

We have talked about freedom of faith or lack thereof with respect to the practice of *jihad* by Muslims. But what about Muslims who want to renounce their faith? Are they given

---

140 Ayaan Hirsi Ali: The Global War on Christians in the Muslim World", *World News.* http://www.thedailybeast.com/newsweek/2012/02/05/ayaan-hirsi-ali-the-global-war-on-Christians

141 Greg Musselman, "Paying the Price in Pakistan", *Voice of the Martyrs,* 4.

freedom to choose based on their own convictions? Whilst enlightened Muslims do tolerate, although not openly approve, family members becoming apostates, tolerance is not the norm. Instead, apostasy is considered to be worthy of death, an unforgiveable sin, unless recanted. The tragic reality is that the threat of being murdered for changing faith keeps many Muslims from taking the plunge or from retaining their faith in Christ. Respecting of the human will is not in the vocabulary of conservative Muslims. Justification for their intolerance to religious freedom comes from sources like *Hadith Sahih al-Bukhari* 9:83:17 which declares:

> The blood of a Muslim who confesses that none has the right to be worshiped but Allah and that I [Muhammad] am His Apostle, cannot be shed except in three cases: In retaliation for murder; for a married man who commits illegal sexual intercourse; and for the one who reverts from Islam [apostate] and leaves the Muslims.[142]

The case can be made that there have been largescale turnings to Christ in some countries like Iran, Indonesia and Algeria because of the oppressiveness of the Islamic State. Thus Garrison concludes that "while the tools of jihad and sharia law have certainly been used to advance Muslim territory, today's Muslims are increasingly repulsed by a religion that imposes its will with force."[143]

Fatalism in Islam Devalues Human Worth

Perhaps the most common phrase spoken by Muslims around the world is *in sha Allah*. It essentially means "if God wills". If a teenage Pakistani girl hopes that she will end up having her marriage arranged with a particular boy, she will be sure to lace her conversation with *in sha Allah. Qadr*, or predetermined

---

142 Cited in David Garrison, *A Wind in the House of Islam*, 28.
143 Ibid, 244.

destiny, is a Muslim doctrine that proclaims that all human behavior occurs according to Allah's will (e.g. Sura 18:29). While Muslims teach human responsibility for their actions, there is also a strong food coloring of fatalism in the mix. A number of times in conversations with Muslims about the meaning of "sin", they will express the idea that if they yield to temptation then God somehow did not keep them from yielding. Something is a 'sin' if one gets caught. It is as if Muslims have a view of the sovereignty of God that is taken to the nth degree so that in fact there is no or little human culpability for behaviour whereas the Bible teaches the paradox of God's control of all things and yet human responsibility for attitudes and actions. The Christian view of humankind presupposes that the ability to choose for humans is fundamental to who they are. To take the right to decide what to believe—whether that decision is based on truth or wistful thinking—is an inalienable right founded on the fact of our being made in God's image.

The Muslim Who Dared to Call God Father

One of the bestselling Christian biographies of the late 1970s was the true story of Madam Bilquis Sheik, from a high society Muslim family of Pakistan, who came to faith in Christ in a dramatic way. One of her most telling statements revolved around the prayer beads that she grew up meditatively fingering, one bead for each of the 99 names of Allah, only the camel supposedly knowing the one hundredth. When she became aware that Jesus was more than a prophet and was the human-divine expression of God's love for people, she spoke of being able to call upon God as Father, a name for God she found missing in Islam. I had the privilege of chauffeuring her around for speaking engagements in Toronto in the early 1980s and probed for myself to see if her amazing story was really true or just some sort of a publicity stunt. After scrutinizing her in different settings and engaging her in conversation over a couple of days, I could see that she was authentic.

Her story parallels that of many Muslims who come to faith in Christ as they realize the love of the God who created them in his image. What many of God's People do not realize as they hear about the statistical growth of Islam is that the number of those coming to faith in Christ from a Muslim background far outweighs the number from Christian backgrounds converting to Islam (most of Islamic growth anyhow comes from biological growth, not conversion growth; Muslims tend to have much larger families than Christians do and this is a real dilemma in continental Europe). What you do not hear about too often is the large number of Muslims who become followers of Jesus in sub-Sahara Africa, who came to faith in large numbers in the 1960s in Indonesia (the most populous Muslim country), and currently do in Bangladesh, in Algeria and in Iran, to name a few. By the end of the 20th century, there had been a total of 13 movements of Muslims of 1,000 baptisms or 100 churches within a two decade period. Since the death of Muhammed almost 1,400 years ago to the end of the 20th century an additional two could be identified but after the first 12 years of the 21st century an additional 69 such movements had emerged.[144]

A recent study of 750 Muslims who became Jesus followers between 1991 and 2007 included an extensive questionnaire on a basic question: *What attracted you to follow Jesus?* The respondents were from 50 ethnicities in 30 countries from all regions of the Muslim world.[145] The top ranked influence was the *lifestyle of Christians* as compared to Muslims. One of those striking differences pointed to was love versus animosity, such as described by an Egyptian respondent who contrasted the love

---

144 Ibid, 18.
145 "Why Muslims Follow Jesus", Dudley Woodberry, Russell Shubin and G. Marks, *Christianity Today*, 80-85.

of a Christian group on campus at an American university where he studied with the unloving experiences he had at a university in Medina, Saudi Arabia. Some respondents noted loving Christian marriages. Now I am not trying to cast aspersions on Muslims stereotypically because I have met scores of Muslims who are charming, hospitable and generous. I also realize there are many problematic Christian marriages and that hatred can be found anywhere because we are fallen creatures living in a fallen world regardless of our worldview. There are good-living Muslims and disappointing Christians. But a pattern is a pattern.

Muslims Are Making the Choice to Follow Jesus

A decade ago I had the privilege of serving in ministry alongside of BMBs (Believers from a Muslim Background)—especially Arab BMBs. What precious people they are. I have met scores of them in North Africa, the Middle East, and to a much lesser extent, in the Arabian Peninsula. Many of them are cautious but eager witnesses to fellow Arabs about their newfound faith. One family from Tunisia told me a story of a Tunisian *imam*[146] who had viewed their TV program from Cyprus which was in the Tunisian dialect of Arabic. In that TV program they had shared how they had come to faith in Jesus Christ. Amazed that there were Tunisians who believed the same thing he was gravitating towards, the imam got in touch with the program hosts via email and thus began his journey to a solid faith in Christ.

After coming to faith, he was disowned by some of his family (his wife became a follower of Jesus though) but he was a man of courage, perhaps in part because he was older and felt he had nothing to lose. Among other things, he found opportunities to talk about Jesus and quote the Bible in his mosque.

---

146 An *imam* is a Muslim cleric, much like Christian pastors or Hindu priests, meaning "the one up front". They give the sermon in mosques.

Returning to her homeland for the first time in many years a few years ago, one of the TV presenters, Fatima,[147] had the opportunity to visit this imam in a town distant to Tunis. After Fatima opened up the scripture in Arabic to him for hours, he told Fatima: "I lost two daughters but God gave me four other children. Please give my greetings to my son, Abdul [Fatima's believing husband], and tell him to keep telling the world and not be afraid." Fatima came to encourage the imam but he ended up encouraging her.

People will make life-changing choices in the face of danger because they are not robots whose wills can be forced; they are made in God's image. Conditioning and culture exercise considerable influence on our choices but our hearts and our heads are more than the sum total of nature and nurture factors.

One of the most riveting stories about bonafide Muslims who have come to faith in Christ in our time is that of Nabeel Qureshi.[148] Hailing from the same Arab tribe as Muhammed, the Qureshis, by the age of five Nabeel could recite the last seven chapters of the *Qur'an* by heart in both Arabic and English. While a freshman at Old Dominion University in Virginia, he was befriended by a Christian. Ridiculing David for reading his Bible, Nabeel was surprised that this guy neither retorted angrily at his challenges but could also provide reasonable answers to his rehearsed Muslims arguments against Christianity. After becoming good friends and investigating the claims of Christianity over his next three years at university, he became convinced of its credibility and so accepted David's advice to study Islam with the same open mind. Doing so, he found himself wavering in his conviction as to Islam's authenticity. As he sought for Allah to reveal the truth to him, Nabeel was

---

147 Name changed for security reasons.
148 Nabeel Qureshi, "Called Off the Minaret", *Christianity Today*, 95-96.

shaken to his core over the next year by one vision and three dreams. He realized he had a tough choice to make about following Jesus even though he now believed in Jesus. After weeks of struggling, he finally knelt beside his bed and gave his life to Christ. As expected, this shattered his family who to this day lament their son's decision. Nabeel is now an itinerant speaker with Ravi Zacharias International Ministries.

Walk a Mile in Their Shoes

I have a lot of sympathy for many Muslims I meet. While the world gasps in shock at the *fatwahs* levied as a result of the Danish cartoons satirizing Mohammad, or at the slaying of the Dutch filmmaker Theo van Gogh in 2002 who printed Quranic verses on the naked bodies of women in his film, *Submission*, or at the 11 deaths stemming from reaction to the *Charlie Hebdo* satirical depiction of Muhammad in the November 2011 edition of the magazine, I believe there are limitations to free speech. Freedom of self-expression does not trump all state- or self-censorship. Hate crimes are already fairly universally recognized for things like denying the Holocaust and white supremacy rhetoric. Human rights libertarians unfortunately feel that being true to oneself, no matter how unfair or vulgar the public display of self-expressions is, is tantamount to a divine right. What about old-fashioned common decency? Making fun of the Prophet in the extreme way it has been done makes a mockery of treating fellow human beings as divine image-bearers. It disrespects their deeply-held core worldview beliefs. To the extent it has been done regarding Muhammad, and other religious figures deeply loved by devotees, such as Jesus being portrayed in a movie as having an erection on the cross, it is going too far. I empathize with Muslim fury at the self-indulgent disrespect of "the free press" even though I would never condone murder and even though I believe in the right of free speech. I also empathize with the Muslim desire to obey God's laws and do not want them stereotyped as submitting to the law of God blindly any more than I would want Christians who claim that their salvation is by grace apart from works of the law being vilified as people who feel they can live any way they want without divine consequences.

Free Speech but with Limits

Restating what I have just said, freedom of speech and expression, while being a right that stems from our great value in being image-bearers, is not as foundational a right as freedom to life. It is limited by other freedoms. The freedom of religion. The freedom to be truthful. If God is light and in whom is no darkness (1 John 1:5), his passion for truth is embedded within the human DNA, too, and needs to be the standard that all human being should live by, as imperfectly as we do. Freedom of expression "lies in the service of the will to truth".[149] Social networking has made the unfettered vilifying of innocent people possible and as common as flies on roadkill. Freedom of expression has too easily been made synonymous with my individual rights, regardless of how they infringe on someone else's as if being true to one's feelings is more important than truthfulness or social responsibility. With the rapid urbanization of the world have come crowded living conditions that contain multicultural, ethnic and religious diversity as never before experienced in human history. Without lapsing into political correctness—which is no free speech at all—we must recognize certain limitations on our freedoms of speech.

---

149 Vinoth Ramachandra, *Subverting Global Myths*, 122.

Before We Get Too Critical of Islam

The Western (or postmodern) World cannot be smug in assuming it is enlightened vis-à-vis Islam. Muslim disenchantment with Western civilization has its roots in our own disregard for what it means to be made in God's image and to be truly human. What once longtime resident of Egypt, American Mike Kuhn, observes, resonates with me: "While it may be easy to cast blame on Islamic fundamentalism, we must resist the urge to look outside ourselves for a scapegoat to our societal dilemma. A movement of radical Muslims will never succeed in destroying our civilization unless our civilization has already been undermined by a massive defection from its values and foundational tenets."[150] Especially Christians need to be careful that we do not justify profiling and stereotyping of Muslims in our own society, deflecting from healthy self-criticism. To not look reflectively at our own prejudices and inconsistent expressions of love of our neighbor, instead automatically demonizing Muslims, would be to behave like Aesop's Fox. Remember him? Noticing some ripening grapes on the vine just out of reach, he leaped unsuccessfully to try and reach them. Once he realized that he could not reach the grapes no matter how hard he tried, he slunk away, muttering, "I'm sure they're sour anyway." Let us not look for a scapegoat for problems within our own churches and culture. Just because there may be a few 'sleepers' in the flood of Muslims refugees to the West should not absolve us from our responsibility to provide shelter and a fresh start for them in our midst; most of them are ordinary human beings who only want to take care of their families and who want to live in peace, embracing their new homeland and the freedoms it affords. More about this issue in chapter 6.

---

150 Mike Kuhn, *Fresh Vision for the Muslim World*, 217.

An analysis of postmodern culture is fittingly what we turn to next as we assess to what extent contemporary cultures and religions mirror the biblical worldview of what it means practically for humans to be made in God's image.

CHAPTER 4
Postmodern Society and the Deification or Trivialization of Humankind

Long before the emergence of postmodern culture in the 20th century, a young woman, with two small children, recently widowed, perched on a bridge abutment staring at the dark waters beckoning her below, a river in Ecclefechan, Scotland. The year was 1815, noted for the celebrated victory of Wellington over Napoleon, but immaterial to Jane Lucretia D'Esterre, contemplating suicide. Before throwing herself off the bridge, she happened to look up and observed a young farmer working his plough in tidily straight furrows on the far side of the river bank. Fascinated by the farmer's pride in his workmanship and listening to him whistling hymns while straining at his work, she gradually was pricked in her conscience about being so absorbed in herself as to contemplate suicide when two young children were dependent on her welfare. Stepping down from the bridge, she returned home and resolved to find happiness in God's purpose for her life.

A few years later she remarried, to the youngest son of the famous Dublin brewer, John Grattan Guinness. Grattan was a follower of Jesus and later became one of the two founders of a mission to the Muslims of North Africa, 'Mission to the Kabyles and Other Races', in 1881, which became North Africa Mission in 1887 and Arab World Ministries in 1987, which I had the privilege of leading between 2002 and 2010.[151]

Why do I share this story, which has nothing to do with postmodern times, as gripping as it may be? Because it reveals that there is something about the human spirit that sings when an overarching purpose in life is embraced. Finding life's purpose resonates within us because human beings are made in the image of God. That is certainly my testimony. Philip Hughes put it this way: "A conscience at harmony with his Creator's will is the true pulse beat of humanity. Only when the human will is one with the divine will can man be his authentic self."[152] Identifying purposeful existence with being made in God's likeness takes us back to Genesis 1.

Life Full of Purpose Because Image-Bearers

After revealing in Genesis 1 that this last created earthly creature named Adam was an image-bearer of God himself, in the next breath God assigns Adam and his offspring a purpose, a task, a calling if you will: "Be fruitful and multiply and fill the earth and subdue it and have dominion over the fish of the sea and over the birds of the heavens and over every living thing that moves on the earth" (Gen. 1:26b). In the verse after it is revealed that humans are God's image-bearers, we find, then, a reiteration of the undergirding principle for living life

---

151 This story is recounted in Os Guinness' book, *The Call: Finding and Fulfilling the Central Purpose of Our Life.* The woman of this story was his great-great grandmother. I met Os Guinness, a famous Christian writer, over lunch in 2007, and presented him with a book called *The Desert Is Alive,* telling tales of faith from the Arab world, in memory of his ancestor and encouraged him by telling him that the 125 year old Arab World Ministries was larger now than at any time in its long history and that Arabs were turning to Christ in larger numbers than ever before since the days of Muslim expansion into North Africa and the Middle East.
152 *The True Humanity,* 60.

in terms of a meta-narrative of purpose larger than ourselves. Some commentators maintain that to associate earth-tending with what it means to be made in God's image is reading into the text what is not there. However, the immediate context is so critical to interpreting Scripture correctly (to hermeneutics) that I believe we are safe to conclude that being made in God's image, in part, has something to do with living life in light of our God-given purpose. Being made in God's image, as we have expounded, is about **why** God created us not **what** the content of the image of God is. The metanarrative of history, according to the Bible, is that God created human beings in his image so that they could have a loving relationship with him and accomplish his intentions for planet earth.

Some have called this purpose the "cultural mandate".[153] By being "fruitful and multiplying" we find our *raison d'etre* for fashioning the social world of families, nations and institutions like schools. The other aspect of this mandate, found in the words "subdue the earth" gives us the impetus to steward the natural world. Looking after the earth. Making the best possible use of it. Not dominion over the earth in the sense of domination, as the rendering of *King James* Version of Genesis 1:26 might imply.[154] Tending the earth is understood to imply not only physical work but all of the social and multi-layered cultural milieu we have come to associate especially with urban living.[155] It is the working out of the implications of verse 26 in its first expression in Genesis 2:15 that gives rise to human significance in our daily toil ("The Lord God took the man and put him in the Garden of Eden to work it and take care of it").

---

153 Nancy Pearcey, *Total Truth: Liberating Christianity from its Cultural Captivity*, 47; Millard Erickson, *Christian Theology*, 510.
154 Ronald Sider, *The Scandal of Evangelical Politics*, 211-212.
155 It is worth remarking here that while the first humans were placed in a garden the permanent residing place of humans will be the New Jerusalem, a city.

A parallel passage to Genesis 1 is found in Psalm 8. There the wonder and glory of God the creator of the universe are unfolded. The puniness of humankind is contrasted with God's greatness. But the relative greatness of humankind is acknowledged: "What is mankind that you are mindful of them, human beings that you care for them? Yet you have made them a little lower than the angels and crowned them with glory and honour. You made them rulers over the works of your hands; you have everything under their feet" (vv. 4-6). Notice the purpose assigned to humans placed alongside their status in the creation hierarchy. There is a purpose for which humans are made; there is an overarching narrative that their existence should square with. It is not that being made in God's image is synonymous with our cultural mandate. But the reason why we were created in God's image, in part, is to demonstrate his rulership on the earth which is noticeably at odds with the purposelessness purported by postmodernism for humankind. As Kilner explains it, "Creation in God's image is about God's intentions, not a statement of current or lost attributes. It encompasses many intended attributes, rulership over creation being one of many."[156] And so, accordingly, the Psalmist declares: "The highest heavens belong to the Lord, but the earth he has given to mankind" (Ps. 115:16).

Humans Are Designed to Live Life with a God-given Purpose

Our creator fashioned us in part so that we might carry out purposes intended to fulfill his plan to bring glory to himself on this planet and to do so it required that we were made in his image. Image-bearing is a means to a larger end. Consider these Scriptures hinting at this very thing (italics and bold font are my addition to highlight the causal nature of our creation):

---

156 *Dignity and Destiny*, 207.

- ➤ "For we are God's handiwork, created in Christ Jesus **to do good works**, which God prepared in advance for us to do." Ephesians 2:10
- ➤ "But you are a chosen people, a royal priesthood, a holy nation, God's special possession, **that** you may declare the praises of him who called you out of darkness into his wonderful light." 1 Peter 2:9
- ➤ "May God be gracious to us and bless us and make his face shine on us—**so that** your ways may be known on earth, your salvation among all nations." Psalm 67:1-2

No Meta-Narrative According to Postmodern Thinking

However, post-Christian and postmodern society, emerging first in the Western world, but becoming increasingly a global phenomenon because of things like the expansive reach of the Internet and the global popularity of Facebook, MTV, YouTube, Instagram and Twitter, posits that there is no metanarrative to life.[157] To speak of an overarching "Truth" or "Purpose" to life, as conditioning and defining all of life, of ontological meaning, in contemporary society meets with widespread cynicism, skepticism or hostility. What transformed Jane Guinness' life would be scoffed at today, or at least snickered at politely, as being nothing more than misguided zeal, perhaps a psychological blanket she wrapped herself in to weather her life-threatening circumstances.

Enlightenment has come to mean 'deconstructing' so-called metanarratives. A father of postmodern philosophy, Jean-

---

157 I admit that I am somewhat a product of postmodern culture and that some generalizations are made here about postmodernity.

Francois Lyotard, defined postmodernity as "incredulity toward metanarratives".[158] Such is postmodernism.[159]

This suspicion of the unseen dimension of spirituality stemmed in large part from the age of Enlightenment where what could not be proved through scientific evidence was spurned as being non-factual. Modernity, with its undying faith in what could be empirically proven, sidelined the religious to non-factual at best, superstitious at worst. In a sense postmodernity or postmodernism might have been predicted because of the increasingly recognized limitations of science in forming a comprehensive worldview. Its inherent weaknesses are well-delineated by theologian Poythress when he observes that "scientific investigation, narrowly conceived, does not prove materialism. Rather materialism arises from confusing two distinct moves: (1) the narrow scientific strategy of focusing on what is material and (2) the claim that the narrow focus is all that there is."[160] Postmodernism, though, arose out of a recognition of the limitations of science to prove and offer a grand explanation (a meta-narrative) of all reality. Thus, Vinoth Ramachandra is probably right in coming to this conclusion: "Postmodernism is simply modernism come home to roost. A movement that sought to guard the objectivity of truth from theological 'interference' has ended up doubting the very concept of truth. A movement that glorified in reason and exalted it above divine revelation has come to spurn the rational in every area of life. A movement that began with the divinization of self has culminated in the loss of that very self."[161]

---

158 Cited in David Lundy, *Borderless Church: Shaping the Church for the 21st Century*, 33.
159 I provide a succinct survey of postmodernism in my book, *Borderless Church*, especially in chapter 3. Little has changed in this worldview in its core concepts over the decade since the book was written.
160 Vern Poythress, *Inerrancy and Worldview: Answering Modern Challenges to the Bible*, 29.
161 *God That Fail: Modern Idolatry and Christian Mission*, 12.

In effect, what this means about truth is that it is perceived as a social construct, serving the purposes of interpretative politicized interest groups, whether they be feminist, white-male, evangelical, political parties or governments. Words like "spin" or "play" are used to describe the speech or actions of politicians, for instance. To quote postmodernist philosopher, Richard Rorty: "Truth is made, not found."[162] Instead of the truth setting us free, we have become free to manufacture our own truth. Postmodernists would side with Pontus Pilate as Jesus came before him to be tried for rebellion against Rome, who asked Jesus rhetorically, "What is truth?"

A suitable symbol of such a worldview might be the black swan. For thousands of years people were convinced that all swans were white. Not so as it turns out. Nassim Taleb in 2007 coined the expression "black swans" to convey his thesis that although we are trained to believe there is an order to our lives, that the future is predictable, in fact it is quite random and chaotic.[163]

The Flattening of the World

The impact of globalization, on the face of it, seemed a portent for flattening the world, as political commentators like Thomas Friedman articulated. Unpredictably, several decades on, the opposite has occurred. Rather than flattening, as in Macdonalizing, the globe, the particularities and heterogeneity of the planet have flourished. As one theologian observed: "Particularity rather than universality is the defining characteristic of the 21st century. We share experiences via global media but interpret contextually and locally. Pluralism, complexity, paradox, chaos are words that define the current state of affairs."[164] In other words, global

---

162 Cited in Nancy Pearcey, *Total Truth*, 242.
163 *The Black Swan: The Impact of the Highly Improbable*.
164 Barry Taylor, "Culture since 1985", *Missiology: An International Review*, 149.

accessibility to knowledge, culture, values, art, religion, etc. has not created consensus about universal truth or absolute values but skepticism that there is such a thing. Universals are out, particulars are in. Exclusivity is cold, inclusiveness is hot. Homogeneity does not excite, diversity does. The only reality we can be sure of, many conclude, is that within each person meaning and values have to be discovered. Individuals create their own moral universe. One hour of TV may inform one's value formation as much as an hour listening to a sermon. Who can say that someone who considered a topic five minutes ago for the first time and wrote a blog about her findings is not as wise on the subject as someone whose article is also posted on the Internet but who got her doctorate in the field? Ironically, then, globalization has fostered postmodernism.

Notwithstanding the flourishing of diversity in spite of globalization, other globe-spanning problems are driving us together. We need common solutions to things like global warming and peace-threatening instability in the Middle East.[165] For instance, the Millennium Assessment, first prepared by the United Nations in 1995, noted that 60% of the world's ecosystems are under serious threat due to things like more land being devoted to agriculture since 1945 than during all of the 18th and 19th centuries combined with deforestation in the tropics alone denuding an area the size of Greece every year.[166] Deforestation accounts for 20% of CO2 emissions.[167]

Driving us together as well is the ubiquitous influence and reach of technology—digital and otherwise. We've spoken of India often in this book and of its half billion poor. Yet, there are 900 million mobile phone subscribers in India. Nor do Indians lack savvy on how to use mobile phones smartly! An Indian favourite

165 Naomi Klein, *This Changes Everything: Capitalism vs. the Climate*.
166 Thomas Friedman, *Hot, Flat and Crowded*, 24-25.
167 Ibid, 189.

is the "missed call", where one makes a phone call for only two rings and then turns off the call, thereby signaling something like "start dinner, I'm on my way home". Mobile phones are used as torches, scanners, as an alternative to YouTube (callback features where the audio can be listened to without needing to be connected to the Internet), and FM radio. Thus a simple villager living in a mud hut can be connected to a wider world.

Such access to cultures and stories from around the world creates empathies to realities other than our own and a wondering if indeed the world and worldview we inhabit is the centre of the universe and explanation of ultimate reality. Ergo the postmodern perspective. A relativistic attitude to everything is seen as the sure sign of enlightenment.

The Unpopularity of Monotheism and Religion, Period

Except for the practitioners of Islam, Christianity, Sikhism and Judaism, you might be hard-pressed in Western cultures to find many people who accept the thesis that there is only one God and one way to God. Relativism holds sway. Indeed, it is more likely to be the case that agnosticism has hardened into "all religions are wrong", at least in urban European and intellectual North American circles. So claims pastor and author Timothy Keller in saying, "When I first came to New York City nearly twenty years ago, I more often heard the objection that all religions are equally true. Now, however, I am more likely to be told that all religions are equally false."[168] Such a worldview is actually atheism.

Charlie Hebdo theology, though, is not as liberating and unbiased as assumed. All worldviews, even the ones that say all narratives

---

168 Keller, *The Reason for God*, 9.

are relative and therefore all should be critiqued unfettered, are sectarian and limited because all make faith leaps, whether or not that is perceived. Postmodern democracy, it seems, is drifting towards being more about freedom from religion rather than freedom to choose one's religion. It is about freedom to speak with political correctness and not freedom of expression. Sure, it argues, there are limits to science, but we must start with the premise that evolution, actually a substantially unproven and flawed philosophy, is true. Postmodernism creates its own philosophical and social straitjackets. Philosopher, Ramachandra, observes that "the atheism of our present age is really a preoccupation with individual consumption and an indifference to the deeper issues of life and death. It hides behind a casual talk of 'tolerance' that is usually a respectable term for apathy."[169]

A big court battle in Quebec in the past few years occurred as a result of the government of Quebec ruling that Loyola High School, a Jesuit institution in Montreal, had no right to teach Catholicism from a Catholic perspective but had to follow the more secular provincial "Ethics and Religious Culture" program. The school spent seven years fighting this ruling in the courts until finally the Supreme Court of Canada overturned the provincial government's ruling. Its stance was that neutrality toward religion also means neutrality toward non-religion.[170] The school's principal, Paul Donovan, in being interviewed by the *Convivium* journal publisher, observed: "You can be as secular as you like but leave room for those who are still religious."

Toronto talk radio host, John Moore, speaks for many of his listeners when he voices these words: "I can't speak for all non-believers but I have neither a holy book nor hymnal. I observe

---

169 Vinoth Ramachandra, *Gods That Fail*, 47.
170 Peter Stockland, "Law, Loyola and the Common Good", *Convivium* (Volume 4, No. 20), 8-12.

no special holidays and attend no services. My atheism is simply an absence of religion in my life. Outside of leaving me a few hours to myself on Sunday mornings this absence is not some kind of void that must be filled with something else."[171]

Sentiments similar to these are expressed across the pond in the UK by columnist for *The Times*, Matthew Parris, who acknowledges his Christian upbringing but then plainly states that "I'm sure religion is wrong". Unrepentant in declaring his atheistic colours, he rants:

> Look at the evangelical movement in America... . Look at the Religious Right in Israel. Look at fundamentalist Islam. What they share, what drives them, the tiger in their tanks, is an absolute, unshakeable belief in an ever-present divinity, with plans for nations that He communicates to the leaders, or would-be leaders, of nations. They are the very devil, these people, they could wreck our world, and their central belief in God's plan has to be confronted. Confronted with passion. Confronted because, and on the ground of that, *it is not true*.[172]

Having lived five years in the UK in the first decade of the 21st century, it is my impression that hostility to "religion" is more hard-bitten and extensive in Europe than in North America.

If God is believed in within this postmodern world, unless you are an adherent to a global religion, you would tend to cut and paste from different sources to create your own designer religion. It would be a mistake to think that spirituality is not cool just because traditional religions are avoided like the plague and considered "boring" or "irrelevant". Strolling through a *Chapters* bookstore in Mississauga, Ontario recently, I could not help noticing that while the company had a separate book case

---

171 "John Moore: The New Atheist Just Doesn't Care", http://news.nationalpost.com/2015/03/26/john-moore-the-new-atheist-just-doesnt-care/
172 Matthew Parris, "Shout Your Doubt Out Loud, My Fellow Unbelievers", *The Times*, 19.

for Christianity, one as well for Eastern Religions, and one for Islam, it had three book cases for New Age writings, alongside of which were two for self-help materials.

My father and my mother died within seven months of each other recently. They were fine believers. In the middle of all this, one of their eight children doggedly second-guessed the care of my parents that one of my brothers provided lovingly and sacrificially over the course of a decade. In one of the few heated exchanges between these two siblings, my brother called the arm chair critic sibling "evil" (this sibling had disavowed the Christianity we were raised in unlike the support-providing brother). That seemed to trigger a response that was treated as being more shameful than the bullying of my parents that this sibling consistently indulged in. Another sibling, also not a practicing Christian, told me "evil" was a horrid thing to be called, that calling someone evil, as my support-providing sibling had of the critic, was to "depersonalize" that person. This sibling was more upset by that choice of words than the haranguing of my parents.

The fact is that Christians do call some behaviour "immoral" and the 10 Commandments a baseline to judge character. Conviction that there is such absolute truth itself is increasingly called "immoral" and an enemy of fundamental human rights. But to be made in the image of God does mean that God shaped all human beings with the capacity to distinguish between right and wrong (cf. Rom. 1 and 2). In the deconstructing world of postmodernism, claims to truth and morality are purported to be power plays. But to say all truth claims are power plays is in itself an absolute statement that could be just a power play.[173] Christian apologist Daniel Clendenin summarizes the postmodernist's relativistic dilemma:

---

173 Tim Keller, *The Reason for God*, 38.

It becomes impossible in this scheme of nonjudgmental toleration to judge and reject many intolerable practices—widow burning, temple prostitution, child sacrifice or female mutilation. One might object to them as distasteful or unpleasant, but it is no longer possible to call them morally wrong in an absolute sense. Quite the contrary; in pluralism one is obliged to affirm the cultural validity and value of such religious practices.[174]

Postmodernists hold to firm convictions such as to save the planet. To end child labour. To stop sex trafficking. That is commendable. However, without societal boundaries established about what is and what is not moral is to invite chaos and anarchy. There has to be some meeting of minds on what the most people in a nation-state decide is the basis for functioning in corporate community. Usually democracy is understood to be the most progressive way of coming to commonly accepted standards.[175] Unfortunately, in postmodern, Western society, the pressure to avoid absolutes has led to marginalizing of those segments of society, like the church, that hold to such things. As one political commentator observes: "You [Canadians] live in a land where freedom is detached from truth. And you, too, will be expected to concede that detachment, whether at university or in civil and social and even family affairs. That detachment is rapidly gaining the positive sanction of law, especially where it touches on religion."[176]

Perhaps the best way to counter that frowning on what is perceived as a lack of inclusivism is 'common sense', now the enemy of the 'objectivity' of relativism (cf. what Rom. 1 has to say about the way nonbelievers suppress knowledge of the truth about God based on what they observe in the natural

---

174 *Many Gods, Many Lords*, 102.
175 See chapter 6 for a fuller discussion on what the common good might look like in a pluralistic democracy.
176 Douglas Farrow, "What is Truth?" *Convivium* (4:21), 14.

world). Nancy Pearcey puts the role of rational dialogue in faith-bearing this way: "The task of evangelism starts with helping the nonbeliever face squarely the inconsistencies between his beliefs and his actual experience."[177]

Democracy also means that Christians recognize that there are limits to how much morality should be legislated. Religious freedom, in reverse, means that countries with a strong Christian history, like the USA, are right not to protect unduly certain Christian conceptions of morality in law. Some of these morality issues, like polygamy, are complicated. Is the right of consenting adults to enter into polygamous marriage strictly an individual freedom of conscience issue (right now before the courts in British Columbia) or is freedom of religion a collective right which has some commonly accepted boundaries of morality which do not include polygamy?[178] If we are made in God's image, is it not common sense to consider some moral values as not being open for discussion, like toleration of murder, pedophilia, rape of women, and stealing? If God has created us in his image to function in the world he had created for us to live in (and rule or shape), does it not make sense that "there is a "continuity of categories" between God's mind, ours and the structure of the world."[179]

Newton's discovery of the law of gravity after noticing an apple fall from a tree in his garden in Lincolnshire, which my wife and I visited with fascination, was not a freak accident of the mind. If truth were known, a good case can be made that much of Western civilization and liberalism are borrowing unconsciously

---

177 *Total Truth*, 314.
178 Kevin Boonstra and Peter Stockland, "Point and Counterpoint: Why Should Christians Promote Religious Freedom?" http://www.cardus.ca/comment/article/2761/point-and-counterpoint-why-should-christians-promote-religious-freedom
179 Nancy Pearcey, *Total Truth, 315.*

from the Judeo-Christian worldview that still undergirds many of our values and mores, like ancient Roman ruins in North Africa speaking of a former great empire. Poet W.H. Auden called societal values held by an unbelieving public but which would not have come into existence without Christian or Jewish faith, "Christian heresies".[180]

Postmodernists Tend to Think Monotheistic Religions Are Intolerant

A big misunderstanding about monotheistic religions exists. Islam, Christianity, Sikhism and Judaism hold to there being one true God. Period. Full stop. Many people think that to claim that there is only one true faith is intolerant and to preach that is to undermine an individual's self-determination, as we have stated. Hostility to monotheism is frequently an *a priori* viewpoint of those influenced heavily by a postmodern worldview of relativism (read most of European and North American society). The basic line goes something like this: "I don't have any objection to you believing what you want to. That's cool. But to say that your beliefs are superior to mine is wrong. Aren't all religions basically trying to say the same thing differently because of cultural diversity?" In a way, this clamour against there being only one faith in light of the multiplicity of faiths is baffling philosophically. We have so many examples of the opposite being true without taking the biblical explanation of Romans 1 and 2 at face value—the most complete biblical explanation of the variety of world religions but only one truth. One is that after the first three moves in a game of chess there can be up to 121 million different moves. Yet, there is only one right move to end the game.

---

180 Os Guinness, "Turning the Tables", *inContext*, 20.

However, the critique of Christianity simply does not hold up to close scrutiny. In Canada, the most frequent objection I get to Christianity in talking to people about faith is that *all religions are basically the same and therefore equally valid* or *equally invalid.* However, in dismissing Christianity because of its exclusivist tenets, instead holding to a relativistic view of reality that there is no one absolute explanation about the nature of ultimate things, such people are taking a philosophically untenable position. They are making an absolute statement (that there are no absolutes) which is impossible to hold to if there are no absolutes like they claim. Christianity will have to be dismissed on some other basis. If something is true or false, it will need to be refuted or validated on its own claims.

The right of all human beings to decide such faith issues of their own volition is dependent on a view of humankind that says that we are made in the image of God. Ironically, there is a lot of misunderstanding about what freedom of choice really means. What it does not mean is:

- All "truths" are necessarily equally valid
- Exchanging different points of view is inherently coercive and intolerant
- Heart choice can be imposed[181]

Disenchantment with Religion but not Spirituality

Christian Millennials are leaving the church in droves.[182] Or never showing up in the first place. They imbibe the spirit of postmodern culture in part because they are shaped unconsciously by postmodernity. They are not skeptical about

---

181 I am indebted for the observations made in the bullet points to Elmer Thiessen, *The Ethics of Evangelism.*
182 Millennials or the Millennium Generation are also called Generation Y and refer to those young adults who were born any time from the early 1980s to the early 2000s. They follow Generation X chronologically.

God or their relationship with him but about organized religion. Somewhat discerningly, they see the church as politicized. They want leaders who are authentic whereas their baby boomer parents are more interested in leaders who are competent and charismatic, who get things done. Millennials want preaching that is vulnerable, where the pastor shares from his own experiences, even struggles, and not a three-point alliterated sermon that seems predictable and even "canned". They feel like the agenda of the church is more about getting them committed to the church program and less about community and discipleship. They think they can feel God's presence more in a forest or at a Starbucks with friends than in a Sunday service surrounded by stain-glassed windows. They feel they get their craving for community outside the four walls of the church building.

Unfortunately, due to postmodernist distrust about the power of reason to explain everything, preeminence has been given to experience, feelings, impressions and emotion as being better detectors of truth and error. For the Christian that has meant an unconscious or conscious discounting of the mind in spirituality and discernment of truth. The heart is seen increasingly as an instrument of feeling.[183] Narrative and story-telling preaching is gobbled up and didactic preaching is undigested—as if it was unbiblical. The Gospels are spiritual but Paul's epistles are dated.

Among younger adult people in general, there is a distrust of the institutional church. A survey conducted in 2001 by the Spanish Centre for Sociological Research found that the Church was identified as the most distrusted social institution in Spain by 32.8% of the respondents, even higher than political parties (30.8%) or the army (22.2%)—this being a conservative Catholic

183 Gregg Elshof, *I Told Me So*, 69-70.

country.[184] Millennials find distasteful the hype that surrounds Christian subculture, especially in the USA, when using such talk as "we need to get our country back" or "vote only for evangelical politicians if you want to return America to being Christian". Chapter 6 will delve into the issue of whether there can be such a thing as a Christian country as it relates to human rights. Yancey invites Christians to resist attitudes or language of the Inquisition or Crusades when he exposes such short-sightedness in these words: "The very things we disapprove of in Islam [the blending of religion and states], some Christians still find tempting; they too seek political power and a legal code that reflects revealed morality."[185] Postmodern secularists and agnostics see all religion as too politicized. Religion is tainted with its own self-serving agenda for the benefit of its own membership and power-holding is the frequent perception, they maintain.

One other reason for why Millennials are abandoning institutional religion is because of their hyper-individualism. Within postmodern cultures, the individual becomes the centre of her universe. Faith that is real is strictly personal. "Religion" is about a collective spiritual experience and that is suspect. "Spirituality" is personal and meaningful whereas "religion" is about church, dogma, and formal institutions. And so young adults talk about being into spirituality but not religion. The realm of faith has been divided artificially into private and public spheres—yet another form of the theologically-incorrect sacred-secular division of life.[186]

---

184 Cited in Les Cowan, "What Is Truth? Religion, Relationships and Reality in Postmodern Spain", *Evangelical Missions Quarterly*, 451.
185 Philip Yancey, *Vanishing Grace*, 258-259.
186 Nancy Pearcey, *Total Truth*, 116-118.

The Selfie Has Replaced God

And so the individual, at least in the less collectivistic and more postmodern cultures of the West, circumscribes her understanding of reality by being at the centre of the orbit herself. God may not be even a reference point on the orbit perimeter, but her friends are—and perhaps family. The popularity of taking photos of oneself on smart phones has taken the world by storm. To me it is symptomatic of Western civilization's and youth culture's preoccupation with self. The deification of self, where God orbits around us rather than we around God, has risen to new heights since the 1980s when New Age teaching resonated with an increasing proportion of Europe and North America. Whether it was Shirley MacLaine proclaiming that "God lies within" or Oprah Winfrey touting the latest self-help book, the supplanting of God with oneself has morphed into bragging about the number of friends we have on Facebook or Tweet followers.

Many postmodernists would subscribe to singer Van Morrison's philosophy: "I have never joined any organization, nor plan to. I am not affiliated to any guru, don't subscribe to any method and for those people who don't know what a guru is, I don't have a teacher either."[187]

Sensing the hollowness of contemporary culture to satisfy inner longing for meaning and ethical behaviour, cultural Jew and *NY Times* columnist, David Brooks, went on a journalistic quest to discern what had changed in culture. In an interview about his findings, he claims that the moral fabric of society changed shortly after World War II and not in the cultural revolution of the 1960s as many sociologists and others suppose. It was then,

---

187 Quoted in Cowan, 455.

Brook, argues, that the notion of sin became outdated. He says in his interview that

> In 1950, the Gallup organization asked high-school seniors, "Are you an important person?" Back then, 12 percent said yes. Gallup asked the same question in 2005, and 80 percent said yes... . Our economy encourages us to promote ourselves with social media, to brand ourselves and get "likes". In theory, we know humility is important, but we live in a culture of self-promotion.[188]

Celebrity Culture

Celebrity culture is just another expression of the virtual deification of the human being. Instead of God being at the centre of the orbit, it is oneself—or the Beyoncé or the Lebron James one wants to become—even if only for five seconds of YouTube fame. Other gods have taken the place of the only living God. Celebrity culture perhaps began with the death of Princess Diana in 1997. She represented an anti-establishment figure and the pop star status spirit of the emerging postmodern world. Ironically, "the Peoples' Princess" was buried on the same day as a true saint and lodestar died in India, Mother Teresa. But Mother Teresa, who sacrificed her life for the poorest of the poor of Calcutta, hardly figured in the news headlines of that day or days that followed at all. Narcissism is 'hot' and self-denial is 'not'.

Rights Are About the Individual Only

Along the way, the idea of the common good has become somewhat passé in the rush to protect individual rights in the postmodern world. The idea of "love your neighbour as yourself" is perceived as a threat to personal freedom. Society becomes a conflagration between competing individual rights.

---

188 Interview of David Brooks by Jeff Haanen in *Christianity Today*, 64.

Ideology is assumed to be political in motivation and so taken with a grain of salt. Each 'ism' has to be deconstructed so that the kernel of truth is finally revealed—or more likely no truth at all, much as an onion peeled back is found to have no centre. It is estimated that over 800,000 searches per month on the Internet are logged in as "How can I get what I want?" The secrecy of the Internet unmasks the inherent selfishness of the postmodern heart.

Unabashed Consumerism

Sunday morning in 'Toronto the Good', as the city was once nicknamed, has had rush hour style traffic on its main highways like the 401 many hours of each day seven days a week for at least the past decade. Before that, though, it was normal for major Toronto highways to be virtually deserted Sunday mornings as people used them primarily to get to church, and most people's churches were nearby to where they lived. Today it is not that people are in a hurry to get to church on time but getting to a new place of worship, the shopping mall. While church attendance is in decline, mall parking lots fill up rapidly by mid-day on Sundays. Toronto routes are clogged by 12:00 noon. Expansive mall parking lots are jam-packed by mid-afternoon.

Unfettered consumerism is symptomatic of the age. It is aligned with the unabashed single-minded pursuit of pleasure as the chief end of man in the twenty-first century. Enjoying the pleasures of satisfying the five senses is not wrong in itself (1 Tim. 4:4). But to live for week-end pleasures and mall-hopping has received fresh expression, and provided an outlet only satisfied for a few hours snatched furtively in the work week by gaming or surfing pornographic websites, which one can satisfy through binge indulgence on the week-end. This pursuit of pleasure as the end game has created a "major cultural crisis ... carried to all four corners of the world on the wings of globalization processes".[189]

The subprime mortgage crisis that triggered the Great Recession in the USA and elsewhere really was a function of greed and catering to a mindset that made living above our means respectable. Baby boomers' parents (the buster generation) mortgaged their futures by saving for their children's higher education, but baby boomers themselves largely declared that the key to the American Dream was getting a cheaper subprime rate for their unaffordable upgraded suburban homes.[190]

Why are Yoga and New Age teaching so popular on Wall Street and in corporate management circles? Could it be because it is a conscience-salving blend of Eastern mysticism and capitalism? In our rush to justify rampant consumerism, we have fashioned gods we can manipulate. Our debt level in North America is but a reflection of the why-defer-gratification-when-you-can-have-it-all-now greed that grips our world.[191] Do we really need the latest Apple product when we already have a smart phone and a laptop computer? People don't need suits and dresses to go to work in a casual world so much anymore so why not have five purses, all costing as much as the dresses used to, and 15 pairs of shoes, also double the price that we used to pay for them because 'the brand you wear reveals the real you'? No longer can mid-winter be survived without an all-inclusive holiday in the Caribbean or North Africa on a sandy beach in a four- or five-star resort regardless of the huge mortgage we have on our house. The list of consumerism gone wild like a teenage boy

---

189 Miroslav Volf, *Allah: A Christian Response*, 217.
190 Thomas Friedman, *Hot, Flat and Crowded*, 38-41.
191 The average household debt in Canada grew in 2015 to $60,100, a jump of 64% in a little over a decade according to Statistics Canada. The number of indebted homes between 1999 and 2012 increased from 67% to 71%. US household debt is 125% of annual income. Similar debt burdens are found in a number of European countries.

being given the keys to the family car for the first time grows longer and longer year by year.

These are really old idols wrapped up differently. The human heart remains the same; we cannot point a finger at postmodern generations. Unadulterated materialism. Love for the world. Like desire for sex outside the bounds of marriage, if an interest in possessing things material evolves to obsession, it is spiritually destructive (Luke 16:13; 18:18-22).

We can see the ruinous power of defining happiness in terms of our material possessions by the bizarre behaviour exhibited in TV hit shows like *Storage Wars*, where people have so much stuff they have to spend a fortune they do not have to house the overflow of their possessions in storage lockers. Storage locker companies have become big business in North America. University of Toronto anthropologist, Katie Kilroy-Marac, is currently researching our society's accumulation of junk, which she claims has become a health hazard across North America.[192] In 2013 hoarding was classified as a mental illness by diagnostic manuals for psychiatrists. In a consumer-centric culture, stuff seems to be the new food, replacing dieting as the fad of early 21st century. It is symptomatic of an age that has surrendered fulfilling God's intentions as his image-bearers for a mess of potage. Postmodern culture has trivialized what it means to be truly human.

Suffering spiritually, the postmodern generation has become, on the one hand, more consumer-driven than their pampered baby boomer parents. That said, it is dangerous to over-simplify, because a whole segment of Generations X and Y have become cause-focused and want to simplify life. More about that shortly.

---

192 Cynthia Macdonald, "Our Problem with Stuff", *University of Toronto Magazine*, 26.

The story is told in India of a guru who was so pleased with his disciple's progress that he left him on his own in a mud hut where he lived simply, begging for his food. After his *puja* every morning, the disciple washed his loincloth and hung it out to dry. One day he discovered that his loincloth had been eaten by rats when he ventured for a time away from his hut. The villagers gave him another one after he begged them for help. However, the rats had a field day with that one too! So he wisely got a cat, who ate the rats, but now he needed milk for his cat and so he begged and got a cow. But the cow needed fodder. So he decided to till and plant the land around his hut. Needless to say, this shrunk his time for devotions so he hired servants to tend the soil. Overseeing the servants became such a chore that he married so that his wife could split the chores with him. After some time, the guru's disciple became the richest man in the village.

One day the guru stopped by while on pilgrimage. He was shocked at the transformation of the mud hut into a stately mansion complete with servants. "What's going on?" he enquired of his disciple.

"You won't believe this, guru-ji", the disciple replied to his mentor. "There was no other way to keep my loincloth."

With no moral absolutes in postmodernity, the idea of greed or covetousness seems old-fashioned. The tenth commandment is out-of-date. Greed has become respectable.

Bent heads are not signaling prayer to the God who is but attentiveness to a Smart Phone as people scroll through the latest online ads. Trivia associated with celebrity gossip and sporting events stream past our glazed eyes on the worldwide web. Our consumer culture has inoculated us against things that matter.[193] We have not only deified humans but we have also reduced them, we have turned our back on the potential that comes with being made in God's image. We have trivialized our existence. Time is filled with trivial pursuits.

Many years ago, when I was living in Lucknow, India, a local pastor told me of a villager who had come to his church to be baptized. Like others going through the waters of baptism, he was encouraged to come in simple white kurta and pants. As this man was being lowered under the water in the baptismal tank, he suddenly realized he had rupee notes lodged in the inside pocket of his kurta. Fumbling at his inside pocket, he yanked the rupee notes high in the air just in time for them not to get soaked. As he was lowered below the surface of the water, only the fistful of money raised in the air was seen by the congregation observing the baptism. Like him, many Christians have not allowed their money to be baptized, especially those growing up in the postmodern world.

The Deification of Diversity

As we have seen, to be made in the image of God means that we are designed to appreciate unity (relationship with 'the other') but also diversity (our individuality). The three-in-one God is not three different gods but the One God. But the One God is also three Persons. While the oneness of the human race is celebrated globally, such as on Earth Day when we all try to turn out the lights for one hour together, or at the quadrennial Olympics, much more is made today of our diversity, whether that is to admire transgender people or feminism that gives non-white women deference to speak for all females. We have become transcribed by the god of endless options and the

---

193 Philip Yancey, *Vanishing Grace*, 203-205.

novel. Diversity trumps uniformity. The particular overrides the universal. 'If it ain't broke, break it' is the battle cry.

This trend is no more apparent than with consumer products. Whole coffee chains like Starbucks were founded on the core value of providing the consumer with a multiplicity of choice in how your caffeine and coffee bean were delivered. "Double, double" and "vanilla nonfat cappuccino one sugar" became a language everyone understood.

Why is our demand for choice a moral issue? Because it becomes a way of insisting on total freedom from all restraints. A British social commentator, Barry Cooper, captures this spirit of exalted diversity well when he says, "We worship the god of open options. And he is killing us... . He promises you freedom from *all* gods, *all* responsibilities. 'Keep your options open', he says. 'Worship me, and you do not have to serve anything or anyone. No commitment necessary. Total freedom.'"[194]

Deification and Trivializing of Humans Coexist

An argument can be made that postmodern culture both deifies and trivializes the individual and that is what we are contending here. Philosopher Ramachandra puts it this ways:

> Here it seems that postmodernism is simply modernism that has come home to roost. A movement that sought to guard the objectivity of truth from theological 'interference' has ended up doubting the very concept of truth. A movement that glorified in reason and exalted it above divine revelation has come to spurn the rational in every area of life. A movement that began with the divinization of self has culminated in the loss of that very self.[195]

---

194 "Imprisoned by Choice", *Christianity Today*. 54-55.
195 *Gods That Fail*, 12.

The trivializing of the individual is discerned in different ways. One example is the proliferation of shaming through social media. People's lives are carelessly being destroyed through abusive online potshots lobbed like a hand grenade from a distance to avoid hand-to-hand combat, as if those being criticized are not real people. Sexting is rampant is Western culture. To relay sexually compromising photos teens exchange on their Smart phones with one other friend confidentially is then forwarded to all those in the friend's network so that the pornographic images become viral. What should be treated as an indiscretion and dealt with discreetly is disrespectfully forwarded around for thousands and even millions to gawk at. The soaring rate of suicides among teenagers caught up in pornographic scams has become a legendary topic in our shameless and sick society. The trivialization of human life has removed what have been hitherto thought of as decent and normal moral boundaries of respect for another human being. It's as if there is no distinction between the virtual worlds, such as in video gaming, and the real world of time and space inhabited by flesh and blood human beings fighting real wars. With sophisticated graphics, realistic characters and complex strategies, the virtual world has become more believable to those addicted to video games and becomes a preferable pastime to hanging out with friends, playing sports or even watching TV with others. Human interaction becomes trivial to those compulsively spending five or more hours per day in gaming. Sitting down to an evening meal as a family in the West has become an increasingly rare thing.[196]

---

196 This disintegration of the extended family has been chronicled for example by Phyliss Tickle, *The Great Emergence: How Christianity Is Changing and Why* (Grand Rapids: Baker Books, 2008). She traces the breakdown of the family and collective consciousness to the arrival of the car, which, for instance, took families away from gathering on Sunday afternoons on the front porch with grandma after church, 85-87.

Speaking of social media, the idea of friendship, of Jonathan-David relationships (non-sexualized) has become blurred with the casual acquaintance engendered in digital human connection. Friendships have become trivialized when we are more concerned about the number of 'friends' we have in Facebook rather than the quality of the relationships. Communication has been reduced to 140 tweetable bites.

What is Intolerance?

If no overarching truth or ultimate purpose is posited, then of course it seems intolerant to try and convert people to one view of life or another. It used to be that 'proselytizing' was perceived as moral if done with ethical means—when not engaged in with pressure tactics like offering inducements to change religions (e.g. access to a job by inclusion in the reservation system in India). Today it is not just the 'means' that is under the microscope but also the 'end'. Both can be perceived as intolerant, if not immoral, by those we have described here as postmodernists. Some of the conversion tactics of Christendom in the Middle Ages were immoral—such as the forced conversion of Saxons by Charlemagne in the eighth century. But can we call normal discourse that involves the effort to persuade another person, politely, who holds to a different worldview, inherently intolerant?

Here are a handful of reasons why not.

- **To make a rational argument to someone is not in itself brainwashing.** Most of the beliefs anyone holds are the result of persuasion (e.g. parents with children about whether it is right to wrong to steal a friend's IPad). There is no excuse for argumentativeness or sarcasm or haranguing. But respectful exchanging of ideas is part of what it means to be social beings and reflects an interdependent world; we are not as autonomous as we would like to think we are. As individuals we do not adopt values and views in a vacuum. We are rational beings. To appeal to our minds is respecting what it means to be human and to be humans who are innately social.

- **Judgment and criticism in the face of opposing viewpoints is inevitable.** To say 'Jesus is the only way to know the one God' is very different than to say 'there is no real difference between Jesus, Buddha and Krishna'. Both philosophical positions cannot be right. To call one arbitrarily intolerant or worse, arrogant, is to make a judgment call, which in itself is a subjective form of criticism. Statements and viewpoints that are different from each other should not be avoided just because they create an intrinsic tension between two engaged minds. They should be contrasted rationally and dispassionately.

- **To accuse someone speaking of ontological necessities, where things like guilt, God, the after-life and sin are talked about, as being emotionally manipulative is itself judgmental.** Emotions are a part of what we are as humans and so there is no such thing as pure objectivity, in the sense of appeal only to reason in discourse.[197] Some topics like sin or death will automatically trigger feelings. Should they therefore be taboo topics? We already anesthetize people enough from harsh realities of life by things like having closed caskets at funerals so people do not have

197 I am indebted for the developing of my ideas here to Elmer Thiessen in *The Ethics of Evangelism* and Donald Carson in *The Gagging of God: Christianity Confronts Pluralism* (Grand Rapids: Zondervan, 1996). See also Ajith Fernando, *The Christian's Attitude toward World Religions* (Wheaton: Tyndale House, 1987), 147-158.

to stare death in the face. To extend such social taboos to calm and collected conversation is over-reaching common sense.

Postmodernism has *de facto* made certain subjects taboo. Instead of a modern focus on **how** discourse is conducted, tolerance is measured by **what** the position on the subject is. If you think marriage should not be permitted for gays, you are by default bigoted. If you believe in one true God, you are intolerant. Donald Carson laments the trend of political correctness: "Exclusivism is the one religious word that cannot be tolerated. Correspondingly, *proselytism* is a dirty word. One cannot help observing a crushing irony: the gospel of relativistic tolerance is perhaps the most "evangelistic" movement in Western culture, demanding assent and brooking no rivals."[198]

The confusion about the difference between *style* (is the method of discourse and communication respectful and non-manipulative?) and *substance* (is the content of the communication true or false, right or wrong?) fails to respect human powers of volition. If the Son of God did not seek to convince a fallen world of his messiah-ship and divinity by leaving the courtrooms of heaven in a blaze of glory, forcing people to believe in him through a demonstration of shock and awe, instead humbling himself by becoming fully human in ordinary circumstances (Phil. 2:6-8), should we not in our postmodern world be slower to police choices of the mind and soul?

So What Is Tolerance?

Tolerance has more to do with the attitude we bring to an exchange of ideas than the content of the message. We can be humble around people who differ from us in their viewpoint

---

198 *The Gagging of God,* 33.

because none of us is infallible. We all have intellectual blind spots. We all are finite. We all are impacted by our environment, family nurturing, education and cultural background so that it is virtually impossible for anyone to come to questions about the ultimate origins and meaning of life without philosophical presuppositions or subjectivity. Some aspects of the philosophy of deconstruction have merit. Such tolerance acknowledges that not only 'me' but 'all' are made in God's image and should be treated with respect.

Ethicist Elmer Thiessen points out that until recently the notion of *tolerance* had to do with enduring or putting up with people (from the Latin *tolerare*), not obnoxious ideas. That is, tolerance allowed us to separate the ideas from the person stating them abstractly so that we could object to an idea while still exercising restraint against the person holding that view. Today, more and more, it is the person, not just their idea, that is pilloried.[199] We've become intolerant of people whose ideas we oppose, not just their ideas. This is accentuated in many spheres where tolerance was the norm previously, such as in American politics. Recently, the public behaviour of US presidential candidate, Donald Trump, has underscored this trend.[200] Disturbingly, his take-no-prisoners tactics have resonated with the voting public. The US system of government is somewhat paralyzed because a party that has a difference set of ideals than yours is dismissed automatically. No longer being willing to separate the person from the issue has heightened the tensions and created extreme partisanship. Such vilification of humans is yet another sign of a cultural slippage away from a biblical understanding of what it means to be made in God's image where civility and respect should be instinctive.

---

199 *The Ethics of Evangelism*, 106-107.
200 Actually there has been a long history of histrionics in American politics but not as bad as now for decades.

Gentle means of persuasion are clearly called for in the Bible. In encouraging Christians to share their faith convincingly, one of the original twelve disciples exhorts us to "always be prepared to make a defense to anyone who asks you for a reason for the hope that is in you, yet do it with gentleness and respect" (1 Peter 4:15b-16a). Similarly, Paul reasons: "Have nothing to do with foolish, ignorant controversies; you know they breed quarrels. And the Lord's servant must not be quarrelsome but kind to everyone, able to teach, patiently enduring evil, correcting his opponents with gentleness" (2 Tim. 2:23-25a). Qualifications for church elders include "not quarrelsome" (1 Tim. 3:3). The Bible respects human rationality, the individuality of decision-making and truth-bearing; collectively these godly principles shine a spotlight on the fact that humans are made in God's image.

We do not have to hit people over the head with the truth. We do not want to imitate Lucy of Peanuts comic strip fame who set up a booth once with a sign that read "Questions Answered: 5 cents". We are dealing with real people. We balance truth and love in our manner of communication. Now that is true tolerance.

The Good News about Our Society Not Believing in God

The good news is that although the percentage of people in the postmodern West not believing in a divine being is climbing, that trend is not indicative that of a lack of searching for deeper meaning in life. You would think most postmodernists would embrace the attitude of the apostle Paul. If God does not exist, Paul mused, we should eat, drink and be merry because tomorrow we die (I Cor. 15:32). But surprisingly more than a few postmodernists are not hedonists or existentialists. Former American Vice-President and renowned global warming spokesman, Al Gore, said: "The accumulation of material goods is at an all-time high, but so is the number of people who feel an emptiness in their lives."[201] Countless numbers of them seek meaning through an altruistic attitude of "giving back" or "giving forward"—as the mainstream expressions go. It may mean that a Bill Gates gives billions for the betterment of clean water and eradication of diseases like malaria. Agnostics and atheists may not treat human life as sacred because they do not believe in a god let alone that we are made in a good and loving God's image. But they would be scandalized, in an uproar, and lobby feverishly to prevent pedophilia from being legalized. They may not agree that nature declares the glory of God (Psalm 19) but they will chain themselves to redwood trees to save primeval forests.

During the Ebola plague outbreak that hit West Africa in 2014, the medical community from different parts of the world converged on the scene of the plague. Remarkably, despite the risk of imminent death, many doctors and nurses who were not religious at all joined the teams that spelled each other off on the ground in spite of the high risk that they could die from exposure to Ebola. Not only was the SIM missionary, Nancy Writebol, who almost succumbed to Ebola, at the forefront of battling the disease in the hot zone in Africa, but numerous non-Christian activists and Doctors without Borders humanists, let alone national medical personnel, heroically risked death. Humans cannot help being moralists. Those who insist that the Christian god should have made all people to always choose good if he really existed, when genuinely being troubled by the reality of evil in the world so as to conclude that either God is all powerful but not loving or that God is love but not all powerful, do not realize the logical inconsistency of denying an objective moral law because evil cannot exist if there is not a

---

201 Cited by Philip Yancey, *Vanishing Grace,* 154.

good to compare it with. Moreover, God cannot do anything that is logically impossible or mutually exclusive. Particularly with reference to this issue, the good and holy God cannot create a being (the human) who can respond to him freely in love without giving that being the ability to make independent choices. In doing so God must limit some expressions of his omnipotence and sovereignty. God freely chose to limit his innate control of all things in order to enable the possibility of love, love that could reciprocate freely his great love.[202]

How can we really be sure God desires to enter into a relationship with us in light of all the suffering in the world? In his seminal book, *The Cross of* Christ, John Stott concluded that the best proof that God really loves us is the death of Christ. At one point, he puts it this way: "Because he [God] loved us, he came after us in Christ. He pursued us even to the desolate anguish of the cross where he bore our sin, guilt, judgment and death. It takes a hard and stony heart to remain unmoved by love like that."[203]

Like many before and after her, Mother Teresa looked at the cross of Christ and reassured herself that this was proof that God is love and desires a personal relationship with human beings. She was particularly exercised by the words of Christ on the cross: "I thirst". These two words came to symbolize for her not only physical thirst but the emotional thirst of God for a loving relationship with human beings, those Christ had died for. And so she made "I thirst" the symbol of the Sisters of Charity, those words being emblazoned in every chapel of the charity. She always maintained that "God thirsts for us and humanity thirsts for God."[204]

---

202 Ravi Zacharias, *Jesus among Other* Gods, 117.
203 83.
204 Philip Yancey, *Vanishing Grace*, 104.

Yancey summarizes this conflicting data for the postmodernist well:

> Instinctively we do not live with utter indifference. We judge some things more beautiful than others, some acts more meaningful than others. We fall in love, we care for helpless infants, grieve when relatives die, prosecute murderers— in a thousand ways we live as though life has meaning, as if love, beauty, truth, justice and morality are not just arbitrary concepts but somehow real. We make choices as if they matter, despite all the modern thinkers who declare just the opposite.[205]

Here is where Christians can strike common cause with postmodernists. Rather than focus self-righteously on how their core values are skewed towards the selfish and narcissistic, we might empathize and converse at the same starting point about things we share in common. It is the demonstration of our hearts (love for God and for our neighbor) and with our hands (practically helping neighbors) that will in some cases enable sceptics to sort out their head questions (intellectual or emotional qualms) about our faith. This is why Indian Christians campaigning to right the wrongs suffered by Dalits alongside enlightened high caste friends is so important. It is why American Christian academics and Muslim academics join hands in their "Common Ground" manifestos to fight terrorism.

Postmodernists Are Believing and Being Transformed

France has been at the cutting edge of philosophical shifts in Western world civilization for centuries. Postmodernism is believed to have begun in France through the thought of Jean-Francois Lyotard. It is almost as rare for French atheists or Catholics to become evangelical Christians as it is for the crown

---

205 Ibid, 57.

jewels to be stolen from the Tower of London. Guillaume Bignon is, however, bucking the trend, like so many young postmodern adults in the Western world today. A proud French atheist, he was into sports and female conquests as a young man. One day, he hitchhiked home from the beach and was picked up by two American young ladies who were lost and wanted directions. One of them turned out to be a practicing Christian.

Finding her not only physically attractive but intellectually engaging, Guillaume pursued a long distance dating relationship with her. Wanting to disabuse her of her vibrant faith, he began to pray into thin air, "If there is a God, then here I am. Why don't you go ahead and reveal yourself to me? I'm open." A sports injury a couple of weeks after first uttering this prayer prevented Guillaume from using his Sunday to play volleyball. So he decided to visit an evangelical congregation in Paris, like one might a zoo. This led to an engaging, lengthy conversation with the pastor afterwards. What followed was unexpected, the awakening of his conscience. Soon he understood why Christ had to die—for him. There in his apartment near Paris Guillaume placed his trust in Christ. He became passionate about studying his new-found faith, moved to the US, went to seminary and ultimately obtained a Ph.D. in philosophical theology.[206] Postmodernity found God.

Kirsten Powers Found More than the White House

On a different continent another postmodern person found God. Kirsten Powers grew up in Alaska with a nominal Episcopal family. By her early 20s Kirsten had begun vacillating between agnosticism and atheism. From 1992 to 1998 she worked in the White House in the Clinton administration. Later, on settling in New York, still involved in politics, Kristen ended up dating a

---

206 Guillaume Bignon, "My Own French Revolution", *Christianity Today*, 96-97.

man who was a follower of Jesus. Although strongly resisting his efforts to share his faith with her, she relented one Sunday and went to church with him. There, although most of the service left her cold, she was riveted by the compelling and intellectually rigorous sermon by Timothy Keller. So she decided to come back to hear him again. Before long listening to Keller on Sunday became the highlight of her week. Kristen then began to read the Bible for herself. Little by little she came to see that the case for Christianity was airtight in comparison to that for atheism and agnosticism.

Over a period of almost a year she continued her spiritual journey, finally ending up in a Bible study group on the Upper East Side of New York. She spent the next few months wrestling to get away from God but, as she put it, "slowly there was less fear and more joy [for] the Hound of Heaven had pursued me and caught me—whether I liked it or not". Today Kristen is a contributor to *USA Today* and a Democratic commentator at Fox News. Postmodernity found God.[207]

---

207 Kirsten Powers, "The God I Can't Write Off", *Christianity Today*, 103-104.

CHAPTER 5
Jesus: The Full Image-Bearer

Did you know that you blink an average of 25 times every minute? Blinks are only one-fifth of a second long which explains why we do not always know when we are blinking. Therefore, if you drive for five hours on a road trip at an average speed of 40 miles per hour, you will drive ten miles with your eyes closed. Christians, like all people, can be blind to many things.[208] As it relates to the subject of this book, humankind being made in the image of God, we may miss the obvious. That is, to discover what God intended us to become as a result of his prior work in creation in making us according to his image. Why God makes us in his image is that we might become like Jesus.

The New Testament is very clear about this purpose for our creation. Romans 8:29 plainly describes why God created us in his image: "The Son stands first in the line of humanity he restored. We see the original and intended shape of our lives there in him" (*The Message*). Jesus himself made this revolutionary statement: "Anyone who has seen me has seen the Father. How can you say, 'Show us the Father'? Don't you believe that I am in the Father and that the Father is in me? The words I say to you I do not speak on my own authority. Rather it is the Father living in me doing his works'" (John 14:9-10). To understand what it means to be like God, we best look at Jesus.

---

208 Attributed to Chuck Swindoll.

Jesus: The One Whose Humanity Demonstrates God's Intention for Us

To be fashioned in God's image makes it possible for human beings to become like Jesus upon entrusting themselves to him and the salvation he offers. To be fully conformed to the image of God's Son is the new trajectory we are launched on (2 Cor. 5:17).

That being the case, we need confidence in the real humanity of Christ. Divinity taking on humanity is not a two thousand year old idea because, without peering at parallels in other religions such as the *avatars* in Hinduism, the Jews already believed that Yahweh had visited the earth in human form in OT times in what theologians call theophanies (e.g. to Gideon on his father's threshing floor in Judg. 6:11-24). NT interpreters of the life of Christ, particularly the apostle John, perhaps the closest of the twelve to Jesus, correlated Christ's pre-incarnate divine existence with his incarnation on earth. As I have sometimes done in talking at the door of my home with Jehovah's Witnesses going door to door, who deny the deity of Christ, in comparing John 1:1 with John 1:14 we come away with no other conclusion than that Jesus Christ was the Man-God, to speak the 'plain truth'. There, Scripture states that "in the beginning was the Word and the Word was with God and the Word was God" (verse 1). Then, as that passage goes on to say, "the Word became flesh and dwelt among us" (verse 14).

The eternality of Christ and yet his time and space limitation as a human being finds similar expression in Islam. You see, Muslims believe that the *Qur'an* is eternal as God's Word and yet also is found, the same Word, in the revelation given to Muhammad in the written word which now makes up the Muslim scripture.[209]

The most visceral description of Christ in human terms in Johannine writings is the introduction of 1 John where Christ is referred to as "that ... which we have heard, which we have seen with our eyes, which we looked at and our hands have touched—this we proclaim concerning the Word of life" (v. 1). In other words, John knew how human Christ was because he lived up close and personal with him for three years. Perhaps that was why John also used *soma*, the normal Greek word, for a physical body, to identify Christ (John 19:38). Not surprisingly, this *soma* needed to quench thirst (John 4:6-7), was tired (John 4:6-7), could not do miracles by physical power alone (John 5:30), experienced grief (John 11:35) and died (John 19:33). Not only did John portray a very human Christ but he also made the complete humanity of Christ a test of orthodoxy (1 John 4:1-3).[210]

We could say that rather than asking the question "Is Jesus as fully human as we are?" we should ask the question "Are we as human as Jesus?" After all, each one of us is tainted with sin (Ps. 14). If Jesus was indeed human while he walked on this earth, then by looking at him we can see how we are meant to be when unsullied by sin. In fact the argument has been made that one reason Christ came down to earth as a human was not just to save us from the penalty of sin but to show us how to be an authentic human being the way God designed us to be, made as we were in his image. The great mystic Frederick

---

209 The Muslim belief in the eternality of the *Qur'an* and yet its expression in time and space in the written book can be a good witnessing platform in helping Muslims comprehend the human and divine co-existent natures of Christ.

210 Robert Morey, *The Trinity: Evidence and Issues*, 294. The ancient heresy that plagued the early church whereby Christ's humanity was not accepted was Docetism.

William Faber (1814-1863) said as much in his writing, such as with these words:

> Of such consequence was it to the happiness of man that he should know how to behave himself as a creature that it was necessary the Creator should take a created nature, and come himself to show how to wear it. This one of the many known reasons of the sublime mystery of the Incarnation was that the Creator Himself might show the creature how he should behave as a creature.[211]

Reflecting on this way of describing the necessity of the incarnation of Christ as enabling humans to know "how to wear" our humanity, we might think of it in terms of the analogy of footwear where, to increase ease of walking, some people, especially older ones, get orthotics to mold their footwear to fit the exact shape (or misshape) of their feet. In that we are sinners with imperfect 'feet', the 'molding' provided by Christ enables us to walk as properly-expressed humans.

The Importance of Understanding Jesus as Fully Human and Fully Divine

Both for Muslims and Hindus—let alone for those raised in a Judeo-Christian milieu—it is critical to grasp the necessity of the full divinity and full humanity of Jesus. Accepting his full humanity is not enough. Islam accepts Christ's humanity but not his divinity. Likewise the Jehovah's Witnesses and other sects down through church history like the Arians do not struggle with the human Jesus. Christology is a crucial issue in coming to correct conclusions in anthropology ('anthropology' as in the theology of humankind) because if Christ was not fully human then he could not have been our substitute, dying in our place (1 Tim. 2:5; cf. Heb. 2:17) and if he was not fully divine

---

211 "The Creature and the Creator" in Richard Foster and Emilie Griffin (Eds.). *Spiritual Classics: Selected Readings on the Twelve Spiritual Disciplines*, 356.

he could not have provided the holiness necessary to make a perfect offering for sin. He had to be fully divine but that is not our precise concern here as it relates to our theme about the image of God in human beings. Suffice it to say here, "a Mediator between God and man who is not fully God or not fully human is like a bridge broke at either end."[212]

As it relates to the subject of this book, if Jesus were not fully human, we would not comprehend how to live up to our status as those made in God's image. Kilner puts it this way:

> The image of Christ provides the standard for how God intended and intends humanity to live out its status. In Christ alone, as perfect God and human being, not only the status of God's image but also the standard of God's image are completely fulfilled. That is why Christ is the only one the Bible's authors consistently affirm *is* the image of God—the exact representation of God (Hebrews 1:3)."[213]

Humans, then, are made *according* to God's image, as we explicated in chapter 1, but begin to *become like* Christ upon regeneration.

Speaking of Hebrews 1:3 as in the above quote, the only use of the Greek word *character* in the NT is found here and translated as "exact representation". Jesus was the exact representation of God. The word's usage in Jesus' day was with reference to a stamp or impress made by a die or seal. It could refer to the stamp making the impression or to the impression itself.[214] Thus, we would not be remiss in concluding that Christ was both the image of God but also the standard for people being transformed into this image.[215] Reinforcing the appropriateness of coming

212 Robert Morey, *The Trinity: Evidence and Issues,* 301.
213 *Dignity and Destiny*, 143.
214 J. Gess, "Image", Colin Brown (ed.), *Dictionary of New Testament Theology*, Vol. 2, 288.
215 John Kilner, *Dignity and Destiny*, 67.

to this versatile interpretation of "exact representation" in describing Jesus are the words following them: "of his being". They translate *hupostaseos*, indicating that God's very essence or nature is in view, according to the meaning of this Greek word. Jesus was the exact representation of God the Father's being. Christlikeness is our goal because Christ was a genuine human being while he lived on this earth, plus rightly being equated with God because he was and is God, the second person of the Trinity. We cannot become gods but we can acquire more and more of the character of God through Christ to the extent that he intends that replication.

Other Scriptures attesting to the two natures of Jesus Christ while he lived on this earth are Romans 9:5 ("Theirs are the patriarchs, and from them is traced the human ancestry of the Messiah, who is God over all, forever praised"), 1 Timothy 3:16 ("The mystery from which true godliness springs is great: He appeared in the flesh, was vindicated by the Spirit, was seen by angels, was preached among the nations, was believed on in the world, was taken in glory"), 2 Thessalonians 1:12 ("We pray this so that the name of our Lord Jesus Christ may be glorified in you and you in him, according to the grace of God and the Lord Jesus Christ")[216] and Philippians 2:5-11 (this latter passage is probably the most convincing and familiar to us).

The Designation "Son of God"

To over one billion Muslims, the word "Son", as used in Scripture to refer to Jesus, is evidence that the Christian God had conjugal relations in order to produce a son. They assume that if Jesus

---

216 According to Robert Morey, *The Trinity: Evidences and Issues*, since the phrase "our God and the Lord Jesus Christ" has only one definite article for two names of the same case separated by the word *kai*, meaning that the same person is in view (pp. 342-344), which is called in Greek NT study the Granville Sharpe Rule.

was the Son of God and "begotten", then he must be the by-product of the procreative act of God the Father with Mary, the 'Mother of God'. But "Son" in Scripture is metaphorical, much in the same way that in the *Qur'an* Muhamad is called in one text "the son of the road". Of course, Muslims do not take this text literally—nor do Christians about Christ being called the Son of God. That title refers to the second person of the Trinity who, with the Father and the Spirit, are in a familial-type profound harmony and love which finds its best human, but imperfect, expression in the family. The Sonship of Christ does not presuppose a sexual activity as taught by Muslims about what Christians allegedly believe happened between God the Father and Mary the mother of Jesus.

"Begotten" as used with respect to Christ (John 1:14, *AV*, but translated as *one and only* in the *NIV*), comes from the Greek word *monogenes*.[217] It also is a metaphor, not to express a physical beginning as in a human birth or even the result of a divinity and a human having sex as found in Hinduism, but the "one of a kind" uniqueness of Christ. It is meant to capture the sense of "eternal generation", of the eternal and timeless Word which we recognized when made flesh as the human being
.

---

217 "Only begotten" is also the old English translation of *prototokos* with reference to Christ in Hebrews 1:6: "And again, when God brings his *first-born* into the world..." We also find the term in Revelation 1:6 in describing Christ: "Jesus Christ, who is the faithful witness, the *first-born* from the dead..." In the former reference, we know that "first-born" does not mean the fruit of procreation because nowhere else in Scripture is there any suggestion that the Father has more eternal sons. In the latter usage, it is more self-evident that Christ, as risen from the grave, appearing in his post-resurrection body, is the first-of-a-kind. There will be no more like him until the rapture of the church when human beings will assume their promised glorified bodies like their forerunner's, Christ (1 Thess. 4:14-17). According to K. H. Bartels, "Only" in Colin Brown (ed.) *Dictionary of New Testament Theology*, Vol. 2, the idea of "only begotten" as a translation of *monogenes* goes back to Jerome using *unigenitus* in the Latin Vulgate to counter the Arian claim that Jesus was not begotten but made (p. 725).

Jesus (John 1:14), but who existed always as the second person of the Triune Godhead. Thus, for example, the Nicene Creed describes the Son as "begotten, not made". As Volf elucidates: "The eternal Word or Son is not a being next to God, but is of one essence with God."[218] While on earth Jesus was one undivided essence with God just as he was eternally with the Father. Two Persons with the third, the Holy Spirit, but one God. Eternally co-existent.

Reinforcing the Christian, as opposed to Muslim, view of Christ's being begotten is the fact that the second half of *monogenes* is not derived from the Greek verb "to beget", *gennao*, but from the adjectival form of *genos*, meaning "origin, race, stock".[219]

C. S. Lewis explains "begotten" this way:

> As soon as I begin trying to explain how these Persons are connected I have to use words which make it sound as if one of them was there before the others. The First Person is called the Father and the Second the Son. We can say the First begets or produces the second; we call it *begetting*, not *making*, because what is produced is of the same kind as himself. In that way the word Father is the only word to use. But unfortunately it suggests that He's there first—just as a human father exists before his son... . The Son exists because the Father exists; but there never was a time before the Father produces the Son.[220]

It is not our purpose here to make a thorough-going case for the intertwined divinity and humanity of Christ, his "two natures", as the early church sought to carefully describe the Word made flesh. There are exceptional resources for defending this orthodox Christian doctrine. For those who want to delve into this critical topic I would recommend Millard Erickson's three chapters on the deity (chapter 32), the humanity (chapter 33)

---

218 *Allah: A Christian Response*, 133.
219 E. F. Harrison, "Only Begotten" in Walter Elwell (ed.), *Evangelical Dictionary of Theology*, 799.
220 *Beyond Personality*, 24.

and the unity of the two natures (chapter 34) for a clear, concise but comprehensive examination of Christology—including the early heresies that plagued the emerging church.[221] Suffice it to say at this juncture that the incarnation of the Son of God was about gaining human attributes as opposed to giving up divine ones. Philippians 2:6-7 then is talking about Christ in being born in a manger laying aside his heavenly privileges for the period of his earthly existence. He was not giving up his deity, as some suggest, but emptying himself of his divine rights. He became functionally subordinate to his Father while on earth but did not empty himself of his divine nature. Moreover, the man Jesus did not press the 'enter' key for divine behaviour on some occasions and the 'enter' key for human responses other times but was acting always as one divine-human person. In the gospels, sometimes we see his humanity revealed. At other times we see his divinity revealed.

We might grasp this complexity by an analogy. Suppose you were the world's Olympic champion sprinter but now must enter a race designed for two people, a three-legged race. Your one leg is tied to a partner. Do you think your ability to win the race has been hampered by this change of circumstance? Of course it has. Your physical capability has not changed but your ability to run nearly as fast has been severely hampered.[222] So too did Christ accept for 33 years the limiting of the exercise of his kingly authority and power in that "when the set time had fully come, God sent his Son, born of a woman, born under the law" (Gal. 4:4). That temporary setting aside of his divine rights is seen poignantly in his 40 days of temptation in the desert when he is tempted by Satan and he counters by saying that he could call down thousands of angels to help him if he chose to avoid the full fury of temptation as a human being.

---

221 *Christian Theology* (Grand Rapids: Baker Book House, 1986), 683-738.
222 Ibid, 135.

The Designation "Son of Man"

While Christians and Muslims are more familiar with the aforementioned term "Son of God" to refer to Christ, in fact Christ called himself "Son of Man". The term is found 69 times in the Synoptic Gospels and 13 times in John's Gospel. Christians have understood this term to be a self-identification by Jesus with his humanness. But Christ also used this term to refer to his heavenly status: "No one has ascended into heaven except he who ascended from heaven, the Son of Man" (John 3:13, *English Standard Version*). Similarly, John 6:62 says, "Then what if you were to see the Son of Man ascending to where he was before?"

Furthermore, when we consider that Jesus would have consciously borrowed this term from its usage in the OT in Daniel 7:13-14, it meant more than his humanity. He was referring to his divine authority and status and of his Messiahship. In the book of Daniel the "son of man" is given everlasting dominion, glory, and the Kingdom by the Ancient of Days.[223] Other references that suggest Jesus had more in mind in assigning himself this title than his humanity are when he claims to be able to forgive sins (Mark 2:10), reveals his redemptive mission (Mark 10:45), claims authority over the Sabbath (Mark 2:28) and reveals his exalted place in heaven (Matt. 19:28). Christ was fully human and fully divine.

Becoming Like Jesus

Our goal as we are re-created in Christ is to become more and more like him. 2 Corinthians 3:18 describes this earthly process: "And we all [born again Christians are being addressed], who with unveiled faces contemplate the Lord's glory, are being

---

223 R. G. Gruenler, "Son of Man" in Walter Elwell (Ed.). *Evangelical Dictionary of Theology*, 1034-1036.

transformed into his image with ever-increasing glory, which comes from the Lord, who is the Spirit." The verb translated as "transformed" is in the passive voice (and the one we get "metamorphosis" from), indicating that people cannot change themselves, but that the change comes from outside of themselves. The Charles Williams translation of the phrase in that verse indicating the transformation taking place is "being transformed ... from one degree of splendor to another", wonderfully phrased. Yes, it involves our cooperation with the Holy Spirit (we are to abide in Christ who is abiding in us – John 15:5) but we are "born from above" and it is his "grace" at work within us in the midst of our brokenness and frailties (2 Cor. 4:7; 12:9). The image of God in such people does not change but people change. The degree of glory changes but not the image, to clarify what is going on another way.[224] The purpose of our creation is condensed elsewhere this way: "Whoever claims to live in him must live as Jesus did" (1 John 2:6).

That progressive process of sanctification, or as described here, transformation into Christ's likeness, is established repeatedly in the NT. One such passage is Colossians 3:1-10. Believing on Christ results in our new resurrected life (v. 1) and union with him (v. 3). These events-actions are described in the past tense. They are decisive, not to be repeated. Like justification, our new identification happens once and does not change. But the process of becoming like we have been made forensically at one point in time is progressive. Our "new self" is "being renewed in knowledge in the image of its Creator" (v. 10; cf. Col. 1:16 where Christ is described as the one who created us). Who is this Creator who is being described but "Christ [who] is all and is in all" (v. 11)? The image we are transformed into, then, is not God the Father's but Christ's.[225] Status and standard are related

---

224 John Kilner, *Dignity and Destiny*, 142.
225 Ibid, 144.

but two different things. Picking up the same thought is 1 John 3:2 which affirms that we are "God's children now" and will be found fully transformed to the likeness of his Son when we die or are raptured: "but we know that when Christ appears we shall be like him, for we shall see him as he is".

The great 20th century American theologian, Carl Henry, summarizes the correlation between the image of God in humans and the image of Christ in humans succinctly: "The God-man assuredly exhibits the divine intention for man, and the glory of redeemed humanity will consist in full conformity to Christ's image. In the past a type of Christian rationalism has sometimes unfortunately emerged, seeking on the basis of anthropology alone, independently of Christology, to delineate man's true nature and destiny."[226] In other words, we cannot look within human beings (which the social science fields of anthropology and psychology do, for example) to discover what the image of God means but within Christ (which Christology and soteriology do). The gospels, in particular then, become our textbook for discerning what true humanity actually should look like, because there we find the life of Christ described in four different and complementary ways.

What Stands Out About Christ as Human?

Since Christ was fully human and therefore, like all of us, represented God's intentions for humankind (because from birth found in his image – Gen. 1:27), but who also lived a perfect, sin-free life, he demonstrated what the "normal human life" should look like. It is just that our sinfulness, connected with our fallenness and our willful selfish choices, have made Jesus' humanity appear abnormal. God's image in humans has been made invisible by our rebellious sinfulness, just as a severe

---

226 Carl Henry, "Image", *Evangelical Dictionary of Theology*, 546.

case of rheumatoid arthritis corrupts the normal appearance of the human body with its crippling symptoms but does not change the fact that the afflicted person still has a real body; we have been corrupted—but as we believers in Christ are slowly but surely being transformed by the Holy Spirit's presence and activity within us we acquire more and more of the image of Christ. We are not only to imitate Christ ("be ye perfect even as your Father which is in heaven is perfect"- Matt. 5:48, *AV*) but we are "in" Christ and therefore have the capability to and his help in positive change: this explains why the apostle Paul could say that "I no longer live but Christ lives in me" (Gal. 2:20). The constant refrain of the pastoral letters in the NT is to live as if you are who you are in Christ already (Eph. 4:17-24; Gal. 5:1; Col. 3:1-3).

It reminds me of a century-old story of an elderly woman who was extremely tight with her money. Her neighbours were surprised, then, when she had her home wired for electricity. Weeks later a meter-reader noticed that her meter showed very little power usage and so he asked her if she was using her power. "Of course", she replied. "Each night I turn on my lights long enough to light my candles and then I turn off the light switches." She was not living in light of her power resources. As Christians, we too can live as if we were not really alive in Christ.

But, then, we are bound to ask, what distinctive traits or behaviors can we highlight as aspirational standards for us in seeking to fully express our desire to be like Christ in his humanity? There are four qualities in particular that strike me as worthy of pursuing in our imitating Christ (alternatively we could have reflected on each of the fruits of the Spirit in Galatians 5 since they represent the full-orbed character of Christ).

Christ Always Did His Father's Will

First of all, **Jesus was the only human who ever has lived who always did his heavenly Father's will**. He described his life passion this way: "My food is to do the will of him who sent me and to finish his work" (John 4:34; cf. 5:30; 6:38). We might think this orientation would unmask Christ as being unusually task-oriented, kind of a left-brained, Type A personality. However, we discover him repeatedly taking time with people, as when he interacted with children instead of sticking to the disciples' air-tight schedule. Or in making crack-of-dawn time to commune with his heavenly Father in spite of a frenetic wave of ministry (Luke 4:42; note the busy schedule he had the day before and in the day that unfolded following his communion with his heavenly Father). Toward the end of his earthly ministry, Jesus could say with confidence that "I have glorified you [his heavenly Father] down here upon the earth by completing the work that you have given me to do" (John 17:4, *Williams*).

He was tempted in every way that humans can be yet without sinning (Heb. 4:15). But his humanity did not distract him from being single-minded. To be fully human must mean, in part, then, to have tunnel vision in seeking to please God, kind of like Paul stated was his primary motive: "We make it our goal to please him" (2 Cor. 5:9). We shed off the good in order to give ourselves to the best, much like a world-class runner tries to wear the lightest and most aerodynamic clothes and shoes she can in order to be at her competitive best. Such single-minded Christians live by faith not by feelings, choosing to do what is right whether they feel like doing it or not. They instinctively recognize proud and selfish thoughts and motives giving themselves instead to the good, just and self-sacrificing, bringing every thought captive to the obedience of Christ. There is a toughness to their character that spurs them on to die to self, counting the cost to follow our Lord, not denial in the sense of giving up chocolate during Lent season but of death to the self-seeking inner purposes and pulls. Steely resolve to do God's will but the sort of softness and love towards God that triggers obedience. Jesus himself taught that the litmus test of that tender-heartedness toward God, true love in other words, was our obedience: "Anyone who loves me will obey my teaching" (John 14:23).

Christ Loved People without Reservation

Secondly, **Jesus was not only followed because he was the great miracle-worker but because he unreservedly loved people.** The epitome of that love for fellow humans was expressed in his self-sacrifice through crucifixion; as Jesus himself said, "Greater love has no one than this: to lay down one's life for one's friends" (John 15:13). He wept with compassion at the death of his friend, Lazarus. He was moved deeply in his spirit when looking out over a lost Jerusalem (Matt. 9:36 – the term for "moved" here means "to be moved in one's internal or visceral organs", a strong image of deep feelings being experienced). He had empathy for the grieving (Luke 7:13). The depth of love reciprocated by those around him is revealed in the moving story of Mary Magdalene extravagantly pouring expensive lotion on his feet. To be fully human, Jesus demonstrated, is to love well. That quality is what leads us to be model fathers or mothers. A cherishing husband (husbands are to love their wives "as Christ loved the church" – Eph. 5:25). A friendly and helpful work colleague. To be self-giving. To be a good listener. To be relational even if by personality we are wired to a left brain, analytical and directive style sort of person.

Over the Christmas season, my wife and I saw the musical, *The Phantom of the Opera*. I was struck in a way I had not been two decades ago when I saw the original stage musical that it was the facial disfiguration of the "phantom of the opera" that caused him to feel no-one could ever love or accept him. We all desperately seek the love of others because that is essential to being human. When we cannot get it, the sense of loss and loneliness can lead to desperate behaviour as it did the phantom of the opera.

Relating it to the theme of this book—in recognizing all human beings to be made in God's image—we tend to shy away from the despised and lowly in society. Our capacity for compassion seems too easily to be skin deep. For the Dalits in India. For street people in London. For those on welfare in Philadelphia. For refugees in or from the Middle East. In contrast, the magnificent love of God is glimpsed in his help of the defenseless and in light of him being identified as the Father of the fatherless (Ps. 68:5). To be fully human is to love well including loving the loveless ... and so it won't hurt to reflect on how Christ loved as we seek to pay the "debt of love" we owe each other (Rom. 13:8). As John Calvin phrased it: "There is but one way in which to achieve that which is not only merely difficult but which is against [fallen] human nature: to love those who hate us... . It is that we remember not to consider men's evil intentions but to look on the image of God in them."[227]

Christ Lived Sacrificially

Thirdly, **Jesus lived sacrificially**. When I was single and lived in India, I was on an outreach team that travelled from village to village and bazaar to bazaar. I kept a diary for four years and in reviewing it one time noticed that there was one year when I slept in over one hundred different locations, almost always in my sleeping bag, oftentimes on a bare church sanctuary floor. The King of Glory remarked that "foxes have dens and

---

227 *Institutes of the Christian Religion*, Book III, Ch. 7, sec. 6.

birds have nests, but the Son of Man has no place to lay his head" (Matt. 8:20). To be fully human, then, is to "crucify the flesh with its passions and its lusts and to put on the Lord Jesus Christ". It is not about being an ascetic like Irish monks of the 6th century who stood in icy ocean water up to their necks while reciting the Psalms. It is about not letting doing God's will be detoured by the possibility of our suffering. Hughes put it this way: "By his act of total self-denial Christ, who is himself the Image of God, showed us what it means for man to live according to his constitution in the image of God".[228] We die to self and therefore become alive to God and experience our full humanity as joyful and free followers of Christ. If that means that we do what it takes to come alongside those who are suffering and neglected because, like Christ, we empathize and love the unlovable, like a Mother Teresa, we embrace that way of life. I fear for Western world Christians who have lived so comfortably and securely that they have closed themselves off to God possibly leading them to even a modicum of physical or emotional suffering in order to do his bidding. My wife and I were shocked in 2002 when we left the pastorate in Toronto to return overseas to work with Arab Muslims and were told by several of our Christian friends and congregants, "Oh, if God told me to do that I could not do it."

Christ Embodied Humility

Fourthly, **Jesus was humble**. If there was one virtue that Christ exhibited that seems the least embodied by humans, at least in the Western world, my sense is that it would be humility. Why just this morning in my Bible readings I was struck by Christ's humility in taking on human existence, although very God, in these remarkable words: "For you know the grace of our Lord Jesus Christ, that though he was rich, yet for your

---

228 Philip Hughes, *Christ the True Image*, 50.

sake he became poor so that you through his poverty might become rich" (2 Cor. 8:9). The magnificent one who created the world "emptied himself" of heavenly prerogatives by becoming human (Phil. 2:6-8). Meekness or humility is also listed as a fruit of the Spirit (Gal. 5:23) and a desirable virtue (Gal. 6:1; Col. 3:12). Conversely, pride is severely condemned in Scripture (Prov. 16:18-19; 6:16-18; 29:13).

A modest earthly comparison is this. If someone has been used to leadership, to being in charge, which I have had the privilege of (or awesome responsibility of – Heb. 13:17) for over three decades as a mission executive or senior pastor, and then stepped aside to let others take the lead, he or she knows how challenging that can be. It is one thing to know the model of servant leadership that Christ demonstrated theoretically or to have written a book on servant leadership but quite another to submit to others and to empower them by not second-guessing them and becoming a follower.[229] That gap can only be overcome by possessing or acquiring genuine humility. Many people used to power never get beyond theoretical servanthood correctness. Many leaders never learn to let go, and so finish poorly, because they do not relinquish the reins of power soon enough nor intentionally mentor their successor (nor know how to do ministry without power).

Great conductor Leonard Bernstein once had this to say about the way some musicians had the tendency to be *prima donnas,* "The second fiddle. I can get plenty of first violinists but to find someone who can play the second fiddle with enthusiasm— that's a problem. And if we have no second fiddle, we have no harmony."

---

229 David Lundy, *Servant Leadership for Slow Learners.*

Simple Dalit villagers have no difficulty in embracing Jesus as both human and divine, as their guru, both powerful and humble. He is their "good shepherd". One who knows his sheep by name (John 10:3); he is not a distant leader. They sense his gentleness, his humility. They see he endured humiliation in his human existence to cover human shame, and so identifies with them in their shame; he was "a man of sorrows, acquainted with grief" (Isa. 53:4). He is a leader who has walked a mile in their shoes (Heb. 12:2). They comprehend that "part of the horror of human suffering is to be unheard, forgotten, and nameless" and so can relate to Christ hanging on the cross outside the city gates, abandoned and scorned (Heb. 13:11-13).[230] They know he will not brow-beat or threaten them, he is so approachable. Is it not said of him that "a bruised reed he will not break, and a smoldering wick he will not snuff out" (Matt. 12:20)?

They have the *bhakti* devotion to Jesus that they used to express for their village deities. But now they know that Christ is with them in their hearts and in heaven as the God-man described in Hebrews 4:15 as the one defending their cause in his function as High Priest who is not "unable to sympathize with [their] weaknesses, but who in every respect has been tempted as [they] are, yet without sin." They know he weeps and intercedes and comes alongside of them through the Holy Spirit in their suffering. Later on in being grounded in their faith they are not at all surprised to learn that the Creator God does not ignore them when they pray (Isa. 25:8) nor forget their tears (Ps. 56:8). Moreover, they intuit what the Word of God says, that at the end of time God will wipe all tears from their eyes (Rev. 21:4). Little wonder that tens of thousands of them have put their trust in Christ since the turn of the century.

---

230 Christopher T. Wright, "Lamentations: A Book for Today", *International Journal of Missionary Research*, 59.

A parallel resonance between Jesus and the Dalits is found in the story of American slavery and the emancipation of slaves in the mid-1800s. The spirit of Afro-American slaves was seen in Harriet Beecher Stowe's wildly popular book of that era, *Uncle Tom's Cabin,* the best-selling book of the nineteenth century in the USA (apart from the Bible), which depicted Jesus as black, meek and mild, at times.[231] The Negro spirituals have retained their popularity for over two centuries and speak to the profound way the African-American slaves identified with Jesus as their fellow and uncomplaining sufferer: *No one knows the trouble I sees; No one knows but Jesus* is an example of some of the words from one of their choruses.

How counter-intuitive this humility is to the self-assertiveness and selling of oneself characteristic of the postmodern world style of leadership. Or of the public posturing instinctive of those from honor-based cultures. The theologian Donald Carson describes meekness or humility this way: "The person characterized by these virtues will be generous in his estimates of others, slow to take offense, well able to bear reproach, consistently above mere self-interest."[232] Sounds like Philippians 2:1-5. And 1 Corinthians 13.

Muslims struggle with the deity of Christ in part because of how they feel his crucifixion could not have happened to an all-powerful one. How could God allow his son to be slain at the hands of an angry mob; they associate a suffering leader with weakness. All over the world, the humility expressed in the servanthood of Jesus has been seen to be counter-cultural yet revolutionary in its impact.

---

231 Richard Mouw and Douglas Sweeney, *The Suffering and Victorious Christ,* 77.
232 *A Model of Christian Maturity: An Exposition of 2 Corinthians 10-13,* 44.

The Imitation of Christ

As we reflect on Christ's peerless life, if you are like me, you are easily dismayed at how far short you seem to be in your journey toward Christlikeness; it seems an impossible standard of humanness and holiness to achieve in this life. Sure, we get instantly perfected (glorified) at Christ's return but what about our sanctification in this life? Did we not expect that upon conversion somehow we would become 'good' people overnight, as if grace were infused into us at the moment of need or automatically like solar panels heating our homes when the sun comes out? Here is where we need to come to grips with the importance of our effort of cooperation with the Holy Spirit. This human responsibility in our sanctification might be compared to the middle voice of verbs in the Greek language of the NT. In English we have only the active voice of the verb (the subject does the action — "The girl **took** her dog for a walk.") or the passive voice (the object does the action not the subject — "The girl **was dragged** by the dog as they went for a walk."). However, in the Greek language, verbs also have a middle voice. A verb is in the middle voice when both the subject and the object of the action are heavily involved in the action. Similarly, in our desire to become like Christ, it would be fallacious to assume that it is all God's work or conversely that it is all up to us to be sanctified. The transforming change is from God but we are expected to cooperate: "Work out your salvation with fear and trembling for it is God who works in you, both to will and to work for his good pleasure" (Phil. 2:12b, 13, *English Standard Version*).

Dallas Willard has captured this dual dimension involved in becoming Christlike well in his seminal books on spiritual formation. He summarizes his thesis in these words: "Spiritual formation for the Christian basically refers to the Spirit-driven process of forming the inner world of the human self in such a way that it becomes like the inner being of Christ himself."[233] While he sees that "process" as initiated by God and his grace, it nevertheless involves our intentional commitment of body, soul and spirit to the outworking of what the Spirit is and wants to pour into us as we seek to:

- Transform the mind – "To bring the mind to dwell intelligently upon God as he is presented in his Word will have the effect of causing us to love God passionately and this love will in turn bring us to think about God steadily. Thus he will always be before our minds."[234] – Romans 12:2
- Transform the body – "God made [our body] for good. That is why the way of Jesus Christ is so intentionally incarnational. The body *should* be cherished and properly cared for, not as our master, however, but as a servant of God. For most people, on the other hand, their body *governs* their life. And *that* is a problem. Even professing Christians, by and large, devote to their spiritual growth and well-bring a fraction of the time they devote to their body, and it is an even tinier fraction if we include what they worry about."[235] – Romans 12:1
- Transform the social dimension – "Love is not a feeling, or a special way of feeling, but the divine way of relating to others and oneself that moves through every dimension of our being and restructures our world for good.... Above all, we who follow Jesus must understand that a couple of hours per week of carefully calibrated distance in a church setting will be of little

---

233 *Renovation of the Heart: Putting on the Character of Christ*, 22.
234 Ibid, 106.
235 Ibid, 160

help, and may only enforce the patterns of withdrawal that permeate our fallen world."[236] – 1 John 3:14

- Transform the soul – "The correct order that the soul requires for its vitality and proper functioning is found in the "royal law" of love (James 2:8), abundantly spelled out in Jesus and his teaching. That law includes all that was essential in the older law, which he fulfilled and enables us to fulfill through constant discipleship to him."[237] – Psalm 19:7

Someone I know well is mystified as to why she seems sincerely to want to pay her bills on time and live within her means, not going into the mountain of debt that has plagued her for decades, but refuses to live a total lifestyle that leads to that sort of outcome. Similarly, we should not be surprised that the spiritual life works any differently. Constantly in Scripture we are exhorted to do things like "train yourself to be godly" (1 Tim. 4:7) and so it is evident that we are no more *recreated* to be spiritual automatons than we were *created* as human beings in the first place. God desires a relationship not a robot. In this vein Willard contends:

> So, those who say we cannot truly follow Christ turn out to be correct in a sense. We cannot behave "on the spot" as he did and taught if in the rest of our time we live as everyone else does. The "on the spot" episodes are not the place where we can, even by the grace of God, redirect unchristlike but ingrained tendencies of action toward sudden Christlikeness. Our efforts to take control *at that moment* will fail so uniformly and so ingloriously that the whole project of following Christ will appear ridiculous to the watching world.[238]

---

236 Ibid, 183, 189.
237 Ibid, 215.
238 Dallas Willard, *The Spirit of the Disciplines: Understanding How God Changes Lives*, 7.

So in thinking about the ways of cooperating with the Holy Spirit in transforming us into our full humanity in Christ, we should not be surprised that the Bible provides insights into 'means of grace' that engage our body, soul and spirit so as to change ingrained bad habits and behaviour. These time-tested disciplines which shape godly character include but are not limited to the following:

- ✓ Reading Scripture daily to know God and to know how to obey him – 2 Timothy 3:14-17
- ✓ Praying intentionally and habitually – Ephesians 6:18
- ✓ Worshiping God on our own and collectively – John 4:23; Colossians 3:16
- ✓ Engaging in Solitude – Luke 6:12
- ✓ Fasting – Matthew 9:15
- ✓ Memorizing of Scripture – Psalm 119:9, 11
- ✓ Meditating – Psalm 119:148
- ✓ Studying/Reading – 2 Timothy 4:12
- ✓ Confessing sin – 1 John 1:9; James 5:16
- ✓ Practicing Silence – James 1:19
- ✓ Celebrating God's Goodness – 2 Samuel 6:12-16
- ✓ Serving – Colossians 3:23[239]

Exerting Ourselves in Seeking Sanctification is not Legalism

Ever since the Reformation, the church of Jesus Christ has been wary of any form of legalism corrupting her understanding of being saved by grace alone. The book of Galatians makes clear that grace plus works is not a basis for being justified by faith, salvation being grace-based alone because of the finished and

239 The most well-known evangelical overview of the spiritual disciplines is *Celebration of Discipline* by Richard Foster. In my book, *Servant Leadership for Slow Learners*, chapter 6 is a description of my own imperfect efforts at practicing the spiritual disciplines.

efficacious work of Christ on the cross on our behalf. Jesus himself denounced the Pharisees for seeking righteousness through their good works and warned of the leaven of the Pharisees. Furthermore, Paul was the chief NT spokesman for not corrupting free grace with dead works: "Therefore do not let anyone judge you by what you eat or drink, or with regard to a religious festival, a New Moon celebration or a Sabbath day. These are a shadow of the things that were to come; the reality, however, is found in Christ" (Col. 2:16-17; cf. Rom. 9:16; Eph. 2:8-9)). However, it is my opinion that Western world Christians, for the most part, are not guilty of confusing grace-righteousness with works-righteousness but of the need for works and sterling effort in living out our faith after our conversion as the only reasonable response to that gift of eternal life. On the grace-works continuum we are guiltier not of legalism but of antinomianism (lawlessness). In this regard Willard maintains that

> The presence of the Spirit and of grace is not meant to set the law aside, but to enable conformity to it from an inwardly transformed personality. We walk in the spirit of the law and the letter follows naturally as is appropriate. You cannot separate spirit from law, though you must separate law from *legalism*—righteousness in terms of actions... . Grace does not set law aside except on the point of justification, of acceptance before God.[240]

As we have just sought to demonstrate, the outworking of our faith in becoming more like Christ requires intention and effort even though it is God's transforming power at work. Again we turn to Willard who observes that "the problem of spiritual formation... among those who identify themselves as Christians today is not that it is impossible or that effectual means to it are not available. The problem is that it is not intended. People do not see it and its value and decide to follow through with it.

---

240 *Renovation of the Heart*, 215.

They do not *decide* to do the things that Jesus did and said."[241] In our concern to avoid the asceticism of monasticism we have ignored the classical value of the disciplines for spiritual formation that Protestants, at least, have associated with the wrong-headed works-righteousness of Roman Catholicism. But the above-mentioned biblical tools are a means of grace intended by God for enabling Christ to be formed in us (Gal. 4:19).

Freeing the Individual to Become Christlike Includes Belonging

As individuals created in God's image recalibrate their fallen humanness through Christ so as to fulfill their God-given potential, they will need to belong, to have the support of the visible community to which in their conversion they became part of invisibly, the Body of Christ, what we call 'church' (1 Cor. 12:13). Virtually we have already made a case for the importance of church for the follower of Jesus in chapter 1 when we talked about the image of God being partly about community because God is not only a unity but three Persons and that social orientation is embedded in how we are created. Also in the bullet point above that refers briefly to the transformation of the social dimension, collective identity is what is meant.

That said, we often struggle in identifying with God's People as found in the local church. We already touched on this issue in the chapter on postmodernity and the way that Millennials have abandoned the church in droves. Scarred by interpersonal conflicts and hypocrisy over the years, we might describe church as a bunch of porcupines getting together to stay warm. Church seems to mimic to many young people the fighting they observed between their now divorced parents.

---

241 Ibid, 91.

Nevertheless, church has also been a place of inclusion for us. We felt accepted when as a new Christian we realized that we were surrounded by mature believers who did not look scandalized when our language betrayed our unsanctified, wet-behind-the-ears state. It dawned on us that the wall of exclusion had been broken down as we stared around the room at the other members in our newly embraced small group and realized that the group represented the ethnic diversity of our community and yet we were still likeminded. We rejoiced in our forgiveness and acceptance in the Body of Christ when we confessed our failures before another brother and he did not blink as he extended the grace of God openhandedly.

Interestingly, our witness becomes effective to the unchurched when they see how much we love other believers (John 13:34-35). Why is that the case? Because it reflects the nature of God who is Three-In-One in community. Meaningful community is what humans long for, as we explained in chapter 1. It represents the reality of who they are as being created in God's image.

A Radical Way to Express Christ's Love

An aspect of the development of Christ's character marked by love is the ability to forgive. One man's intimate reflection on this subject is germane to our understanding of how we express Christlikeness as God's People. Miroslav Volf, Christian philosopher and theologian, was forced into military service for a year in the former communist Yugoslavia in 1983, and subjected to repeated interrogations there for being suspected as a spy. His search for healing from the bitter memories and unforgiving spirit that plagued him following his traumatic interrogations prompted his book *The End of Memory: Remembering Rightly in a Violent World*. Early on in his deliberation about how as a Christian he ought to deal with the injustice perpetrated against him, he makes this telling statement: "To triumph fully, evil needs two victories, not one. The first victory happens when an evil deed is perpetrated; the second victory, when evil is returned."[242]

Revenge is not the Christian way he realized, nor sweet. When people are not treated as if they matter and are manhandled, the desire for revenge is overpowering. It explains why tribal feuds in Africa destabilize countries like Rwanda for generations and result in genocide. It explains unhelpful tensions between Christians and Muslims of the Arab world a millennium after atrocities perpetrated by both sides in the Crusades occurred. It explains why a century and a half after the American civil war, many African Americans still do not trust the white man. Love, too often, seems to be a many splintered thing. In the church, though, above all else, this is the laboratory where we can practice the art of forgiving people and learn the love which is patient, kind and which bears all things.

Healing and Forgiveness in the Face of Injustice

Applying this principle to specific communities and peoples we have focused on, if the Dalit Bahujan rises up against upper caste power holders as the tide turns, what can assuage their resolve to shift from being victims of injustice to perpetrators of injustice? How can the cycle of mistrust and mistreatment between Caucasian-Americans and Afro-Americans be broken? How can aboriginals experience healing from their abuse in the residential schools in Canada? What can permanently sublimate the bitterness and mistrust between the Irish and the English? The simple but truthful answer is Jesus. It is possible to be a human and forgive the most appalling mistreatment; did not Jesus hanging on the cross in excruciating agony say to his persecutors, "Father, forgive them, for they do not know what

---

242 *The End of Memory*, 9.

they are doing" (Luke 23:34)? Healing from post-traumatic stress disorder or victimization will not be an automatic thing, Christian or otherwise. But God's forgiveness experienced through Christ gives us an edge in overcoming incipient bitterness. The Holy Spirit now resident in us frees us to be counter-cultural in seeking reconciliation and healing in broken and abusive relationships. Furthermore, the help of God's people in community can give us the strength to do what would be more difficult on our own.

The standard the spirit of Jesus calls and empowers us to embrace is expressed in these practical attitudes and actions and to be developed in the fellowship and community of the local church involves:

- ❖ Speaking the truth in love (Eph. 4:15 – the victim may be tempted to exaggerate the wrong done)
- ❖ Being mindful of one's own human weaknesses when given the opportunity to exact justice (Gal. 6:1-2)
- ❖ While naming and blaming truthfully and accurately, choosing not to require punishment for named crimes committed ("Love covers a multitude of sins" – 1 Peter 4:8)
- ❖ Forgiving those who violated us ("forgiving each other, as the Lord has forgiven you" – Col. 3:13)

Living out these principles will set us free and will demonstrate that we really believe all people are made in the image of God. That difficult process of forgiving the unforgiveable is developed and nurtured in the local church.

Summarizing this mindset, Volf states:

> When we forgive those who have wronged us, we make our own God's miracle of forgiveness. Echoing God's unfathomable graciousness, we decouple the deed from the doer, the offense

from the offender. We blot out the offense so that it no longer mars the offender. That is why the non-remembrance of wrongs suffered appropriately crowns forgiveness.[243]

Jesus bore our reproach, the just dying for the unjust. Therefore, to exact a pound of flesh, to insist on strict eye for eye justice may never bring societal healing and redemption. Volf reminds us that "Christ did not only die in solidarity with sufferers, but also as a *substitute for offenders*." [244] Keller calls this form of justice "generous justice" and posits in his book by that title that Christians are not always required to exact strict justice but have the choice to add in a pinch of mercy.

The cycle of hatred and conflict is not likely to be fully resolved with the meting out of strict justice. We see that, for example, in the way that survivors of the Holocaust sometimes have been known not to forgive those who did the unspeakable and unimaginable; cultivating permanent memory of wrongs suffered seems not to reflect the nature of the God who remembers our sins no more (Ps. 103:12). It is broken only when unconditional grace is extended to those who do not deserve it, just as we, deserving God's eternal punishment for our rebellion and transgression, have been recipients of unconditional grace. God loved us while we were yet sinners, not after we got our act together (Rom. 5:10). There will come a day—at the Last Judgment—when unrepented sin of those who crushed image-bearers of the divine will be exposed and full justice executed ("The sins of some are obvious, reaching the place of judgment ahead of them; the sins of others trail behind them" – 1 Tim. 5:24). This capacity to forgive will not come for the victimized overnight and may involve relapse. But persevering will make all the difference in the continual renewing work of

243 Ibid, 208.
244 Ibid, 115.

the Holy Spirit (1 John 4:4). As the Ethiopian proverb goes, "The donkey may have died but we do not abandon the journey".

A capacity to forgive is critical in treating all human beings with dignity because they are made in God's image. It also philosophically acknowledges that humans are fallen creatures. This aspect of creation theology informs our treatment of our very enemies. Found in the image of God and fallen. Perfect humanity blurts out, "Forgive them, Father, for they know not what they do." A forgiving spirit is fundamental to becoming like Christ.

Christian Tolerance of Pluralism

Given the fact that all of humankind is made in God's image, it is not consistent faith-practicing for Christians to squelch religious pluralism and multiculturalism. We've already touched on that subject in chapter 4. History bears out the relative tolerance of Christianity. Where is Christianity's centre of gravity (unless you are Roman Catholic)? You can be a Christian in Mali or Minnesota and feel equally identified with your faith, which is universal in scope but cultural in expression. In contrast, Islam has Mecca as its holy city and the *Qur'an* is untranslatable from Arabic without losing its inspired quality, according to most Muslims; it is very culture-bound. So are Judaism, Buddhism, Confucianism and Hinduism.[245] For example, Hindu Scriptures should not be read out loud by anyone other than in Sanskrit, a language reserved for forward castes and especially the priests. As Lamin Sanneh, himself a former Muslim, originally from Gambia, now Professor of History and World Christianity at Yale University, has so persuasively argued, the translation of the Bible into the vernacular all around the world has paved the way for it to be embraced in every culture and for Christianity

---

245 Ibid, 41.

to be a truly universal religion.[246] And why should it not be a universal religion, for it mirrors the reality that resonates with all people, who are all made in God's image? There is diversity in the godhead and so we should expect it in humans. The diversity in creation itself speaks to us about God's love of difference, variety and complexity. God loves colours but is colourblind so to speak.

Free To Become All We Were Meant To Be

My experience is that only when I submitted my life unreservedly to Christ while a student at the University of Toronto did I really begin to discover who I was as a person. That 'leap of faith' did not obliterate my personality but actually liberated me to be my true self as Christ came inside by the Holy Spirit to transform me. Change was not overnight and sometimes involved painful decisions and change of habitual behaviour but I have never found the cost of following Christ to be too steep to bear. In dying to self I have become more fully alive. Why possible? Simply because Christ is the most completely human being who ever lived, if we can be so bold as to make that statement without being misunderstood. He is the image of God and therefore as we become Christlike we become more of what God intended us to be as those made in his image. It is through dying to the old person's fallen and self-absorbed ways and yielding ourselves to Christ that we experience the life of the resurrected Christ (Romans 6 explicates this process and identification with Christ well). This real life experience of transformation and yet fulfilment individually is expressed in the otherwise baffling words of Jesus:

> "Whoever wants to be my disciple must deny themselves and take up their cross daily and follow me. For whoever wants to

---

246 *Disciples of All Nations: Pillars of World Christianity* (New York: Oxford University Press, 2008).

save their life will lost it but whoever loses their life for me will save it" (Luke 9:23-24).

Look at it this way. If someone you knew was ignorant about salt and you gave her a few grains to taste and told her that most people use it in their cooking, she might react by worrying that all dishes must taste the same as that sharp taste she had just experienced. But we would smile knowingly and assure her that the effect of adding salt, unless too much, is quite the opposite. It actually brings out the distinctive flavour of the food. Christ invading our lives is much like that. He fulfills us and satisfies us, not destroying our personhood.[247] Jesus: the full image-bearer.

Yes, that lifelong journey to become like Christ and so better reflect God's image can be scary to begin at the outset, or along the way, when we comprehend that being freed from the penalty of sin by trusting in Christ to forgive us does not mean God wants to leave us the way we are. Paul the apostle wrestled with this in Romans where he expounds so carefully and clearly the justification and peace with God that come by faith and not by works/good behavior. He seems to hesitate after chapter 5 which makes explicit that all of our past, present and future sins have now been forgiven because of Christ. It is as if Paul then realizes that one logical conclusion of the truth of justification is that this knowledge can lead to the presumption that the believer in Christ is free to sin all the more. Hence he writes chapters 6 and 7, returning to his glorious theme of the implications of justification by faith in chapter 8. We wrestle and falter with the push and pull of our world and its attractions. We see our feet of clay and compare that with the words of Jesus to his followers that their righteousness needed to be greater than the righteousness of the Pharisees. But then we remember the underlying grace characterizing our relationship with God. So

---

247 I am indebted to C. S. Lewis for this analogy in *Beyond Personality*, 62-63.

we return to the straight and narrow road of seeking to do God's will and discovering the abundant life. That grace frees us to set the bar high. That underlying grace is kind of like the all but invisible screen behind home plate in baseball that protects the crowd close to the playing field from being hit by stray foul balls. It is only visible from certain angles. The screen is fully effective even though invisible.

High Standards but High Hope

When we look at the life of Christ and see the standard of humanness we are to live up to, it seems impossible, like trying to hit a golf ball when you have Parkinson's. Who can always do God's will, be so gentle and humble, love so unreservedly and live so selflessly? We might feel like Joseph Parker, an accomplished pianist who treated himself one evening in London to a concert for the great pianist, Paderewski. Parker was so stirred by the performance that when he returned home, he shouted to his wife, "Bring me an axe! Today I heard great music for the first time. By comparison what I can do amounts to nothing at all. I feel like chopping my piano in pieces!" Parker did not follow through on his threat although he knew he could never rise to the level of Paderewski's brilliance by simply following his example. He would need Paderewski's very hands and soul. Similarly, although we can never live up to Christ's standards, we can move in the right direction because He lives inside of us and is helping us grow and be transformed into his likeness.

CHAPTER 6
Seeing People with the Eyes of Jesus: Human Rights and Restoring Dignity[248]

Shortly before his death the legendary film maker of blockbusters like *The Ten Commandments* and *The Greatest Show on Earth*, Cecil B DeMille, mused on the human spirit while observing a beetle morph into a dazzling dragonfly as he lazed on the water in a canoe. He rambled:

> [The beetle's] glistening black shell cracked all the way down his back. Out of it came a shapeless mass, quickly transformed into beautiful, brilliantly colored life. As I watched in fascination, there gradually unfolded iridescent wings from which the sunlight flashed a thousand colours. The wings spread wide, as if in worship of the sun. The blue-green body took shape. Before my eyes had occurred a metamorphosis—the transformation of a hideous beetle into a gorgeous dragonfly, which started dipping and soaring over the water. But the body it left behind still clung to my canoe. I had witnessed what seemed to me a miracle. Out of the mud had come a beautiful new life. And the thought came to me, that if the Creator works such wonders with the lowest of creatures, what might be in store for the human spirit?[249]

---

248 Ethical Issues not covered in this chapter which are germane to the subject of this book include euthanasia, capital punishment, eugenics, post-biological existence, environmental care and genetic engineering.

249 Http://www.templehayes.com/the-message-of-the-wate-beetle/

Indeed, what a difference it would make if we perceived people in such a transformed way. Instead of seeing humans as 'beetles', or existing solely as a combination of chemicals, but as 'dragonflies', distinctly and beautifully made in God's image. In fact, we need to see people the way Jesus did. Apart from his actions as he walked the length and breadth of Palestine, recorded in the gospels, we see the way Jesus looked at people by his first public speech, given in the synagogue of Nazareth. There he applied the Messianic prophecy of Isaiah 61:1-2 directly to himself: "The Spirit of the Lord is upon me, because he has anointed me to proclaim good news to the poor. He has sent me to proclaim liberty to the captives and recovering of sight to the blind, to set at liberty those who are oppressed, to proclaim the year of the Lord's favour" (Luke 4:18-19). If we took Jesus' attitude and actions in relation to fellow human beings as a blueprint for our 21st century understanding of human rights and the implications of what it means to be in God's image, we surely could not go too far wrong.

Even in this one statement of Jesus, corroborated repeatedly by his behaviour, we comprehend that every single person matters. All human beings are made in God's image and equally so, as we have sought to articulate here. Whether you are in prison as a thief in Jakarta or a middle class American living in a bungalow surrounded by a white picket fence in Jacksonville, whether an oppressed Dalit mother fetching water on your head from the nearest village pond near Baroda or a Caucasian woman headed for work in a smart business suit in Boston, or whether a physically disabled child unable to go to school or a world class athlete with the world as your oyster, Jesus loves you. Jesus affirms your human worth. He sees you as made in the image of God. He sees your potential. "For God so loved the world". Given these truths, what difference should it make in our behaviour?

Human Rights Are Mainstream Values

The biblical worldview that includes the foundational principle that humankind is made in God's image has shaped western civilization and still does to some extent. In public speeches Abraham Lincoln described the American Declaration of Independence as upholding the biblical view that all human beings were created equally. Martin Luther King a century later pointed to the same document and the same Bible as the rationale for the equal treatment of blacks and whites. But today the cry for human rights and social justice is not particularly associated with the Christian community. Millennials in particular have taken up the cause of global social justice whether steeped in a Christian worldview or not. Emerging adults lobbying for social justice is as popular as viewing cats playing the piano on YouTube. Unlike the political scene in Great Britain when William Wilberforce began his uphill battle to bring about abolition of slavery, today's politicians are socially aware and engaged, whether as Green Party anti-pollution activists or as anti-human trafficking advocates following International Justice Mission on Twitter.

When Do Human Rights Begin and Choices End?

We live in a day and age when the fanaticism of certain extreme ideologies threatens the sustainability of global civilization, reflected on particularly in chapter 3. There is a heightened tug of war going on, a kind of clash of civilizations, between those who want to restrict freedom of speech and religion for the sake of minimizing violence and maintaining a secure world and those who brook no rivals to their own ideology to the point of being willing even to shed blood, perpetrate torture or impose imprisonment. Even as I enter these words on my computer, the news in my homeland is rife with talk about the federal government tabling legislation that will grant greater surveillance privileges to our equivalent of Homeland Security in order to make for greater success in the war on terror, and the reaction from the leader of the opposition party and civil libertarian groups who say that the proposed legislation will erode basic freedoms of privacy and speech. What human rights are inviolable, if any? What can we agree on whether or not we hold to a biblical worldview about the divine image-bearing of humans?

As we talked about in chapter 1, human rights flow out of how and for what purpose God has made us. We saw other inklings of how we should then live side by side as persons who are individuals and in community. Some rights are not embedded in the social contract forged in each society. Others are. Respect for the rights of fellow human beings is engendered in the simple commandment Jesus gave his followers to "love your neighbor as yourself". The right to worship as we please, or not at all, is inferred in Scripture by such things as the parable of the wheat and the tares (weeds) where Jesus says that the tares should be allowed to remain in the field with the wheat until harvest time (Matt. 13:30) which suggests that freedom of religion is a basic human freedom. Certainly the right to life is grounded in image of God theology and so we can argue that the right to a basic level of food is also a human right.[250] The right to a fair trial is explicitly taught in Scripture (Deut. 17:6). And so forth.

Three winters ago we had a terrible ice storm in Toronto which resulted in power going out all around the city as tree branches crashed into power lines. Our condo building got hit with a 12 hour blackout. That would not have been so upsetting if we were living in India as we did in the 1970s and faced massive power cuts every day so that we got used to keeping candles at close hand. In the recent ice storm, scurrying to find our emergency

---

250 Ronald Sider, *The Scandal of Evangelical* Politics, 134-135.

candles and battery-powered flashlight, our rooms eventually lit up and we felt safe again. In like manner, the crucifixion of Christ illuminates the darkness surrounding suffering and evil in the world. It reveals a God who is so committed to not overturning his act to create freely responding beings to love him that he allowed his Son to suffer the indignities, shame and searing agony of crucifixion, thus making right what had been skewed and lost by the Fall. The all-powerful Creator of the universe suffered in our place. This exchange of honor for humiliation, of the crown for the cross, shows us the way in not allowing ourselves the fleshly inclination to impose our faith or values on others. It patiently waits for others to be convinced and captivated by Love and Truth as we live in a Christlike way and prayerfully in their presence.

The Church Is Not the State

The problem with Christians being judgmental of people and societies that do not hold their views is that they apply OT laws and morals governing the theocracy of Israel (state ruled by God) on all contemporary citizens. How many times have we heard pastors and Christian leaders calling their nation to turn from its wicked ways, humbling itself and praying? But that is a prayer directed to the people of Israel and not to a modern nation state. The United Kingdom can repent collectively and politically about as much as Brits are likely to overthrow the monarchy. We treat morality injunctions and exhortations intended for the church as a theocracy wishing to impose NT principles and practices of the church on surrounding non-Christians. But modern political states and societies are pluralistic in composition; church and state are separate animals—which even Jesus recognized when, in looking at a Roman coin, he declared that the Jews should render to Caesar the things that were Caesar's and to God the things that were God's. Insisting on the coalescing of moral standards and values into a uniform Christian mold is wrong-headed. It is what Muslim states aim to do (joining mosque and state under Sharia law) but that is not the Christian way.

If God does not force persons outside the covenant community to obey all of the Ten Commandments, for instance, then the State should protect and respect individual freedoms too. How many of the Ten Commandments can actually be made legal in a pluralistic society? Probably only those concerned with murder and stealing. Certainly the first commandment is not enforceable nor the one on coveting. In fact, there is no "Christian" society as such. Imagine my amusement when I first landed in the Philippines in 2004 and while heading into Manila from the airport saw a huge banner above the terminal exit pronouncing that the Philippines was the only Christian country in Asia. Then on a small (official airport) sign underneath that one were inscribed the words "Beware of Pickpockets".

These fundamental moral standards are ones that we should only expect to be fully practiced in the church of Jesus Christ—and even there you would find that things like Sabbath-keeping do not find widespread acceptance. Whatever moral standard you are talking about, in the church you find inconsistent, struggling sinners imperfectly seeking to live holy lives. Then when one factors in the standards Jesus set for his followers in the Beatitudes and in statements like if anyone lusts after a woman in his heart he has committed adultery, or if you are angry in your heart against someone you have committed murder, who can cast the first stone? Christians dare not seek to legislate morality outside of the local church.

A reasonable line in the sand to draw when it comes to legislating morality or rights in a secular state is 'does this value/right/choice do violence or harm to other people'. Just as part of the medical profession's primary ethic in helping people medically is 'do no harm', so the state should promote the common good. Tolerance and the understanding of justice should coalesce around this standard. There is a difference between allowing citizens the freedom to smoke cigarettes in their own homes and allowing Imperial Tobacco to advertise their products on school websites. You should not legislate morality except where it clearly upholds the common good.

That is no easy feat. The present hullabaloo in Ontario over the new provincial sex education update for children in schools, starting with sex education at age 8, is an example. It resulted in large protests by parents in front of the provincial legislature in Toronto. Shortly thereafter 35,000 children were withdrawn from public schools[251] by parents in protest, parents who felt the up-to-date curriculum was a downgrade morally and that sex education should be left to them to teach at home. This furor arose in spite of the existing right of parents to withdraw their children from the classroom when the sex education took place.

The moral teachings of the Bible are designed for our human good nonetheless: "We know the law is good if one uses it properly" (1 Tim. 1:8). Incidentally, right after this statement Paul includes in his list of "lawbreakers and rebels" a number of examples including "slave traders" (verse 10). But it is in the Church where moral standards based on the Bible are to be modelled and accountably followed, and not arbitrarily in society as a whole. That said, it is apparent that God does hold non-believing nations to a certain level of moral expectations. Many places in the Prophets we see God rebuking nations surrounding Israel for their injustices. In Amos 1:3-2:3, for example, God holds Syria, Gaza, Edom and Moab accountable for the evils of taking civilians captive, breaking of treaties, ripping

---

251 Called private schools in the UK.

open pregnant women, and committing indignities to dead people.[252] One wonders at the fate of leaders and the military in places like Syria in light of atrocities perpetrated on their own people. A nation that is smart sticks to a Judeo-Christian ethic if in doubt about the right way forward in a pluralistic context.

Vinoth Ramachandra seeks to strike this balance when he advises:

> A morally and culturally "neutral" state which makes no moral demands on its citizens and is equally hospitable to all cultures and conceptions of the good is logically incoherent and practically impossible. And since every law coerces those not sharing its underlying values, a morally and non-coercive state is a fantasy. Openly recognizing this fact is the first step forward in reconfiguring the nature of politics in any pluralistic society. Christians should not respond by demanding a state that makes no controversial moral judgments but rather by demanding a state that is more transparent in its judgments, precisely so that they can be subjected to wide-ranging public scrutiny and debate.[253]

Complex, isn't it? For Christians to get this balancing act right is about as easy as a 67-year old man with bifocals (me) trying to hit a 92 mile an hour baseball whose spin from the pitcher's mound 60 feet away to the batter's box must be recognized in a split second and responded to on the basis of whether it is a slider, a curveball, a fastball or a change-up. In part, this complexity of living as a follower of Jesus in a fallen world of religious and ethnic pluralism explains why Christians are often viewed as anti-gay, anti-abortion bigots by outsiders even when they are trying to love their neighbours as themselves.

---

252 Timothy Keller, *Generous Justice*, 23-24.
253 *Subverting Global Myths,* 143.

Is Democracy the Best Political System if We Are Made in God's Image?

The above train of thought might lead us to dare ask the question, "Is democracy the right way to establish government if humankind is made in God's image?" Most Europeans, Latinos and North Americans would say "of course". The flag-waving sentiment that democracy is next to godliness cannot verbatim be derived from the Bible. Israel was governed by a monarchy. Jesus told his disciples to render to Caesar, who was an emperor, his rightful due. Democracy is a rather modern invention. Even British democracy evolved over hundreds of years; the Magna Carta was just one step in a long road toward democracy as now expressed. However, what we are finding as time marches on is that democracy both makes allowance for the equality of all people plus the corrupting influence of power on fallen humanity (as Machiavelli declared, 'Power corrupts, absolute power corrupts absolutely'). Another famous statement was made by theologian Reinhold Niebuhr: "Man's capacity for justice makes democracy possible; but man's inclination to injustice makes democracy necessary."[254] We could argue that democracy respects both the image of God within humans and at the same time their fallenness.

Where to Put Our Foot Down

Cobbling together common cause with disparate communities is not easy but far from impossible. Modern political philosophy takes human equality for granted. At least lip service is given to it—such as by most of the 49 Muslim-majority countries which have signed the UN Declaration of Human Rights. Although some of these states might be closet (or openly) anti-American, they subscribe to the words of the US Declaration of Independence

---

254 Quoted in Ronald Sider, *The Scandal of Evangelical Politics*, 140.

of 1776: "We hold these words to be self-evident, that all men are created equal." Never mind that the preamble to that Declaration speaks of the innate equality of all human beings because they are made in God's image.

At the same time, we need to take heed from the Muslim state's policy of *dhimmi*, which is an enforced tax on non-Muslims. It is a severe form of carding (racial profiling in police-language in Toronto) which has no place in a pluralistic democracy. Muslims do not separate religion and politics. Christians need to, though. We cannot mix politics and religion.[255] It is not fair to those who do not share our belief system. By not mixing the two I do not mean we have no right to bring our values to the table in determining what is best for society.[256] We just do not want to do so as political lobbyists for enforced Christianity.

However, while we should not be political exclusivists in a democracy, assuming that only one party or cause automatically represents Christians, we can be cultural inclusivists. We are religious exclusivists, convinced that there is only one way to know God, through Christ. But we are political and cultural inclusivists. Lesslie Newbigin coined this phrase of Christians being cultural inclusivists while religious exclusivists. He was ahead of his time in recognizing that the West had changed; it was no longer a largely Christian world. In an increasingly pluralistic world, he called on Christians to be cultural pluralists.[257] By that

---

255 I do not mean by this statement that Christians should not be politicians. They should. William Wilberforce is an excellent example of how a Christian politician can function in what seems to be a fairly corrupting milieu.

256 This book is not the best place to unpack the issue of how to vote. Let me just say that Christians tend have the reputation for voting habitually for right wing political parties. However, while conservative parties subscribe to virtuous things like hard work, liberal parties uphold societal responsibility to help the poor, also a biblical virtue.

257 Lesslie Newbigin, *The Gospel in a Pluralistic Society* (Grand Rapids: W. B. Eerdmans, 1989).

he meant that the gospel both affirms and critiques culture. There are some aspects of every culture that are good (such as the equal treatment under law of every American) and some that are evil (sanctioning of corporate greed and irresponsibility in not protecting the environment as a necessary restraint on profit). If I might paraphrase Newbigin's big idea to make sure you understand how it relates to the theme of this book, there are certain aspects of every culture that reflect the fact that humans are made in the image of God and some aspects that substantiate another biblical claim—that humans are fallen creatures. So Christians need to laud the things we regard as virtuous in society and encourage all sides of the citizenry to contribute to the debate over the common good and shared values.[258]

A pluralistic liberal democracy is posited by philosopher Miroslav Volf as the best way forward so as to avoid the inevitable totalitarianism of fundamentalist Islam, Communism or Hindutva, which we might view as angry-looking, dark, late-autumn clouds on the horizons of disparate corners of the planet.[259] We also touched on this issue of how to forge a pluralistic society where human freedoms flourish in chapters 3 and 4. While it is felt in some intellectual circles today that monotheism is the chief cause of societal discord and violence, the fact is that some of the worst atrocities of the past century, such as through Stalin, Mao and Hitler, were the fruit of atheism.[260] Instead of monotheists (Christian, Muslim, Jew or otherwise) seeking to impose their view of right and wrong on the society they live in through laws, Volf sees the best way

---

258 Miroslav Volf, *Allah: A Christian Response*, 224-226.
259 *A Public Faith: How Followers of Christ Should Serve the Common Good*, chapter 7: "Public Engagement".
260 For example, the view of monotheism as being inconsistent with global peace is a veiled theme of Samuel Huntington, *The Clash of Civilization and the Remaking of the World Order* (London: Simon & Shuster, 1996).

forward as not the opposite of excluding all religious views from the public realm—which is the way European and North American democratic societies lean, sometimes delineating a clear, sometimes a fuzzy, separation between religion and state. Contrary to what is supposed today, the separation of church and state was historically promoted in order to protect religion from the state, not the other way around.

So, we allow the interplay of Muslim, secular, Christian and all other aspects of society to inform how we should then live together. Faith is not just a private matter. We can no more ask the Muslim minority of our Western civilization to keep their faith in their mosques than we can ask Christians to do so in their churches. Christians are to be salt and light within whatever cultures God places them. There is no one Christian "culture" for the gospel to take root in and find expression in. We are called to remain in the world although not unblinkingly swallowing the world's values (John 17:14-16). As Volf summarizes this train of thought, "Though I agree that God's moral laws have universal validity, I believe they may be imposed as the law of the land only through valid democratic processes and not against the will of the people."[261] I would go a step further and say that this is the only political solution to respecting what it means for humans to be made in God's image. To be made in God's image means the upholding freedom of speech and freedom of religion—the very things that humanitarians are united around regardless of their religious stripe.

So I am not in favour of a complete separation of church and state as many advocate. There is no neutral moral ground. Secular humanism is a worldview just as much as Christianity is. You cannot have "church" only representing personal morality and "state" representing public morality. The thought

---

261 *A Public Faith: How Followers of Christ Should Serve the Common Good*, 144.

is that separating the two works to protect religion from state interference. But that truce has ended up isolating religion, not allowing it to be freely expressed beyond the individual person or the walls of places of worship.

Similarly, to require Muslims entirely to leave their religion at home when they enter the workplace in their job as a pharmacist, maintaining that only a secular workplace is morally neutral, is to dehumanize the Muslim. A pluralistic democracy makes room for everybody as mediated by the give and take dialectic expressed in a pluralistic society. The gay. The Buddhist. The new immigrant. The Christian. The secular humanist. All need a voice in determining what is lawful and just. Whereas the age-old sense of justice was predicated on an innate understanding of right and wrong that would lead to the good life (e.g. Aristotle's notion of justice), contemporary society tends to found it on what the individual freely chooses to be the good life (e.g. as developed over the past few centuries by philosophers such as John Stuart Mill who argued in nineteenth century Britain that government should not intervene with individual liberty unless it brings harm to someone else). Harvard political philosopher, Michael Sandel, maintains that although modern concepts of justice focus on what brings the most freedom for the individual (e.g. whether the state should declare greedy behaviour as wrong or be neutral about that sort of thing), universal moral standards still play a big part in influencing the public's understanding of what is justice.[262] His point? Don't exclude any segment of society in establishing laws and standards of justice. Speaking along these lines in an interview with *Christianity Today*, legal scholars, Stephen Monsma and Stanley Carlson-Thies, observed:

---

262 *Justice: What's the Right Thing to Do?* 8-10.

A political system is not a church. It needs to be fair to everybody. That means respecting different convictions. We don't imagine that all moral views are equally valid or that all roads lead to God. Pluralism is relativism. Ideally, we'll continue to argue vigorously about different principles and work on persuading each other to try a different path. But when we haven't persuaded each other, we need space to live out our convictions... . Principled pluralism acknowledges basic human nature, and the fact that we have to live together, despite our disagreements."[263]

On final analysis, what should govern political decisions that seek to further justice? For the Christian, governments should make decisions that reflect the reality that all human beings are made in the image of God. We are moral agents who freely choose what we consider to be right and wrong, even though as Christians we understand that capability within humans to be warped by our fallenness. We therefore respect the individual to have freedom to live life large except where we have forged a majority consensus as to what limits need to be put on personal freedoms so as to work for the common good.

A Word of Warning

A word of warning about what radical Muslims really believe about democracy. Many fundamentalist Muslims in the West appear supportive of democracy—which includes the preservation, as it should, of their minority religious rights—but really see it as leverage to buy them time until Islam can be established as the dominant political power in the state. When that happens, so the argument goes, there would be no recourse in their view but to see an Islamic state and law emerging, thus spelling the end of democratic states, at least as Western civilization understands it. Elections might continue, as they do in many Muslim states, but they would be only for

---

263 Matt Reynolds interview, *Christianity Today*, 62-63.

show and do nothing, or only slow down, the inevitability of an Islamic theocracy being installed. Their electoral policy has been classically phrased as "one man, one vote, once."[264]

Helping the Poor Practically

Enough about politics. Globally, there is a lot of goodwill to help the world's poor. To help the poor is to enable them to live as more than sub-humans. It means to treat them commiserate with being made in God's image. It means not only being literate about global disparities between the affluent and the poor—but doing something to narrow the gap. There is an Arab proverb that exclaims that "the eye sees far but the hand is short." Can we really claim that to grant people the right to life, freedom of speech and freedom of conscience without giving them the means of livelihood to accomplish these things is to respect them as creatures made in God's image? Philosopher Ramachandra agrees: "The right to life implies access to the resources that sustain life. To speak of the poor as having rights to sustenance implies that what we owe them is not simply charity but justice."[265]

As we have intimated in different ways as we have reflected on the implications of humankind being made in God's image, Christians must give more than lip service to helping the poor. In commenting on Psalm 41:1, which talks about the blessedness of those who "have regard for the poor", Keller notes that the Hebrew word for "have regard for" means to give sustained attention to and then to act wisely and effectively with regard to whatever it is, in this case helping the poor.[266]

---

264 Bernard Lewis, *The Crisis of Islam*, 85.
265 *Subverting Global Myths*, 106.
266 *Generous Justice*, 110.

In North America, we are cocooned from the stark reality that the gap between the rich and poor is widening globally. We see the affluence of our lifestyle within our own culture in comparison even to what our parents experienced and we generalize, thinking that it must be improving everywhere in the world at about the same pace. On the contrary, the gap between nations rich and poor is yawning wider. In the 1820s, according to Jeffery Sachs, there was a differential of 4 to 1 in per capita income between the wealthiest and poorest regions of the world, whereas today that gap is something like 75 to one.[267] Is that fair? Is that a just distribution of the world's resources? To help the poor, as Bono rants, "is not about charity. It is about justice."

If we could question the impartiality of the God of the Bible in any way, it could only be that he has a soft spot in his heart for the poor. The OT Law recognized and provided for the material needs of different groups of the poor (Ex. 23:2-9; Lev. 19:9-10; Deut. 15:1-8). Jesus declared in his first public address that he came to "proclaim good news to the poor" (Luke 4:18). He also so closely identified with the poor that he claimed that to give a cup of cold water to them in his name was tantamount to giving it to him (Matt. 25:35). Akin to this special connection with the poor, in Proverbs 19:17 we read that "whoever is generous to the poor lends to the Lord." What a strong statement.

When Jeremiah the prophet was sent to evil King Jehoiakim to prophesy that he would be severely punished, he compared him with his good father, King Josiah, and said, "He defended the cause of the poor and needy, and so all went well. *Is not this what it means to know me?* asks the Lord" (Jer. 22:13-19). To know God is not about having one's quiet time so much as it is in advocating for the poor, it would appear.

---

267 Cited in Richard Stearns, *The Hole in our Gospel*, 100.

In our minds, we associate Sodom and Gomorrah with profligate living. However, when the prophet Ezekiel, speaking for God, refers to their cardinal sin, he points elsewhere: "Now this was the sin of your sister Sodom. She and her daughters were arrogant and unconcerned; they did not help the poor and needy" (Ezek. 16:49).

If the poor have the same right to life as the affluent do, the quality of their life cannot be disregarded. It is only logical. Sider addresses this integrated view of the rights of the poor, relating it to health care, this way:

> Like the right to food, this right [to health care] flows from the right to life. Every person created in the image of God has the right to the level of health care that the science, technology and wealth of a given time can make available to its members. That does not mean that everyone has a right to identical health care ... but a right to the level of health care that protects life itself and helps the person flourish physically and emotionally.[268]

With the global refugee population reaching epidemic proportions, whether through the ravages of war like the longstanding slaughter in Syria, natural disasters like the massive earthquake in Nepal, or those fleeing religious persecution in Pakistan, can the world stand idly by?

Micro-Enterprise: The Story of Ram

Here's one way to help. Ram Kumar is a middle-aged *Chamar* Dalit who lives near the Indian city of Lucknow. It is thought that about 18% of India's Dalits are *Chamars*. Among their inherited occupations is the skinning of dead cattle, considered an unclean job. Ram is married with four children and lives in a dilapidated mud hut. His job does not provide him with regular

---

268 *The Scandal of Evangelical Politics*, 136.

income and it resulted in none of his children going to school. The family usually had two meals a day.

In 2014 he heard about the program called LAMP sponsored by the Dalit Freedom Network (DFN), which facilitated forming of self-help groups among Dalits with the view to starting small jobs through vocational training and micro-enterprise development. So Ram joined a self-help group near him. Through his association with the LAMP self-help group, whose members chipped in monthly small amounts to a common pot, matched by seed money from DFN initially, so that, in turns, members could receive loans to start up a small business, Ram was able to purchase a water buffalo.

After rearing the calf for six months, his family began to sell milk in their village. They now have a steady and larger family income. As a result of that kick-start, Ram was able to repair the roof of his hut, feed his family three healthy meals per day including a daily diet of fresh milk, and get his children into school.

Why would God be pleased that someone provided the seed money to enable Ram to better care for his family? Why does God defend and look out for the down and out, the marginalized? On the face of it, we can conclude easily enough that if God is love (1 John 4:8), then that's just the way he might be expected to act and feel. Indeed, helping the poor is a reflection of his character. It makes sense that if one child is balanced on one end of the teeter totter and three on the other, the only way to relieve the imbalance and for the kids to enjoy the teeter totter is to sit on the side where the one child is. The rich don't need help. The poor do. It is a matter of distributive justice. It is about compassion. The self-righteous don't need help. Those who have a sense of their own spiritual deficit do. We should not be surprised at this sort of description of the play-no-favorites

God, repeatedly underscored in Scripture: "The awesome God is not partial and takes no bribe. He executes justice for the fatherless and the widow, and loves the sojourner [the refugee or immigrant, for example], giving him food and clothing" (Deuteronomy 10:17b-18).

Not only is God's character the explanation for his preferential care for the poor but so is the fact, germane to this study, that all human beings are made in his image. The mistreatment or neglect of the outcastes of India, the aboriginals of Canada or the squatter dwellers in Manila offends God's sense of justice. God is not only holy and love at the core of his being, as revealed in scripture, but he is just: "He executes justice for the oppressed and gives food to the hungry" (Ps. 146:7). These aspects of God's character in fact cannot be understood in isolation from each other when trying to interpret God's action and intervention in our world.

Balubhai Naran Sandpa is a father of four children in India, a trained carpenter by profession. As he originally had no financial capability to buy his own carpentry tools, he was forced to hire himself as a carpenter's assistant for meagre wages. Even with his wife working as a charwoman, life was so hard that Balubhai could send only one of his kids to the nearby Good Shepherd School. Even though as a Dalit the school only charged him about 50 rupees per month. However, through the Good Shepherd self-help initiative called LAMP, he received a cheap loan of 15,000 rupees so he could buy his own carpentry tools. This gave Balubhai the capability to take up carpentry jobs on his own. Now, Balubhai's business has grown to the extent the he often hires a couple of workers for the large orders he sometimes gets. His chest now swells with pride at how self-sufficient he has become. His loan has been repaid to the self-help LAMP group in his community so that another Dalit can be jump-started into a small business through a micro-loan.

Balubhai's transformation was not just about *what* amount of money he received in the way of a loan but *how* he was helped. Not only was he able to escape the economic indebtedness of a loan shark but he felt that his success made it possible for other outcaste comrades in his village to be lifted out of endemic poverty. Outsiders walked with him through his poverty and not just relieved his poverty. This is showing the love of Christ in action. A love which respects the need for human dignity for we are all made in God's image.

To empower the poor so that they can function in society with a decent place to live and job so they can put food on the table is to enable them to feel like they are made in the image of God. It is not a communist state that we are after, that is to say, equal results for everybody, but equal opportunities. Dalits in India don't want to be given a handout. They want work that is dignified and meaningful. That is what is so important about educating their children. The poor have a right to work. As we have seen, that inalienable right is linked to the Cultural Mandate of Genesis I alongside of the truth that all humans are made in God's image.

Microenterprise Development Makes Possible Private Property Ownership

Included in the reasonable expectations that the poor should have along with the right to meaningful work is the right to own private property (home ownership as we refer to it in the West). It is so fundamental a value that it is embedded in the Ten Commandments (where stealing is forbidden in the eighth commandment). Whenever I read the OT through I am struck by several things, one of them being how painstakingly God divided up the land of Canaan so that every tribe and family of the Israelites was guaranteed private property (e.g., described in detail in the book of Joshua). Reinforcing this right to private property are two further injunctions in Scripture: (1) every 50 years was the Year of Jubilee when land had to revert to its original owners (Lev. 25:10); and (2) slaves had to be released every seven years and given the opportunity to assume viable independent employment (Deut. 15:1-15). Bonded labour, so prevalent in India and other countries, does not respect the fact that destitute people are made in God's image and should not be so despicably taken advantage of as to force them to live in hovels and be landless. I like what the Oxford Declaration on Christian Faith and Economics proclaims: "It is the responsibility of every society to provide people with the means to live at a level consistent with their standing as people made in the image of God."[269]

Haleni is a graduate of the Dalit Freedom Network's women's vocational training program. She was part of a cohort of 20 Dalit women who took the free six-month tailoring course. For several hours a day, these poor women would leave the homes in the villages surrounding the Good Shepherd School to learn how to cut and sew cloth on a treadle sewing machine. Haleni had dropped out of school in Grade 7 because of being forced into marriage. This left her with little opportunity years later to find decent work. Then her husband had a work-related accident that left his lower limbs paralyzed and rendered him unemployable. Workmen's Compensation for someone like him was unknown. Desperate to find a source of income, Haleni enrolled in the vocational training school.

Now with her loan from the LAMP self-help group, she has her own treadle sewing machine and has started a small tailoring business which is bringing in good income for her family. Haleni is able to lift her head up high in the village. She has rediscovered hope in life. Why should she not for she is made in God's image?

---

269 Cited in David Bussau and Vinay Samuel, *How Then Shall We Lend"*, 15.

Is Health a Human Right?

Just as one might argue that to be made in God's image implies the inalienable right to work, the same case can be made that nation states should guarantee a reasonable expectation of health care. Although the 1948 *United Nations Declaration of Human Rights* states that there should be a universal right to medical care, it has not been taken seriously by many member states. In a concomitant manifesto of 1966 called by the UN the *International Covenant on Economic, Social and Cultural Rights*, one of its provisos appealed to member nations to provide the "highest attainable standard of physical and mental health". While the 1948 declaration has been used by international lawyers as a source of general principles, the 1966 covenant is a treaty and therefore binding on all 164 member states.[270] Courts in countries like Columbia, Brazil and India have given legal assent to the right to medical care. Some countries like the United Kingdom, France and Canada have universal health plans that apply not just the letter but the spirit of this standard—but there is a long way to go before such quality of health care is recognized as a universal right.

Learning About Advocacy from the Christian Response to Slavery

While acknowledging that Christians have a stained legacy when it comes to the advocacy and practice of slavery, it would do us well to be objective in our perspective on how slavery really got abolished in most countries of the world and recognize that the driving force for the abolition of slavery came from a Christian worldview and Christian advocates, as we outlined in chapter 5. Their motivation in advocating for the abolishment of slavery

---

270 Alec Scott, "Is Health a Human Right?" *University of Toronto Magazine*, 25.

was commitment to the biblical teaching that all human beings were made in God's likeness.

Movies like *12 Years a Slave* portray slave owners as hypocritical Christians. Yet it was Christian activists like William Wilberforce in Great Britain and John Woolman in the USA who spearheaded the thrust that ultimately toppled slavery. While such towering figures are acknowledged in history books, what is not so well known is that abolitionists based their passionate disavowal of slavery on their understanding of the Bible's teachings on the nature of humankind. Keller makes this case in *The Reason for God* when he argues as follows: "Christian abolitionists concluded that race-based, life-long chattel slavery, established through kidnapping, could not be squared with Biblical teaching either in the Old Testament or the New."[271]

Countering the politically correct version that Christians were complicit in the forestalling of slavery's elimination is sociologist Rodney Stark, as we explored in the last chapter. Like Keller he maintains in *For the Glory of God* that Christians have long held an uneasy peace with slavery and that in fact it is the Muslim World that has the spottiest record when it comes to prolonging and harbouring slavery. In that book he documents how he arrived at this thesis and summarizes his review of the history of slavery with these words:

> The excesses of political correctness have all but erased awareness that slavery was once nearly universal to all societies able to afford it, and that only in the West did significant moral opposition ever arise and lead to abolition. Unfortunately, the typical discussion of slavery, especially in textbooks, gives the impression that it was a peculiarly European and especially American vice, and no notice is taken of the extent that slavery

---

271 64-65.

in times past, or of the substantial amount of slavery that *continues* in many parts of the non-Christian world.[272]

Understandable it is, then, to find Christians today to be in the vanguard of movements opposing anti-human trafficking and various other forms of virtual slavery. Organizations like International Justice Mission admirably attract Christian and general population support, either because they view their work as rectifying universal human rights violations or as restoring to humankind treatment consistent with being made in God's image. Justice advocacy for people trapped in these social conditions is one practical way to help the poor.

Human Trafficking

Speaking of human trafficking, usually of women or children, this crime against humanity has drawn the attention of such notables as Hillary Clinton. Human trafficking represented an estimated $32 billion of international trade per annum in 2013.[273]

Tara Teng gained notoriety in 2012 when she refused to participate in the swimsuit competition as she represented Canada in the Miss World competition, the only one of 118 contestants to do so. She took this stand as a protest against the sexualization of young females, trafficking and over-sexualization of culture in general. She informed the public that the media and consumer pressure put on girls and women to possess a certain ideal physical shape and wear scanty clothing

---

272 291. His chapter 4, "God's *Justice*: The Sin of Slavery", (pp. 291-365) is a scholarly treatment of this subject.
273 "Trafficking", wikepedia.org.

had triggered an epidemic of bulimia and anorexia, and the proliferation of pornography in Western World countries.[274]

In a relatively modest way, Operation Mercy Trust, Indian partner for Dalit Freedom Network, engages in anti-human trafficking rescuing. It is a far more laborious, risky and ineffective charitable activity than rescuing girls by the prevention of trafficking entailed in getting them into Good Shepherd Schools by kindergarten age. Both the curative and preventive efforts are important. Rescue homes have been set up in Hyderabad, Bangalore and Belgaum by Operation Mercy Trust.

Special Needs Children

Akash is now in high school in a Good Shepherd School in India. When first enrolled, he was unable to keep up with his classmates, academically. It became apparent that he was struggling deeply and so his teachers scheduled a meeting with his parents. In that appointment, they admitted that Akash had manifested cognitive difficulties since birth. When the teachers learned about this condition, they provided more hands-on assistance in his classes. Since then, Akash has matched the level of learning of his classmates. Akash's parents were astounded at his progress and so enrolled their younger son, Vikaraman, in school as well.

You can discern a society's degree of congruency with the biblical perspective on humans being in God's image by their attitude to the disabled, mental or physical. Just as a barometer or our arthritis tells us when bad weather is coming our way, social attitudes and governmental comprehensiveness of

---

274 Every year 1,000-1,500 girls in Canada alone die from bulimia or anorexia, and Canadian youth begin viewing pornography on average at age 12. Tara Teng, "We Are Not Commodities", *Convivium: Faith in our Common Life*, Vol. 4, No.22, 17. Similar statistics are found for other Western world countries.

support systems for those who cannot look after themselves inform us about society's view of humanity. Are we defined by our usefulness to society? Are we simply biological machines? We would be remiss to assume that most societies care for their disadvantaged. As recently as 1929, Hitler proposed that every German with a disability be killed. He pushed for 700,000 of the "weakest" Germans to be "removed" per year.[275] Surely D'Souza and Rogers speak for the biblical worldview when they say, "Those who are sick, weak and physically or mentally challenged are a gift to the human race because they call upon our deepest empathies, compassion, and humanity. As human beings they in turn contribute by giving us back our lost innocence, humility and human bonding."[276]

In Brooklyn, New York, there is a school for developmentally challenged children, called *Cush*. A decade ago at a fund raising event, the father of one of the children told the story of his disabled son, Shaya. He made a telling statement as he opened his story. He contended that "I believe that when heaven brings a child like this into the world, the perfection it seeks is in the way people react to the child." He then told the story of how one day when his son and he were watching a game of softball, Shaya told his dad that he wanted to play. So his dad went over to one of the teams' benches and spoke to the pitcher for that team, asking if his son could play.

At first hesitant, the pitcher shrugged and said, "Why not? We're behind six runs in the eighth inning. We've got nothing to lose. He can play short centre field and will bat in the bottom of the ninth." Shaya was ecstatic.

In the bottom of the ninth, with the bases loaded, Shaya came up to bat. His team needed a home run to win, having clawed

---

275 Eric Metaxas, *Bonhoeffer: Pastor, Martyr, Prophet, Spy*, 354.
276 *On the Side of the Angels*, 45.

back two runs in the bottom of the eighth. Astoundingly, the team let Shaya bat. The pitcher did a remarkable thing. He took several steps closer to home plate and lobbed the ball up nice and easy. Shaya swung and missed badly. One of this teammates then came up behind Shaya and standing behind Shaya wrapped his arms around his. They swung at the next pitch together, hitting the ball softly to the pitcher. Shaya shuffled along toward first base. The pitcher could have easily thrown him out but deliberately threw wide of first. The players yelled for Shaya to take second. Again the opposing team threw wide of the bag. On it went, all the players on bases scoring and Shaya lumbering around all the way home to score. The boys cheered madly and lifted Shaya to their shoulders, parading him as a hero.

"That day those boys reached their level of heaven's perfection", their dad tearfully blurted out.[277]

This story brings to mind the words of Jesus when he passed a boy blind from birth and his disciples asked if the boy's blindness was due to his sin or his parents'. Jesus' unexpected reply was that "this happened so that the work of God might be displayed in his life" (John 9:3). All human beings have great value in God's sight because they are equally made in his image. That's why one way to bring social justice to bear on all levels of society is to help those with special physical or mental needs.

New Immigrants and Opening Our Homes

With the unparalleled surge of refugees pouring into Europe and North America from the Middle East since the start of the civil war in Syria, the global church has had to remind herself of the way the Scriptures talk about attitudes to 'strangers' and the ministry of 'hospitality'. The UNHCR (UN Refugee Agency)

---

277 Mark Buchanan, *Hidden in Plain Sight: The Secret of More*, 183-184.

estimates that at the end of 2014 there were 59.5 million externally and forcibly displaced people in the world. In that year they estimated that 19.5 million were refugees, around two million more than in 2013. Including 2015, it is estimated that over four million Syrians have fled their homeland taking up residence chiefly in Turkey (2.072 million), Lebanon (1.078 million), Jordan (628,000), Iraq (247,000 and Egypt (132,000).[278]

The welcoming of the refugee and stranger has a long history in Scripture, and indeed in the cultures of the Middle East where the Bible is historically rooted. For example, we see Abraham welcoming strangers into his tent and preparing a feast for them (Gen. 18). To this day, Arabs extend lavish hospitality to the unexpected visitor. They have a saying that goes something like this: "If you have room in your heart, you have room in your home". Few people know that Oswald Chambers, the famous devotional writer, was a pastor in Egypt at one time and is reputed to have said, "Make your home a highway for God". He may have learned that ministry through his Egyptian neighbours.

The Israelites were explicitly exhorted in Leviticus 19:34 to be kind to the newcomer found in their community: "The foreigner residing among you must be treated as your native-born. Love them as yourself, for you were born in Egypt." Specific commands to provide hospitality to fellow believers are enjoined in the NT in Romans 15:7-9, 1 Peter 4:9 and Romans 12:13, and to the stranger in Hebrews 13:2. Refugees, immigrants and international students are to be treated with kindness and love because, just like us, they are made in God's image and therefore have inestimable value.

---

278 Statistics taken from the UNHRC website.

In terms of migrants (a larger grouping demographically than the refugees identified above), there are over 230 million in the world today, people who by choice emigrate to or live in other nations. Half of them live in ten countries, led by the United States with 45.8 million, Russia with 11 million, Germany 9.8 million, Saudi Arabia 9.1 million, United Arab Emirates 7.8 million, United Kingdom 7.8 million, France 7.4 million, Canada 7.3 million, Australia 6.5 million and Spain 6.5 million.[279]

Sadly, though, Christian homes in the West have become fortresses. We barely let relatives into our family lair, yet alone other Christians, let along unchurched strangers. One organization reaching out to visiting foreign students, International Students, Inc., estimated not too long ago that few of the 600,000 international students in America at any one time ever get inside an American home.[280] Yet unwittingly, perhaps, when we open our homes to international students we are influencing tomorrow's leaders of many developing countries. For instance, Asian students represent 53% of the students studying abroad, with the most coming, predictably, from China, followed by India and then South Korea.[281]

For several years my wife and I invited Chinese-Canadians into our home for meals while we were pastoring the English congregation of a multi-lingual inner city Chinese church in Toronto. We were fascinated to see how many of them went around our condo apartment looking with curiosity at how our home was decorated. Daring to ask one of them once why they did that she blurted out that she had never been in the home of a Caucasian Canadian before, nor had many of her friends in church. Astoundingly, some of these people had been

---

279 http://www.esa.un.org/unmigration/wallchart2013.htm
280 David Lundy, *Borderless Church*, 23.
281 http://www.oeed.org/edu/education-at-a-glance, pdf. 344.

in Canada for decades. Opening up our homes to welcome the refugee or the new immigrant living down the street is a wonderful object lesson to our children about being generous and not self-absorbed; about the need to be attentive and not closed-hearted; about being public-minded (e.g. by sponsoring a refugee) and not only passive tax payers.

While the OT motive for helping the stranger was the Israelites' undeserved redemption (they were once slaves in Egypt), which was to remind them likewise to embrace the normally-undesired alien or stateless, the underlying principle could have just as easily been the fact that humankind is made in God's image. All human beings made in God's image is a timeless truth: in the OT age and for the duration of earthly history. People neglected and despised within cultures, shivering with cold bodies and aching hearts because they intuitively know that there is no good reason why they should not be treated with dignity by their host society. Such neglect, benign or otherwise, is unconscionable.

Canadian society reacted instantly when the picture flashed across media screens in the autumn of 2015 of a dead boy in the arms of his sobbing father on the beaches of Turkey, lost in the Mediterranean when his family's boat, overcrowded with refugees from Syria, capsized and washed up on the shore. Pressuring their government to welcome thousands more than a proposed 5,000 refugees, within days, the newly formed Canadian federal government promised to bring in 25,000 refugees by the end of the year, a seemingly logistical impossibility unless the refugees were not reasonably vetted for security reasons.[282]

---

282 The first 25,000 Syrian refugees ended up being settled in Canada by the end of February 2016.

The Syrian-Canadian aunt of the dead boy, who in the days following the wave of sympathy surrounding the picture which affected viewers so viscerally, spoke of the feelings associated with being a stateless refugee. She declared: "Being a refugee means you feel dead, that you are not a person". Only someone made in God's image would feel this way. That is why a Christian response to the refugee in today's chaotic global politics is a timely way to demonstrate the love of God to those who are not like us, who nevertheless are no less deserving of God's mercy and grace.

We see other tragic examples of human beings being demeaned because their political circumstances have made them stateless or unwelcome. Bangladeshis trapped between India and Bangladesh since partition because neither state wants them. Palestinians without their own homeland. Kurds similarly without their own state and mistreated by Turkey and others. What an opportunity for the church of Jesus Christ to mirror our Savior's love by unconditionally accepting and ministering to them.

Providing Education for the Have-Nots of the World

My heart goes out to the Dalits of India, as you know by now. They represent the "oppressed" that Jesus reached out to while on this earth. You've read a few of the stories in this book of Dalit children who are being given hope and a bright future because of the transformative power of education.

The emergence of the Good Shepherd Schools is an unfolding story of the power of education. As we described those early days of dialogue with Dalit leaders in chapter 2, we learned that it was they, and not the Indian Christian community, that initiated the compelling idea that English-medium schools be started for their children. Not only did the idea of the schools come from the grass roots, but where the schools were constructed was a function of the invitation of the rural Dalits themselves, with priority given to those who provided land for the schools. At the time of writing, there is a long queue of Dalit communities around India which have taken the initiative to invite Operation Mercy Trust India to start a Good Shepherd School in their area. The Dalit leaders are involved in the decision-making and so the reputation of the schools is outstanding around the country because those benefiting from the schools have a sense of ownership about the schools.

That swelling pride is also due, as mentioned above, to the education not being provided free of charge. Each Dalit family has to contribute about the equivalent of $1.00 per month for each child they have in the school and pay for their child's uniform ($33.00 is raised elsewhere). That amount, which would seem trivial to most readers, is as much as a day's wage for a Dalit and so given at some sacrifice. Increasingly, non-Dalit children are being allowed to join the schools and they pay a partial or full tuition fee—based on their ability to pay.[283] The broadening of the social base for students also models the goal that there be no discrimination in the schools on the basis of religion, race, caste or gender. Nevertheless, the bulk of the seats in each school is reserved for the Dalitbahujans as a kind of affirmative action. Richard Stearns, President and CEO of World Vision in the USA captures the importance of providing dignity for the poor in these words: "The poor are not lab rats on whom we can experiment with our pet theories; they are human beings with rich cultural and personal stories of their own."[284] Again, love that is Christ-like must treat the recipients of that love with respect and be practical: "If anyone has material possessions

283 The higher caste students (kept to a small quota) enable the schools to be more sustainable in the long run and not so dependent on foreign money.
284 *The Hole in Our Gospel*, 130.

and sees a brother or sister in need but has no pity on them, how can the love of God be in that person? Dear children, let us not love with words or speech but with actions or in truth" (1 John 4:17, 18).

One practical way that you can apply something you have learned in this book is to sponsor a Dalit child in one of the Good Shepherd Schools sponsored by the Dalit Freedom Network or a similar global organization. Sponsoring one child addresses the question as to what one person can do in a vast sea of underprivileged and poverty-stricken masses globally. Never mind that to help children instead of adults nips the cycle of poverty in the bud by preventative care rather than curative care. Sponsoring a girl protects one minor from human trafficking, less complicated than rescuing a trafficked girl. That is preventative rather than curative child care.

What is the Statistical Impact of Child Sponsorship?

But one overshadowing question is "What is the actual impact of child sponsorship?" Until recently, even though nine million children for various programs valued at $5 billion are sponsored worldwide, nobody had ever empirically investigated this question. Two graduate students in economics worked with a development economist in 2010 to survey over 10,000 students in six countries through USAID funding that took into consideration a number of variables: primary, secondary, and tertiary education; type and quality of adult employment; community leadership; assets owned as an adult.[285] The findings were astounding. Here are a few of them.

> ➤ Sponsorship makes children 27-40% more likely to complete secondary school

---

285 Bruce Wydick, "Want to Change the World?" *Christianity Today*, 20-25. The study is also found in the June 2013 issue of the *Journal of Political Economy*.

- Sponsored children are 50-80% more likely to complete a university degree
- Children sponsored are 14-18% more likely to obtain a salaried job
- Adult children who went through a sponsored education are 35% more likely to obtain a white-collar job

$33.00 per month. That's all it takes to educate a Dalit child with Dalit Freedom Network. The reality is that the average North American earns far more than the Dalits of India, even those who have against all odds risen to the level of the Indian middle class. If you earn $25,000 per year, you are wealthier than about 90% of the globe's population; if making $55,000 per year wealthier than almost 99% of the world's population.[286] I think it is a rare person in the North American cocoon of affluence who cannot afford this sort of commitment—about half of what the average North American spends in coffee shops like Starbucks monthly. There is an African proverb that goes something like this: "If you think you are too small to make a difference, try spending the night in a closed room with a mosquito."

Kamlesh is a 16 year-old Dalit girl who recently graduated from one of the Good Shepherd Schools in India. Piling up an insurmountable debt, her family had been lured into bonded labour by a wealthy, upper caste factory owner, making promise of a loan too good to be true when told that short term work would pay off the family debt if they but worked for him for a few months. Secretly he increased the interest rate on their loan to such an astronomical amount that they faced the likely prospect of never being able to pay it back. Reluctantly her parents allowed Kamlesh to go to the new English-medium

---

286 Based on calculations in 2008 by the World Bank Development Research Group as cited in Richard Stearns, *The Hole in Our Gospel*, 215.

school near their home, knowing that by doing so they would lose some small income from her working.

One day the factory owner closed his business without warning. Kamlesh's parents were without jobs. Kamlesh's mother began to pick up part-time work as a maid in the evenings, while her father got odd jobs as an electrician. Destitute, the family lives in a one-room hut made of mud, sticks and plastic sheets with an open drain outside their door because there are no toilets or sewage system in their slum. Despite these deplorable conditions, they are filled with hope because Kamlesh is doing so well in school. Due to her extreme poverty, Kamlesh had become one of the Good Shepherd Schools' first sponsored children.

Now after completing Junior College, Kamlesh's hope is to become a nurse through further studies and in biology, physics or chemistry. Kamlesh is a living example of the difference $33 per month can make.[287]

Infanticide

From the early days of church history, Christians opposed infanticide because they believed all human beings were made in God's image. They were countercultural in this regard. The Roman Empire did not think twice about abandoning infants; the church in turn rescued them. Murdering one's 0-1 year old child is as ancient a practice as recorded human history and thought to have occurred in every ethnicity known to man.[288] The reasons have remained fairly predictable: extreme familial

---

287 Selecting a child to sponsor can be done online at www.dalitnetwork.org (for USA), www.dalitfreedom.ca (for Canada), or www.dfn.org.uk/ (for United Kingdom). Other Dalit Freedom Network offices are found in Brazil, Sweden, Australia and Germany.

288 We are distinguishing here between abortion and infanticide. Abortion occurs during gestation, infanticide after delivery. Feticide, as one type of infanticide, is considered in chapter 2.

poverty, gender prejudice, postpartum depression, dowry, unintended pregnancy, incest, and rape. Although forbidden by major world religions and legally banned in countries fairly universally, infanticide is still believed to be prevalent in some parts of the world today. It is estimated that 30.5 million female babies are "missing" in China, 22.8 million in India, 3.1 million in Pakistan, 1.6 million in Bangladesh, 600,000 in Egypt and 200,000 in Nepal.[289] The USA has the 11th highest ranking of countries that kill their infants so this is not just a current problem in Asia.[290] At the end of the day, there is an entirely different outlook on the birth of an infant when the worldview of the family embraces the principle that their child is made in God's image.[291]

As mentioned above, not only gender plays a role in infanticide. Birth deformities also sway parents. The line between benign neglect of newborns who are born to die, like one who is an anencephalic infant (born without a brain) and inducing death for babies with Down's Syndrome is qualitatively different. Without going deeply into the issue of euthanasia, we should at least agree that we should not play God. As ethicist Paul Ramsey articulated the issue: "If physicians are going to play God under the pretense of providing relief for the human condition, let us hope they play God as God plays God. Our God is no respecter of persons of good quality... . A true humanism also leads to an "equality of [right to] life" standard."[292]

---

289 Larry Milner, "A Brief History of Infanticide. http://www.infanticide.org/hisory. htm.
290 Ibid.
291 About abortion, without entangling ourselves deeply in this complex moral issue, as it relates to our topic, it should be self-evident that if a fetus is a human being not already born, then it would be morally wrong because all persons are made in God's image. The Bible does use words for the fetus that are used for persons who are already born (Luke 1:41; Ps. 139:13-16; Gen. 25:22; 38:27-30).
292 *Ethics at the Edge of Life* (New Haven: Yale University Press, 1978), 203.

Advocating: Speaking Up for the Powerless

Sometimes I find myself questioning why I should speak up for someone whom I do not know who lives thousands of miles away. What difference does my little voice make? It reminds me of the same sort of sentiment expressed in the movie, *Woman in Gold*, the story of an American Jewess who fled Vienna in World War II whose parents died in a Nazi concentration camp. Sixty years after the seizing of her family's property, including a famous portrait of her Aunt Adele painted by Gustave Klimt, now hanging in the Vienna State Art Gallery, and called 'The Woman in Gold', Maria Altman (played by Helen Mirren) seeks to reclaim the stolen and priceless art. It is a long, uphill battle, pitting her and her inexperienced lawyer against a nation-state which considered this painting a national treasure. At several points in the film, Maria Altman wavers. "Is this arduous, expensive legal battle against all odds worth it?" she ponders. Only the thought of gaining justice and the memory of the powerlessness of her family vis-à-vis the Nazi regime give her the incentive to persevere in the fight and eventually succeed in reclaiming the family art collection, especially the famous painting for which the movie is named. Giving a voice to those who are fighting for justice against all odds is almost always about taking the long-term view, visualizing what success might look like and how the liberated would feel if vindicated.

It may be something as simple as petitioning your Congresswoman or your Member of Parliament for trade with a particular country to be stopped until forcible conversion is ended there and freedom of religion is restored. It may take you a little out of your comfort zone to march in front of the embassy with expatriates from that country who protest the imprisonment of a protester engaged in peaceful civil disobedience. Indian Christian leaders standing shoulder to shoulder with Dalits in

2001 in New Delhi who wanted to become Buddhists increased the trust these Dalits had for Christians: today 3,800 churches among Dalits is one of the unintended consequences of that justice advocacy. Truly "speaking out for the rights of others is perhaps the most powerful form of witness for the gospel. It is also a matter of self-interest, for persecuted Christians are more likely to gain help from people of different faiths if they themselves have stood in the gap for others."[293]

A strong argument can be made that it was the failure of the Lutheran state church in Germany prior to and during the Second World War to confront the evil of Hitler and Nazism that allowed the war to happen in the first place. Dietrich Bonhoeffer's biography reveals how, at every turn, between 1934 and 1939 when Poland was invaded, the church looked the other way when faced with the anti-Semitism, untruthful duplicity and violent thuggery of Hitler's regime, much to Bonhoeffer's agony and that of others who formed a kind of church in exile. Bonhoeffer's civil disobedience led him to become part of the plot to assassinate Hitler that led to his imprisonment and untimely execution by firing squad toward the end of the war. When evil and error are not confronted, the fabric of society and peace are eroded. The prophet in Isaiah 1:17 pleads: "Learn to do good; seek justice, correct oppression; bring justice to the fatherless, plead the widow's cause."[294]

The church is not called to look away. One German dissenter to Hitler's regime who spent eight years in a concentration camp, Niemoller, had this indictment for the German church:

---

293 Joseph D'Souza and Benedict Rogers, *On the Side of the Angels*, 85-86.
294 Eric Metaxas, *Bonhoeffer: Pastor, Martyr, Prophet, Spy* (Nashville: Thomas Nelson, 2010).

"First they came for the Socialists and I did not
      speak out—
Because I was not a socialist.
Then they came for the Trade Unionists
      and I did not speak out—
Because I was not a Trade Unionist.
Then they came for the Jews and I did not speak out—
Because I was not a Jew.
And then they came for me—
And there was no one left to speak for me.[295]

Are Christians Hypocritical in Protesting Oppression of the Dalits?

The argument is sometime made that Christians, of the American South in particular, were complicit in the endorsing and prolonging of slavery. Also that Christian Europe since the Middle Ages had been embracers of slavery. However, the reality is that Christians were in the vanguard for the abolition of slavery, yet alone many other social revolutions for good in the past two millennia, as we have noted earlier. They did so, although far from without exception, because they emulated the loving, self-sacrificing and humble spirit of Jesus.

What academia's Rodney Stark makes clear in his sociological and historical study on slavery, as we have seen, is that there is misinformation and myth on the subject, and that:

1. Evangelical abolitionists like Wilberforce overcame societal and parliamentary resistance to trigger the outlawing of slavery (which most of us know about);
2. Slavery existed on only the fringes of Europe after the decline of the Roman Empire due to a theological

---

295 Ibid, 192.

realization that the Bible really did not affirm lifelong servitude;

3. The New World rise of the slave trade was undertaken in spite of papal opposition;

4. The modern American civil rights movement had its moral justification based by its leaders like Martin Luther King on the Bible, and not so much on secular liberal humanitarian views;

5. The abolishment of apartheid in South Africa in the 1990s did not end in a bloodbath because of the Christian-driven South African Commission for Truth and Reconciliation (many people know about this fact, too).[296]

Sweeping generalizations about Christianity's association with slavery are undeserved. In fact, the Bible forbids kidnaping (Deut. 24:7; 1 Tim. 1:10). The OT form of indentured servitude and bond slavery was quite different than the racist, lifelong slavery practiced in the age of the European empires.[297] While in the NT Paul addressed the issue of slavery in his counselling of Philemon, an escaped slave who came to faith in Christ, whom he implored to return to his master voluntarily, and asked believing slaves to obey their masters (Eph. 6:5-6), the profundity of him treating Philemon as a "brother" and of the emancipating impact of the Gospel (Gal. 3:28; cf. Eph. 6:9) spelled the death knoll for slavery being condoned or even considered as biblically acceptable.

One of the most telling biblical passages that reveals God's attitude about slavery is found in Jeremiah 34. King Zedekiah made a covenant with all the people in Jerusalem to proclaim freedom for the slaves. But before too long the slave owners

---

296 *For the Glory of God: How Monotheism Led to Reformations, Science, Witch-Hunts, and the End of Slavery*, 329-358.
297 Tim Keller, *The Reason for God*, 65, 271.

changed their minds and took back the freed slaves. The word of the Lord relayed by the prophet to the Israelites at that turn of events was severe in nature: "You have not obeyed me; you have not proclaimed freedom to your own people. So I now proclaim 'freedom' for you ... 'freedom' to fall by the sword, plague and famine. I will make you abhorrent to all the kingdoms of the earth" (v. 17 ff.). It is hard to read the Bible and justify slavery. It is not surprising, then, that no less a celebrated author than H. G. Wells insisted: "Christianity has been denounced by modern writers as a 'slave religion'. It was. It took the slaves and downtrodden, and it gave them hope and restored their self-respect so that they stood up for righteousness like men and faced persecution and torment."[298]

Let the Children Lead Them

A phenomenon is happening. Children are socially conscious and engaged as never before in global justice issues, Joan of Arc aside. In the Dalit Freedom Network it is inspiring for those on staff to discover children in the US and Canada who are sponsoring Dalit children in the Good Shepherd Schools. Craig Kielburger, who in 1995 was in grade 7 while researching for a social studies project, discovered the struggle of a Pakistani boy taking a stand against child labour in his country. Craig was aghast to learn that a boy his own age was caught in this wretched practice. As a result, Craig started a youth advocacy movement called "Free the Children". Today this youth network, which continues to work in primary and secondary schools to raise awareness and involvement, has a network of over 100,000 students in about 40 countries that have started 350 schools that have provided education in the developing world for over 20,000 children.[299] Young people want more of a hands

---

298 Cited in Philip Yancey, *Vanishing Grace*, 53.
299 Dave Toycen, *The Power of Generosity*, 23-24.

on approach to helping the needy. It could be the proverbial car wash or garage sale that they get excited about as a platform for raising money. Or it might be the increasingly popular crowdfunding approach using social media.

Kaile is a ten year old girl who was taken by her mother to India to see first-hand how the other half lives. To help them she got involved in doing something practical for Dalit children. Her mother, a former member of Arizona State College Basketball Team, was inspired to raise money for a basketball court at one of the Good Shepherd schools. The two of them signed up for the Mississauga Marathon Run in 2015. Cassandra and Kaile ran together, Kaile for 10 kilometers and Cassandra completed the 42 kilometer entire run. Hands on involvement by children. That's what you call putting feet to your words!

Children will lead them in other ways too. If we give the underprivileged poor children of the world a chance, who knows what will happen to them. Richard Stearns, president of World Vision USA, shares the story of meeting a Korean gentleman in New York who told him how important organizations like World Vision were. He told Richard about growing up in South Korea after the Korean War, destitute. He and his family, he intimated, were helped incredibly by shipments of clothing, food and school supplies from caring Americans. With this edge, he was able to finish school. Today that poor Korean is the Secretary-General of the United Nations, Ban Ki-moon.

Do You Want the Politically Correct Version of Truth or the Truth?

Not very politically correct it may be but the unvarnished truth about the influence of Christianity in history is that where Protestant presence and mission have been virile in the developing world in the past two centuries of the modern

– 229 –

missionary movement, on average such societies are more developed economically and democratically today than other developing countries. Much of this success at modernization was rooted in the biblical worldview that all human beings were equally made in God's image. Thus Eliza Bridgman opened up a girls' school in Beijing in 1864, an unthinkable development at the time. This school later transitioned to being Yenching University and now is China's most prestigious university, Peking University. True, too often missionaries not only brought the gospel but the view that Western civilization was, like cleanliness, they supposed, next to godliness. There is always the danger that we read our present culture's insights gained from social sciences and natural science into our interpretation of earlier history. While training in contextualization and anthropological sensitivities may today be part of the missionary's "Bible", it was not even known about in the time of William Carey, and it would be unfair for us to assume that what would be inappropriate for us to communicate cross culturally is what they too should have considered taboo. At the heart of their motivation was a love for people and a respect for their potential as beings made in God's image. It drove them to abolish suttee, eliminate slavery, reduce indigenous languages to writing, medically treat untouchable lepers, and educate the poor.

In fact, Robert Woodberry, a sociology scholar, created a statistical model that could test between missionary work and the health of nations.[300] His difficult-to-prove dissertation nevertheless led him to this claim: "Areas where Protestant missionaries had a significant presence in the past are on average more economically developed today with comparatively better health, lower infant mortality rates, lower corruption,

---

300 The findings from his 14 years of research were published in the 2012 journal, *American Political Science Review*, which resulted in him receiving major awards including the prestigious Luebbert Article Award for the best article in comparative politics.

greater literacy, higher educational attainment (especially for women), and more robust membership in nongovernmental associations."[301] There are so many anecdotal examples of how mass literacy and education, introduced by missionaries, led to progressive reforms in many societies in the 1800s and early 1900s, from Japan to Botswana to India.

We are globally becoming more engaged with current and longstanding humanitarian issues. The question is: will the church lead the way as it should because she knows that all human beings are made in the image of God? Will you?

---

301 Andrea Palpant Dilley, "The World the Missionaries Made", *Christianity Today*, 39.

Conclusion

Sarasu spent her early childhood making firecrackers in a fireworks factory near the southern tip of India. Her family was Dalit and so they needed her money-earning help. The sort of work she was asked to do required the dexterity and tiny fingers of a child and so girls like her were in demand. It was dehumanizing work because of the danger involved and long hours, 10-12 hours per day six days a week.

One day a community development officer of a Good Shepherd School from the nearby town of Sivakasi happened by and seeing her working there took the initiative to contact her family and arrange for her to attend the Good Shepherd School in Sivakasi. Right from the beginning Sarasu proved to be an outstanding pupil. She consistently ranked first in her class in grades and so her family let her attend the secondary school there as well. A couple of years ago Sarasu graduated and by then had determined to be a teacher like the ones who inspired her in her school.

By now Sarasu not only concluded that she was equal in value to any other human being but had accepted that Christ was the Son of the God who has created her in his image and so she entered her bachelor's degree and finally teachers' college with self-confidence and hope. Again, Sarasu graduated at the top of her class. From being a child laborer she had been transformed into a bonafide school teacher.

Blessed by her education and introduction to a Christian worldview, Sarasu decided to "give back" and so returned to the Sivakasi Good Shepherd School, where today she teaches and models the transformation from the outside-in that education brings and the transformation from the inside-out that Christ brings. She had discovered what it means to be human.

What motivates people in India and globally to reach out to under-privileged Dalits? The president of the Dalit Freedom Network and bishop in the Good Shepherd Community Churches, Joseph D'Souza, eloquently captures that compulsion:

> Our love for the Dalit people is like the love of Christ for them—unconditional. It is not dependent on them coming to faith in Christ. We love people whether or not they choose to follow Jesus. The Hindutva lie is that Christian love always has an ulterior motive—conversion. We love the Dalit-Bahujan people unconditionally. True Christian love is always the agape kind of love—free, unconditional and free. We are therefore able to hold an unwavering faith in the life and teachings of Christ and love all people unconditionally—even our enemies.[302]

That all human beings are made in God's image was expressed simply but profoundly by a freed slave, Frederick Douglass, to his former owner following the American civil war. It is one which captures the heart-cry of millions of people circling the globe, in every culture and people group: "You are a man and so am I. God created both, and made us separate beings. I am not by nature bound to you, or you to me."[303] We are all unshackled by virtue of being made in God's image.

The intellectual and spiritual gap between Christianity and other religions, including that of atheism, is nowhere more profoundly apparent than in our respective views of what it means to be human. Comprehending that we are all as human beings

---

302 *Dalit Freedom: Now and Forever*, 52.
303 Cited in Mouw and Sweeney, *The Suffering and Victorious Christ,* 90.

equally made in the image of God has far-reaching implications for how life should be lived on this earth, as we have seen. It is the only philosophy or ideology or faith that allows humans to live without inherent contradictions and confusion with respect to their self-awareness and behaviour. Acclaimed Christian apologist Ravi Zacharias put it this way: "Religions that attempt to keep the body sacred while denying the Creator's hand are in the same boat as skeptics who try to protect life while saying it is nothing more than matter."[304] I hope that by now you are convinced, if not a follower of Jesus, that to hold human life as sacred makes as much sense as thinking that by running in the opposite direction in a train corridor corrects the dilemma of having boarded a train headed in the wrong direction.

Not only should all human beings be treated with dignity because they are made in the image of God but those who have been re-created (born again) in Christ have the expectation in this life that they can fully align themselves with the purpose of God for them, even more so in the life to come. As Kilner expresses this closing of the gap,

> Christians, in Christ, will ultimately become free of sin and able to be all that God intends for humanity. Nevertheless, they will remain human. So even when they become Christ's image after Christ returns, they will not become all that Christ is as God's image, for Christ is both divine and human. Rather, in Christ people gain the opportunity to realize their specific human destiny—to become fully human.[305]

Maybe you are like me. The stories of lives transformed by a perspectival change as they began to view themselves as being made in God's image, or even more so by discovering the death and resurrection of Christ to radically transform them, are inspiring and motivational. But it is easy to slip into becoming

---

304 Ravi Zacharias, *Jesus among Other Gods*, 69.
305 *Dignity and Destiny*, 235.

weary in helping people (Gal. 6:9). We can get overwhelmed by the need of broken people down the street and around the world. We get donor fatigue.

There is an interesting word in Peter's exhortation to add to our faith "perseverance" (2 Peter 1:5-6). It is *hypomene* and literally means "stand your ground", a military term used to describe a solider not retreating but holding to his position or ground. It calls to mind an unremarkable spy in the movie, *Bridge of Spies*, starring Tom Hanks. He, playing a civilian during the Cold War, was called upon to work on the exchange of an American held in East Germany for a Russian who was stoic in the face of possible life in prison in America. When Hanks, the civilian and also a lawyer, visited the Russian in the jail and came to see how patriotic he was to his homeland, he was curious to know what made him tick. The Russian paused and blurted out, "Well, they just used to call me the standing man. When I was tortured, taking punch after punch, I would not give in and crumble to the ground."

Hanks, playing the lawyer, drew strength from that image and from the spy working for the other side as he gradually formed a bond with him. That became his motivation to bravely move ahead with tricky three-way negotiations between the USA, the USSR and East Germany. Hanks became a kind of "last man standing" in order to gain freedom for both the Russian spy and the American. A "standing man". That's what we are to be as followers of Jesus in working for justice and righteousness. Persevering in the face of difficulties and dissent from power brokers. Making sure that all human beings are treated with the respect and fairness that they are owed by virtue of being divine image bearers.

Works Cited

Adeney, Miriam. *Kingdom without Borders: The Untold Story of Global Christianity*. Downers Grove, IL: IVP Books, 2009.

Ali, Ayaan Hirsi. "The Global War on Christians in the Muslim World". *The Daily Beast*. (February 6, 2012):1-11.

_____. *Heretic: Why Islam Needs a Reformation*. Toronto: Alfred A. Knopf, 2015.

Ambedkar, B. M. *Annihilation of Caste: The Annotated Critical Edition*. New Delhi: Navayana, 2014.

Bannister, Alan and Tanya Walker. *Islam in Context*. Toronto: Ravi Zacharias International Ministries, 2013.

Barnabas Fund. "Hindu Activists Storm Two Christian Schools in India, Demanding Closure". May 14, 2015. https://barnabassaid.org/news/Hindu-activists-storm-two-Christian-schools-in-India-demanding-closure.

Bartels, K. H. ""One, Once, Only" in Brown, Colin (Ed.). *Dictionary of New Testament Theology*. Vol. 2. Grand Rapids: Baker, 1976: 716-25.

Baugh, Sumit, "In the Conversion Noise, the Silence". March 9, 2015. http://indianexpress.com/article/opinion/columns/in-the-conversion-noise-the-silence/99.

Bignon, Guillaume. "My Own French Revolution". *Christianity Today* (November 2014): 95-96.

Boonstra, Kevin and Peter Stockland. "Point and Counterpoint: Why Christians Should Promote Religious Freedom". http://www.cardus.ca/comment/article/2761/point-and-counterpoint- why-should-Christians-promote-religious-freedom.

Bruce, F. F. *The New Testament Documents*. London: InterVarsity Press, 1970.

Buchanan, Mark. *Hidden In Plain Sight: The Secret of More*. Nashville: Thomas Nelson, 2007.

Bussau, David and Vinay Samuel. *How Then Should We Lend? A Biblical Validation of Microenterprise*. London, UK: Christian Transformation Resource Center, 2001.

Calvin, John. *Institutes of the Christian Religion*. (Trans. John McNeill). Philadelphia, Westminister Press, 1960.

Carson, Donald A. *The Gagging of God: Christianity Confronts Pluralism*. Grand Rapids: Zondervan, 1996.

_____. *A Model of Christian Maturity: Exposition of 2 Corinthians 10-13*. Grand Rapids: Baker Books, 1984.

Clendenin, Daniel. *Many Gods, Many Lords: Christianity Encounters World Religions*. Grand Rapids: Baker, 1995.

Cooper, Barry. "Imprisoned By Choice". *Christianity Today* (January/February 2013): 52-55.

Cork, Matthew and Kenneth Kemp. *Why Not Today*. Chicago: Moody Publishers, 2013.

Cowan, Les. "What Is Truth? Religion, Relationships and Reality in Postmodern Spain". *Evangelical Missions Quarterly* (October 2014): 448-455.

Deshpande, G. P. (Ed.) *Selected Writings of Jotirao Phule*. Delhi: LeftWord Books, 2010.

Dilley, Andrea Palpant, "The World the Missionaries Made". *Christianity Today* (January/February 2014): 34-41.

Doniger, Wendy. *The Hindus: An Alternative History*. New York: The Penguin Press, 2009.

Doniger, Wendy and Brian Smith (Trans). *The Laws of Manu*. London: Penguin Books, 1991.

D'Souza, Joseph. *Dalit Freedom: Now and Forever*. Secunderabad: OM Books, 2004.

D'Souza, Joseph and Benedict Rodgers. *On the Side of Angels: Justice, Human Right and Kingdom Mission*. Colorado Springs: Authentic, 2007.

Elshof, Gregg. *I Told Me So*. Grand Rapids: W. B. Eerdmans, 2009.

Erickson, Millard. *Christian Theology*. Grand Rapids: Baker Book House, 1986.

Faber, Frederick. "The Creature and the Creator" in Richard Foster and Emilie Griffin (Eds.), *Spiritual Classics: Selected Readings on the Twelve Spiritual Disciplines*. New Rock: HarperOne, 2000.

Farrow, Douglas. "What is Truth?" *Convivium* (Vol. 4, No. 21): 12-14.

Fernando, Ajith. *The Christian's Attitude toward World Religions*. Wheaton: Tyndale House, 1997.

Forani, Jonathan. "Where Have All the Girls Gone?" *Toronto Star*. (April 12, 2016): A1, A11.

Forward Press. "Dalit Population Growing Faster but Falling Behind Rest of India". (June 2013): 32-33.

Foster, Richard. *Celebration of Discipline: The Path to Spiritual Growth*. London: Hodder & Stoughton, 1984.

Friedman, Thomas. "The Problem Is Islamism". *The New York Times*. (January 23, 2015): 2-4.

_____. *Hot, Flat and Crowded*. Vancouver: Douglas & McIntyre, 2009.

Garrison, David. *A Wind in the House of Islam*. Monument, CO: WIGTake Resources, 2014.

Gess, J. Image" in Brown, Colin (Ed.). *Dictionary of New Testament of Theology*. Vol. 2, Grand Rapids: Regency Reference Library, 1976: 288-289.

"Good Shepherd Health Initiative". April, 2015: 4.

Gopal, Nagara. "Dalit Nation". http://frontline.in/social-justice/dalit-nation/article7447625.ece

Gruenler, R. G., "Son of Man" in Elwell, Walter (Ed.). *Evangelical Dictionary of Theology*. Grand

Rapids: Baker Book House, 1994: 1034-1036

Guinness, Os. *The Call: Finding and Fulfilling the Central Purpose of Our Life*. Nashville, TN: W Publishing Group, 2003.

_____. "Turning the Tables". *InContext* (Vol. 4, 2015): 19-25.

Haanen, Jeff. "Interview" *Christianity Today* (January, 2015): 6065.

Harrison, E.F. "Only Begotten" in Elwell, Walter (Ed.). *Evangelical Dictionary of Theology*. Grand Rapids: Baker, 1994: 799.

Henry, Carl F., "Image of God" in Elwell, Walter (Ed.). *Evangelical Dictionary of Theology*. Grand Rapids: Baker Book House, 1994: 545-48.

http://www.indianexpress.com/article/india/india-others/ dont-want-a-religion-that-only-rejects-us/Jan.26, 2015 .

http://www.prospectmagazine.co.uk/features//Indias-shame

http://www.templehayes.com/the-message-of-the-water-beetle/.

Hughes, Philip. *The True Image: The Origin and Destiny of Man in Christ*. Grand Rapids: W. B. Eerdmans, 1989.

Huntington, Samuel. *The Clash of Civilization and the Remaking of the World Order*. London: Simon & Schuster, 1996.

Ilaiah, Kancha. *I Am Not a Hindu*. Kolkata: Arunima Printing Works, 2012.

International Dalit Solidarity Network. "India: Official Dalit Population Exceeds 200 Million". http://idsn.org/india-official-dalit-population-exceeds-200-million/3/31/2015

Kasturi, Charu Sudan, "Learning Curve". *Hindustan Times* (April 21, 2013): 12-13.

Kaushika, Pragya. "Don't Want a Religion that Only Rejects Us, Say the Aligarh Dalits on RSS List". (January 26, 2015). http://indianexpress.com/article/india/india-others/dont-want-a-religion-that-only-rejects-us

Keller, Timothy. *Generous Justice: How God's Grace Makes Us Just*. New York: Riverhead Books, 2010.

_____. *The Reason for God: Belief in an Age of Skepticism*. New York: Riverhead Books, 2008.

Kilner, John. *Dignity and Destiny: Humanity in the Image of God*. W. B. Eerdmans: Grand Rapids, 2015.

Klein, Naomi. *This Changes Everything*. Toronto: Vintage Canada, 2015.

Kuhn, Mike. *Fresh Vision for the Muslim World*. Colorado Springs: Authentic Publishing, 2009.

Kumar, Abhay, "Untouchability Dies Hard', *Forward Press*. April 2015: 34.

Larson, Warren, "How Islam Sees Itself", in Laurie Nichols and Gary Corwin (Eds.). *Envisioning Effective Ministry: Evangelism in a Muslim* Context. Wheaton: Billy Graham Center, 2010.

Lewis, Bernard. *The Crisis of Islam: Holy War and Unholy Terror*. London: Weidenfeld & Nicolson, 2003.

Lewis, C. S. *Beyond Personality*. London: Geoffrey Bles, 1952.

Lewis, Gordon, "Attributes of God" in Elwell, Walter (Ed.). *Evangelical Dictionary of Theology*. Grand Rapids: Baker Book House, 1984.

Lundy, David. *Borderless Church: Shaping the Church for the 21st Century*. Milton Keynes: Authentic Media, 2005.

_____. *Servant Leadership for Slow Learners*. Carlisle: Authentic Lifestyle, 2002.

Mangalwadi, Vishal. *The Quest for Freedom and Dignity: Caste, Conversion and Cultural Revolution*. Willernie: South Asian Resources, 2001.

_____. *Why Are We So Backward?* New Delhi: Forward Press, 2013.

Mazurkewich, H. "Women's Rights, Women's Plights". *Homemakers* (October 2001):57-68.

_____. "Veiled Threats?" *Homemakers* (October 2001): 45-53.

McGrath, Alistair. *Christian Theology: An Introduction*. Cambridge, MA: Blackwell Publishers, 1994.

Metaxas, Eric. *Amazing Grace: William Wilberforce and the Heroic Campaign to End Slavery*. New York: Harper One, 2007.

_____. *Bonhoeffer: Pastor, Martyr, Prophet, Spy*. Nashville: Thomas Nelson, 2010.

Larry Milner. "A Brief History of Infanticide." http://www.infanticide.org/history.htm.

Mondal, Sudipto. "Rohith Vemula: An Unfinished Portrait". http://www.hindustantimes.com/static/rohith-vemula-an-unfinished-portrait/index.html

Moore, John. "John Moore: The New Atheist Just doesn't Care". http://nationalpost.com/2015/03/26/john-moore-the-new-atheist-just-doesn't-care/

Morey, Robert. *The Trinity: Evidence and Issues*. Grand Rapids: World Publishing, 1996.

Mouw, Richard J. and Douglas A. Sweeney. *The Suffering and Victorious Christ: Toward a More Compassionate Christology*. Grand Rapids, MI: Baker Academic, 2013.

Musselman, Greg. "Paying the Price in Pakistan", *Voice of the Martyrs*. (March 2015): 4.

Nassif, Bradley. "The Meaning in the Monotony". *Christianity Today* (April 2015): 54.

Newbigin, Lesslie. *The Gospel in a Pluralistic Society*. Grand Rapids: Eerdmans, 1989.

Packer, J. I., and Thomas Howard. *Christianity: The True Humanism*. Waco: Word Books, 1985.

Parrish, Matthew. "Shout Your Doubt Out Loud: My Fellow Unbelievers", *The Times* (April 21, 2007): 19.

Parshall, Phil and Julie. *Lifting the Veil: The World of Muslim Women*. Waynesboro, GA: Gabriel Publishing, 2002.

Pearcey, Nancy. *Total Truth: Liberating Christianity from Its Cultural Captivity*. Wheaton: Crossway, 2005.

Pickett, Mark, "Ethnicity, Kinship, Religion and Territory: Identifying Communities in South Asia", *The Journal of the International Society for Frontier Missiology*, (January-March 2015): 23-36.

Pickthall, Mohammed M (Trans.). *The Meaning of the Glorious Koran*. Toronto: New American Library [*sic.*]

Pipes, Daniel. "Jihad and the Professors". http://www.danielpipes.org/498/jihad-and-the-professors/11/2002.

Poythress, Vern. *Inerrancy and Worldview: Answering Modern Challenges to the Bible*. Wheaton: Crossway, 2012.

Powers, Kirsten. "The God I Can't Write Off", *Christianity Today* (November 2013): 103-04.

Qureshi, Nabeel. "Called Off the Minaret". *Christianity Today,* (January/February 2014): 95-96.

Rabanni, Atif, "No End to Untouchability", *Forward Press* (March 2015): 32-35.

Ramachandra, Vinoth. *Gods That Fail: Modern Idolatry and Christian Mission*. Carlisle, UK: Paternoster Press, 1996.

_____. *Subverting Global Myths: Theology and the Public Issues Shaping the World*. Downers Grove, IL: IVP Academic, 2008.

Ramsey, Paul. *Ethics at the Edges of Life*. New Haven: Yale University Press, 1978.

Reynolds, Matt. "Hide It Under a Bushel?" *Christianity Today* (October 2015): 60-64.

Roy, Arundhati, "The Doctor and the Saint", Intro to B. R. Ambedkar. *Annihilation of Caste*. New Delhi: Navayana, 2013.

_____. *Prospect Magazine*. "India's Shame". (November 13, 2014): http://www.prospectmagazine.co.uk/features/indias-shame

Sandel, Michael J. *Justice: What's the Right Thing to Do?* New York: Farrar, Strauss and Giroux, 2010.

Sanneh, Lamin. *Disciples of All Nations: Pillars of World Christianity*. New York: Oxford University Press, 2008.

Sastri, Shakuntala (Trans.). *The Bhagavad-Gita*. Bombay: Bharatiya Vidya Bhavan, 1971.

Scott, Alec. "Is Health a Human Right?" *The University of Toronto Magazine*. (Autumn 2015): 25.

Sider, Ronald J. *The Scandal of Evangelical Politics*. Grand Rapids, MI: Baker Books, 2008.

Singh, Nav. "Against Their Will". *The University of Toronto Magazine*. (Autumn 2015): 53.

Stark, Rodney. *For the Glory of God: How Monotheism Led to Reformation, Science, Witch-Hunts, and the End of Slavery*. Princeton: Princeton University Press, 2003.

Stearns, Richard. *The Hole in our Gospel*. Nashville: Thomas Nelson, 2010.

Stockland, Peter. "Law, Loyola and the Common Good", *Convivium* (Vol. 4, No. 22): 8-12.

Stott, John. *Involvement, Volume 2: Social and Sexual Relationships in the Modern World*. Old Tappan: Fleming H. Revell, 1985.

_____. *The Cross of Christ*. Downer's Grove: InterVarsity Press, 1986.

Taleb, Nassim. *Black Swans: The Impact of the Highly Improbable*. London: Penguin, 2007.

Taylor, Barry. "Culture since 1985". *Missiology: An International Review*. April 2007: 149.

Teng, Tara. "We are not Commodities", *Convivium* (Vol. 4, No. 22): 17-19.

Thekekaekara, Mari Marcel. http://newint.org/blog/2015/07/31/indias-forgotten-cotton-picking-child-labour/

Thiessen, Elmer John. *The Ethics of Evangelism: A Philosophical Defense of Proselytizing and Persuasion*. Downers Grove, IL: IVP Academic, 2011.

Tickle, Phyliss. *The Great Emergence: How Christianity Is Changing and Why*. Grand Rapids: Baker Books, 2008.

Todd, Paula. "Veiled Threats?" in *Homemakers* (October 2001): 45-53.

Toycen, David. *The Power of Generosity: How to Transform Yourself and Your World*. Toronto: HarperCollins, 2005.

Varma, Pavan K. *The Great Indian Middle Class*. Delhi: Penguin Books, 1998.

Volf, Miroslav. *A Public Faith: How Followers of Christ Should Serve the Common Good*. Grand Rapids: Brazos Press, 2011.

_____. *Allah: A Christian Response*. New York: HarperCollins, 2011.

_____. *The End of Memory: Remembering Rightly in a Violent World*. Grand Rapids: W. B Eerdmans, 2006.

Westhead, Rick. "Modernizing India on the Back of Children". *Toronto Star* (March 6, 2010): A25, 27.

Wikipedia.org. "Hindutva".

Wikipedia.org. "Trafficking".

Willard, Dallas. *Renovation of the Heart: Putting on the Character of Christ*. Colorado Springs: NavPress, 2002.

_____. *The Spirit of the Disciplines: Understanding How God Changes Lives*. New York: HarperSanFrancisco, 1988.

Wolfe, Thom and Suzana Andrade. *Savitribai: India's Conversion on Education.* New Delhi: University Institute, 2008.

Woodberry, Dudley. "Terrorism, Islam and Mission", *International Bulletin of Missionary Research* (January 2002): 2-7.

Woodberry, Dudley, Russell Shubin and G. Marks, "Why Muslims Follow Jesus". *Christianity Today* (October 2007): 80-85.

Wright, Christopher. "Lamentations: A Book for Today". *International Journal of Missionary Research.* (April 2015): 59-64.

Wydick, Bruce. "Want to Change the World? Sponsor a Child." *Christianity Today* (June 2013): 20-25.

Yadav, Ashok, "OBC Quota Division: States' Job Not Centre's". *Forward Press* (July 2015): 10-13.

Yancey, Philip. *Finding God in Unexpected Places*. Grand Rapids: Zondervan, 2005.

_____. *Vanishing Grace: What Ever Happened to the Good News?* Grand Rapids: Zondervan, 2014.

Yancey, Philip, and Paul Brand. *Fearfully & Wonderfully Made*. Grand Rapids: Zondervan, 1982.

Zacharias, Ravi. *Jesus among Other Gods: The Absolute Claims of the Christian Message*. Word: Nashville: 2000.